Leadership: All You Need To Know 2nd edition

David Pendleton • Adrian Furnham

Leadership: All You Need To Know
2nd edition

palgrave
macmillan

David Pendleton
London, United Kingdom

Adrian Furnham
London, United Kingdom

ISBN 978-1-137-55434-5   ISBN 978-1-137-55436-9   (eBook)
DOI 10.1057/978-1-137-55436-9

Library of Congress Control Number: 2016938064

Printed on acid-free paper

This Palgrave Macmillan imprint is published by Springer Nature
The registered company is Macmillan Publishers Ltd. London

Foreword by Sir Rod Eddington: Great Leadership Matters

Great leadership matters—from the front line of any organisation to the CEO's office. It is the most important competitive advantage that any company can have. This is as true for organisations of all types—in politics, sport, government and business.

David Pendleton and Adrian Furnham have spent most of their lives understanding what makes leaders tick, and how to make them better at their critical leadership tasks. They have matched their academic knowledge of leadership with a comprehensive practitioners' view of what does and doesn't work in the business world. I've seen their passion for this subject up close for 25 years. In Asia, Europe and Australia, across a number of companies. And across cultures—great leadership has more common denominators than differences as we move from place to place.

Their collective wisdom has been distilled into this book *Leadership: All You Need to Know*. It combines their collective insights with numerous practical examples down through the centuries and across the disciplines.

Both authors have had considerable success as advisors to major companies because they combine the tough messages that come in honest feedbacks with constructive ideas on how to improve and grow as leaders. Understanding your own strengths and weaknesses as a leader is the first step on the journey to growth.

'Are leaders born or made?' is a question often asked. Whatever you might think it is clear all of us must aspire to be the best we can be at our chosen leadership tasks. We all have a lot to learn and the learning process never finishes.

So keep this book at your elbow. The ideas it brings to life are profoundly useful. And it's an enjoyable read along the way.

Sir Rod Eddington is currently Chairman of J P Morgan Australia and New Zealand. Formerly, he ran Cathay Pacific Airways, Ansett Australia and British Airways. He received a Knighthood in 2005 for services to the aviation industry.

Rod Eddington
Melbourne, Australia

Preface to the Second Edition

There is little orthodoxy in the field of leadership. Richard Pascale at Oxford University created, initially for a joke but with serious content and consequences, a map of the published literature on leadership and management from 1950 to 2000. Having the appearance of a geological cross-section of a hillside, the map charted the rise and fall of ideas as reflected in the business and management journals during this 50-year period. It illustrated three patterns clearly. First, that there has been an explosion of interest in these subjects since the 1980s (ten years before the internet) and that the internet created a second growth spurt. Second, that ideas come and go. They make an impact for a while, spawn a flurry of research activity and then disappear from the journals. They may linger in practice but not in the academic world. Third, that there has been no game-changing new idea that has swept all before it. In science, a new paradigm can change a field of study totally as when Einstein revolutionised physics in the early twentieth century. Nothing like that has happened to the study of leadership. The challenge is, therefore, to keep up with a constantly moving target. Pascale called his map 'Business Fads 1950–2000'.

In the first edition of this book, Adrian and I tried to focus on what is key. We dared to describe it as all you need to know because the essential elements are, in our view, few. Yet there is a wealth of new ideas and research constantly emerging in the field of leadership. We too are continuously developing our own ideas and the Primary Colours approach to leadership is maturing and growing. This book aims to keep track of the *key* new developments and to expand, update and refocus as required. Thus, some chapters have been significantly expanded (e.g., chapter 1) and others have received minimal additions (e.g., chapters 3 and 7). Some have been refocused (e.g., chapter 4) and others are new (chapters 8 and 9).

Significantly, since the first edition, our emphasis on teams leading rather than individuals has emerged as a new emphasis in the research on leadership: leadership in the plural. We would be proud if we could claim that we caused this new wave to appear but we did not. The zeitgeist created the wave and we, like good surfers, spotted it and caught it early. Nevertheless, we are pleased to witness its emergence and believe it is likely to be more than a fad since it is a response to the world's increasing complexity and the changed expectations of smart people at work. These contextual effects are unlikely to change. This is explained in chapter 1's new sections.

It is our hope that the new edition continues to prove to be helpful to leaders, those aspiring to lead, consultants and academics interested in leadership.

David Pendleton
Adrian Furnham
London, UK

Acknowledgements

Many friends, colleagues and clients have helped us develop these ideas in many different ways. We both studied together at Oxford in the late 1970s and were enormously helped and encouraged by our doctoral supervisors Michael Argyle and Jos Jaspars. Michael nagged us to complete our dissertations, made learning fun, structured our time and developed our skills in playing charades. Jos developed our understanding of theory and statistics. Both of them believed in us.

Adrian would like to express his gratitude and thanks to Professor Robert Hogan whose imagination, brilliance and generosity with ideas has always inspired him. Adrian would also like to thank his support team at home, Alison and Benedict, for forgiving him spending far too much time in the office scribbling.

For David, colleagues at Innogy (now npower) helped him develop the five leadership enablers (chapter 4): Jon Cowell, Tor Farquhar, Erin Bland and Alan Robinson. Colleagues at Edgecumbe Consulting have worked with the Primary Colours Model for years and several helped brainstorm the approach to chapter 10: Jon Cowell (again), Chris Marshall, Megan Joffe, Jo Beale and Claire Romaines. Colleagues at Oxford University's Saïd Business School also commented on early drafts of the first edition: Kathryn Bishop, Alison McQuater and Professor Tim Morris.

Clients have been helpful, and many are rapidly becoming friends, specifically John Rishton (formerly CEO of Ahold in Amsterdam and of

Rolls-Royce in the UK). From Ahold: Larry Benjamin, Klaas Miedema and Hans Hijne. From ICA in Stockholm: Åsa Gabriel and Kenneth Hagsten. These busy executives gave their time willingly to read and critique early drafts and went way beyond what was reasonable to be helpful. They commissioned, co-designed and participated in courses based on these ideas and pushed for the book to be written. All have now (2016) moved on from these positions but their legacies continue here and elsewhere.

Friends have also pitched in. Sir Rod Eddington is an outstanding leader and has encouraged Adrian and I professionally and personally for over 20 years. Professor Alastair Scotland (formerly CEO of the National Clinical Assessment Service of the NHS), David Haslam (Former President of the Royal College of General Practitioners, Former President of the BMA and now National Professional Advisor with the Care Quality Commission) and Elisabeth Kutt (Taylor), Divisional Director of Bristol's UBHT all read early drafts and provided invaluable feedback, guidance and a great deal of encouragement. Peter Derbyshire gave many thoughtful comments and engaged in substantive debate about the issues.

Finally, David acknowledges the help, support and love of his wife and colleague Jenny Pendleton (King). She is the perfect role model for how to challenge and support simultaneously. She has pushed me to be clearer, more articulate and more disciplined in producing this volume. Her comments have ranged from structure and content to punctuation and grammar. Her confidence in me is limitless and her professionalism exemplary.

Contents

List of Figures

List of Tables

Introduction

Leaders and leadership fascinate us. This is unsurprising given the current state of our world, the news headlines and the continuing uncertainties. As we write this introduction to the second edition of our book, we are coming to the end of a financial crisis but it is by no means over, the Middle East is still experiencing turmoil and threatens to spill over, there is political controversy engulfing leaders in Europe, the United States, Africa and elsewhere and we are coming to terms with disruptive technology that seems to be changing many of the assumptions we make about our lives and our futures. Leaders and leadership are in our media and on our minds every day of the year.

Consider the global nature of change. We are writing in 2016 but we could have been writing in similar circumstances at almost any time over the last 100 years. Consider the second half of the twentieth century and beginning of the twenty-first. In the 1960s many Soviet bloc countries struck out for more liberal treatment only to be crushed by the then Soviet Union. In the 1970s there had been major problems with inflation in many Western nations. In the 1980s many Latin American countries defaulted on their debt and there was a savings and loan (building society) crisis in the USA, where over 700 such institutions went out of business. The Vietnam War lasted from 1955 to 1975 but was most seriously escalated through the 1960s. It altered public consciousness as TV brought the war, for the first time, into the living rooms of the USA where, some assert, the war was lost. TV had military consequences. In the twenty-first century there has been turmoil in Ukraine, Syria, Iraq and continuing tensions in Israel while relations with Iran seem to be changing and the old order in the Middle East seems to be re-forming.

New technologies over the last 150 years have informed the world about the changes happening around the globe in new ways that bring the change increasingly closer and deeper into the consciousness of more people. In the second half of the twenty-first century, computers became more widespread and with them came the technology which brought us to the brink of changing the world for ever—the internet. Indeed, many believe that the awareness of the public in the Middle East was so affected by what they saw on the internet and the world's global media that they finally demanded change from the old and authoritarian regimes in the uprisings of 2011, much as billboard advertising influenced race riots in Watts in Los Angeles in the 1960s.

Earlier, in the 1950s, the Korean War lasted from 1950 to 1953, there was the Suez Crisis (1956) and the potentially disruptive technology of the time was the spin-offs from the start of the space race (*Sputnik 1* was launched in 1957). In the late 1920s and early 1930s there was the Wall Street Crash and the advent of television to change our lives. In the 1890s we were introduced to radio and the possibility of instant coverage of the world's major events.

During the last 100 years there have been two world wars (1914–18 and 1939–45) and conflicts around the globe which have given birth to international institutions designed to provide a forum for international leadership and diplomacy. We have seen the inception and demise of the League of Nations and the emergence of the United Nations. In the 1940s the IMF and World Bank were created in response to the Great Depression and the Second World War as a way to promote monetary cooperation, financial stability and economic growth for all countries. We have seen Communism rise in the Soviet Union and Eastern Europe and we have seen it fall, as symbolised by the toppling of the Berlin Wall in 1989.

We have seen global economic changes. Arguably the nineteenth century belonged to Britain as the British Empire turned the world's atlases pink. The twentieth century belonged to the USA and Japan as they became the dominant economies across the globe. Already the twenty-first century seems to belong to China with its double-digit growth sustained for many years—it had already overtaken Japan to become the world's second biggest economy by 2011. It is believed that China will overtake the USA economically in the next decade or so. The ubiquity of change makes it unsurprising that our fascination with leaders and leadership continues unabated.

In this book we make passing mention of leadership in other realms, but we are principally concerned with the leadership of *organisations* in the public and private sectors. We now know a great deal about effective and ineffective leadership by observing the events around us, but we know a great deal more from the last 100 years of systematic research on the topic. In this book, we describe much of this research and locate the firm and generaliseable findings we can all use as a basis on which to act.

Our definition of leadership is this: *to create the conditions for people to thrive, individually and collectively, and achieve significant goals.* Thus, gardening may be a better analogy than sports or fighting a war. Gardeners have to understand the circumstances in which they are working and work with the elements and the plants to create the conditions for sustainable growth. The difference of course is that, in organisations, leaders are not dealing with plants but with people who increasingly demand a say in how decisions are made!

We will not avoid controversy but we will seek to resolve it, where possible, by reference to sound evidence rather than conjecture. In chapter 1, we describe the history of research on leadership, focusing largely on the twentieth and twenty-first centuries. In this second edition, the research record has been updated and emerging trends in the twenty-first century have been identified. In chapter 2, we show that leadership makes a difference to the performance of organisations. We briefly describe the evidence against this assertion before setting out the overwhelming evidence for it and underlining a number of themes around effective leadership which we will incorporate later in models and suggestions of our own.

In chapter 3 we describe Pendleton's Primary Colours Model of Leadership: a simple means of describing the domains in which leaders must operate and the tasks they need to achieve. We offer the model as a map of the territory of leadership, showing the interrelations between the three domains. In chapter 4, we concentrate on the task of leading that lies at the heart of the Primary Colours Model: of balancing and coordinating the contributions required of effective leadership and we describe five enablers that make the task more likely to succeed.

Chapter 5 makes the case that it is extremely difficult, if not impossible, for any individual to be a complete leader. The reasons are several fold but their implications are important. For years, learning and development specialists in organisations have proceeded on the assumption that all limitations can be turned into strengths. We will suggest otherwise and recommend a different way of thinking about the problem. We will suggest that there may need to be work-*around* solutions as well as developmental actions to work *on* any significant limitation. In chapter 6, we consider the implications for teams. We will suggest that, while complete individual leaders may be hard to find, teams hold the possibility of finding complementary leaders who demonstrate complete leadership together. We will describe several examples of such leaders who have created effective leadership teams and who have achieved a great deal thereby. We will assert that 'we don't need another hero': a leader who tries to be complete alone. Those who try to be so are probably condemned to a career of mediocre leadership.

In this second edition, we have added a new chapter. Chapter 9 is a new chapter on leaders who fail and derail. It started as a section in chapter 8 in the first edition but is now much expanded and developed to shed more light on this remarkably common occurrence with a section devoted to the subject of resilience: how it is to be understood and developed.

Naturally, there are formal propositions about leadership that we also need to address. The first of these is that effective leadership is all a matter of intelligence: that leaders are brighter than most people and the brightest leaders have the greatest success. This is the theme of chapter 7 and the results may give rise to some surprise, since the effect of intelligence on leadership effectiveness is much weaker than most of us might imagine. Similarly, there is the effect of personality on leadership. Intuitively most of us would expect the effect of personality on leadership will be less than that of intelligence, but the reverse is true, as we shall see in chapter 8 which also contains a new section on introverted leaders.

We will occasionally refer to the oldest question of all: are leaders born or made? The answer is unequivocal: both, for reasons we will describe.

In the final chapter 10, we set out a programme of action in the form of a story describing a fictitious character facing the challenges of leadership. It is intended to draw out the key lessons from the rest of the book.

This book is written for leaders in all walks of life, though we hope that we will also find readers among those who advise and consult, train and develop, educate and coach. It is also for those who have to evaluate the quality of leadership in an organisation: executives, non-executives and investors. Different types of reader are likely to want to access the book differently. Leaders, non-executives and investors who want to consider our approach to leadership and its implications, might only want to read chapters 3, 4, 5, 6 and 10 since these are the most practical and original. Those who educate and coach will also need to understand the background provided in chapters 1 and 2 in order to compare our approach with others. Those with a more psychological orientation will need to look at chapters 7, 8, and 9 in addition.

We are attempting to produce a book that is intellectually satisfying but not essentially academic. Accordingly, it has been fully referenced. We want to point out the reasons why a particular approach to leadership is to be followed, not merely to provide practical suggestions. The original working title for the book was *We Don't Need Another Hero* in order to reflect one of the key concepts delineated in it, but our publisher persuaded us to give it its present title to reflect our intention to be evidence based, conceptually coherent and entirely practical.

The evidence we cite throughout the book will draw most heavily on published research, favouring the larger studies and meta-analyses of other published works. This approach makes the best use of the most data. In the attempt to be conceptually coherent, we will suggest models that are simple but not simplistic. In this way we will attempt to make our ideas easily memorable and the more robust for their basis in published evidence. Most of all we will attempt to draw out the practical implications of our suggestions so that our thoughts can make a difference if put into practice.

1

The History of Thinking about Leadership

Introduction

The topic of leadership is controversial. There are those who argue that leadership is greatly overvalued: that the success of organisations derives at least as much from serendipity as from strategy, vision or leadership. They argue that attempts to identify the characteristics of great leaders have proven to be inconsequential or contradictory and that generalise-able lessons about leadership are elusive. We believe that these arguments may have some validity but that they do not represent the overwhelming weight of research evidence; evidence that has become more convincing since the first edition of this volume.

Philosophers, historians, novelists and journalists have always been interested in what makes a great (and a failed) leader: what are their unique characteristics and strengths; allowable weakness and peculiar foibles; and what makes them fall from grace, get forgotten or get lionised for all time? Do special circumstances (crises) throw up certain types of leaders who are only suitable in that situation? Certainly the study of leaders, organisations, countries and empires seem to need frequent updates as yesterday's heroes become today's controversies and tomorrow's embarrassments.

© The Editor(s) (if applicable) and The Author(s) 2016
D. Pendleton, A. Furnham, *Leadership: All You Need To Know*
2nd edition, DOI 10.1057/978-1-137-55436-9_1

World history is littered with examples of leaders in a time of crisis who became a poor leader in a time of stability and vice versa. The history of organisations provides examples of business leaders who are victims of the Peter principle (promoted until their level of incompetence is reached). Thus, is succession planning for leaders really viable, given that circumstances change so often? Key to all these dilemmas is one of the oldest questions of all: are leaders born (with some genetic disposition) or are they made (by chance, learning or circumstance)?

After generations of research effort and observation, there is a lot we know about leadership. There is evidence to answer a great many questions such as what is leadership? Does leadership matter? How are leaders chosen? Who is likely to become a leader? Why do leaders fail? How do leaders build effective teams? And the like. This chapter will describe several attempts to study leadership over time and suggest an emerging story on the basis of which we can begin to understand leadership differently. It will also include a section on followers and followership: a theme that has come into sharper focus since the first edition of this volume.

Disciplinary Perspectives on Leadership

Leadership has always been studied through the lens of different approaches or disciplines. Each brings its own theories, models and jargon and each has a different way of conducting analyses and collects different data. The historian and biographer will approach leadership somewhat differently from the psychologist or psychiatrist, let alone the management writer. They seek out and interpret the data differently. They focus on different causes; offer different explanations. Even within a single discipline there are dramatic differences. This is not to assert the virtues of one over the others. Rather it is to point out the complexity of the topic and the different ways of making sense of leadership.

Consider the multiple ways in which psychologists from various sub-disciplines write and think about leadership. These approaches fall broadly into three categories concerning how leaders emerge, who they are and what they do.

1. *How leaders emerge*

   a. *The biographical approach.* Neo-psychoanalysts have written about famous leaders like Luther King and Gandhi. There have also been fine essays on famous despots who often intrigue readers the most. Psychobiography is a psychological analysis of the conscious and unconscious forces that shape an individual life. Most leaders are complex figures. They often have phenomenal drive and persistence. They overcome adversity and rejection. The biographical approach is often focused on deceased leaders and it can offer new and insightful perspectives on their motives and drives. This is not to be confused with the autobiographical approach where leaders seek to influence how they will be appreciated and remembered: to determine their own place in history before others do it for them.

   b. *The educational or developmental approach.* What creates a leader? What educational experiences, both formal and informal, shaped them? How, when and why did leaders develop their beliefs, skills, knowledge, motivation and drive? This also speaks to the question of training and developing leaders of the future. This approach is about the development of leaders and so frequently focuses on the talented or high-potential group. It addresses the question of what is trainable? Can people be taught to be good or better leaders, and if so, how? It seeks to define both the minimal and optimal preconditions for good leadership on which developmental activities can work to transform potential into fully realised leadership capability.

   c. *The environmental approach.* We shape our environment and afterwards it shapes us, as Winston Churchill once said of the British Parliament. Leaders frequently send out witting and unwitting signals about how they want to be perceived by the decisions they implement about the design and function of the buildings they inhabit. Organisational cultures are frequently typified by such signals as the location of the CEO's office, the differences in office size and furniture found there, the ease or difficulty of gaining access to the Executive suite and the like. Even the layout of the furniture influences behaviour in the office and conversations conducted across desks tend to be more formal than those in more comfortable settings. Leaders create and modify physical environments with psychological and cultural consequences, creating physical analogues of their leadership style and approach.

2. *Who leaders are*

a. *The personality approach.* This is perhaps the best-known approach. Whilst some writers include ability and values under this heading, the majority focus on personality traits. They aim to discover those traits in highly successful leaders that explain their success. The best trait studies look at longitudinal data so that one can separate cause from correlation, but more typically, these studies are correlational and can merely infer causality. This approach has seen a significant revival since the 1980s due to the development of the so-called 'Five Factor' model of personality which has now shown highly significant correlations with both leadership emergence and effectiveness, as we shall see in subsequent chapters.

b. *The clinical approach.* Psychologists, psychiatrists and psychoanalysts have taken an interest in the abnormal, disordered side of leaders which sits alongside their skill and determination and frequently accounts for their drive. Many are known to have both acute and chronic disorders, which they often exploit for their own ends. The psychopath, the narcissist and the manic depressive leader are far from rare. By one definition of abnormal (i.e., the statistical definition) all leaders are abnormal since they are exceptional. The question for the clinical approach is how their problems helped and hindered them both in the journey to the top and their experience once there.

c. *The evolutionary approach.* It has been suggested that leaders tend to be taller, more handsome and fitter than the average person of their age and stage in life. Evolutionary psychologists looking at other animals and our own primitive past have noticed that leaders have always tended to be fit and strong; bright and 'wily'; feared by adversaries; admired by followers. Some physical anthropologists have noted the shape of successful leaders. Whilst we can all think of short, tubby, bald exceptions to the rule, it is also apparent from our elected politicians and from the CEOs of top companies that they are often taller and more attractive than the average person of their age. In US Presidential elections in the television age, for example, the taller candidate has usually won and the idea of a 'commanding presence' persists.

3. *What leaders do*

a. *The cognitive approach.* Cognition is about thinking and therefore involves perception, information processing, understanding, knowledge and sometimes creativity. One essential feature of leadership is decision-making. Cognitive psychologists are interested in all aspects of decision-making from decision-making under uncertainty to decision-making in groups. How do leaders typically make decisions: to hire or fire, buy or sell, advance or retreat? Do they consult others or make decisions alone; do they agonise or act impulsively? What sort of data do they seek before they decide? Perhaps most importantly, do leaders make better decisions than their followers and has high-quality decision-making contributed to their emergence as leaders?

b. *The ideological approach.* Sometimes called the moral approach, it looks at the influence that leaders have been able to wield predominantly through the power of their preaching and message. In history, some of the most enduring and powerful of leaders are those who have crusaded with simple but attractive moral goals. Many have not sought leadership itself but had it thrust upon them—and the question is how they did it. One of the best examples from the twentieth century was Martin Luther King, whose rhetoric was so powerful and whose message so straightforward and just that millions were persuaded to follow his teachings and his cause. King followed in the peaceful tradition of Gandhi several decades earlier—both died for their cause, but their impact has been legendary.

c. *The social approach.* No leader can succeed without followers. Leaders give the led a sense of identity and mission. He or she has to build and maintain morale in groups, which is an intensely social act. The social approach concentrates on inter-personal rather than intra-personal approaches to leadership, seeking to understand how social forces create and maintain, and in due course derail, leaders. In this tradition leaders' abilities to influence and persuade are central and closely observed.

    d. *The work approach.* A great many leadership studies have concentrated on business leaders: how they rose in their organisation and how they changed the structure and processes not only to consolidate their power but achieve great results. This is the organisational psychology of leaders that looks at the interaction of leaders with their board, the media and their customers but most of all with others who work in the organisation. It looks at organisational structure and how leaders in different sectors (e.g., manufacturing, services, banking) may differ in style, temperament and outcome.

Whatever the psychological sub-discipline, however, there are five topics that seem to recur inter alia (Table 1.1).

    In the next section, we will explain how these various themes have emerged through time and the current state of leadership research on which we will seek to build.

Table 1.1 Five recurring topics in the study of leadership

Topic	Unit of analysis	Variables of interest
The leaders	Individual leaders	Their abilities, personality traits, beliefs and behaviours, values, background and pathology
The led	Acolytes, teams and organisations. Followers	Mutual influence between leaders and followers. Their needs and circumstances. The power they invest in leaders and why
Power and influence	Organisational roles and positions	Influence tactics. How leaders acquire and use power. Political tactics
The situation	Environment or context in which leadership emerges, succeeds or fails	Situation effects on leader behaviour; factors defining favourable situations; antecedents and consequences
Leader emergence versus effectiveness	Individuals and/or groups	The route to leadership of individuals or groups; their effectiveness in office; the metrics by which they can be judged

The View through the Rear-View Mirror: The History of Leadership Theory[1]

There have tended to be surges of interest in leadership after great conflicts such as the First and Second World Wars. Great leaders have differed significantly in their approaches, however, and no individual style of leadership seems to be effective in all contexts. On the political stage, the twentieth century saw the brutality of Hitler and Stalin, as well as the peaceful leadership of Gandhi. In the case of organisations, there have been successful centralisers and decentralisers, strategists and tacticians, controllers and empowerers. However, there is a pervading view that leadership influences every aspect of organisational performance and that leaders who stand the test of time cast a long shadow so that much of the organisation is said to be in the shadow of the leader, carrying his or her particular stamp or character.

Pre-twentieth Century

As far back as 380 BC, Plato argued in his *Republic* that those best suited to leadership were those with the greatest knowledge. They were the philosopher kings and their attributes made them effective. These included wisdom, truthfulness, justice, gentleness and a love of learning. Some 1,900 years on from this 'classic' view of leadership, Machiavelli, in *The Prince* (1513) described leaders somewhat less kindly, arguing that appearances were important and leaders must appear compassionate, generous and of great integrity while at heart being self-centred and even cruel. Their aim was first to acquire and sustain their positions as leaders.

Surprisingly, it was the ancient Greeks who had invented the dramatic form which used the 'persona'—a mask which was worn to create an outward appearance which could belie an inner reality. But the philosopher kings were said to be true to themselves: genuinely wise and just according to Plato. Machiavelli's recommendations evoked the mask and

---

[1] This section draws extensively on an excellent summary of the subject by Peter Derbyshire and Dave Peel in an unpublished manuscript from 2009.

suggested its use as a subterfuge or cover for truth in contrast to current theories that emphasise authenticity.

Leadership in the Twentieth Century

There appear to have been six distinct phases in the history of thinking about leaders in the twentieth century. Scholars from very different disciplines—from history and political science to psychology and sociology—have added their particular slant to try to understand the dynamics of leadership (Table 1.2).

We will describe these approaches in more detail below, but throughout these phases of leadership investigation, there has emerged a discernible trend in which old models of leadership might be contrasted with an emergent or new model and this change has reflected a change in Western

Table 1.2 Development of thinking on leadership in the twentieth century

Period	Approach	Dominant ideas
1920s	Trait theory	Leadership can be understood by identifying the distinguishing characteristics or traits of great leaders
1950s	Style theory	Leadership effectiveness may be explained and developed by identifying appropriate styles and behaviours
1960s	Contingency theory	Leadership occurs in a context and is practised differently depending on each situation: hence 'Situational Leadership'
1970s	Charismatic theory	Leadership is concerned with charismatic behaviours of leaders and their ability to transform an organisation
1980s	New leadership/neo charismatic theory	Leadership and management are different. Leaders require a transformational focus which encompasses a range of characteristics and behaviours in addition to charisma
Late 1990s	Emerging approaches (a) Strategic leadership (b) Change leadership	(a) leadership may be understood by examination of strategic decision-making (b) Leadership is inexorably linked to the management of change. Leader behaviours may best be understood in the context of delivering change

societies. In the old compliance-based model, senior managers or leaders created strategy and plans and more junior managers or front line workers operated those plans. The leadership approach depended on the *compliance* of those who were more junior and their faith in, or acceptance of, the authority of their seniors. The emerging pattern is quite different and consistent with a more egalitarian, twenty-first-century society found in more prosperous nations. It is based on *engagement* and the building of commitment in all those involved with the enterprise. Distinctions can be seen along several lines:

- Planning, allocating responsibility and controlling have given way to vision, creating alignment and motivation
- Creating routine, retaining power and creating compliance have given way to embracing change, empowerment of others and building commitment
- The detached rationality of distant leaders who emphasise contractual obligations has given way to leader involvement, the use of feelings and intuition and the pursuit of discretionary effort

The emerging picture, described below, is of leaders who seek to work *with* their employees: creating conditions in which their people love to work and in which, as a consequence, those people choose to work harder and more effectively. This contrasts nicely with the old model in which employees worked *for* their boss who controlled them.

Indeed, there is discernible a distinct tendency for ideas about leadership to reflect strongly the mores of their time. Thus, at the start of the twentieth century, society in most industrialised nations was clearly hierarchical and great disparities existed between those regarded as entitled to govern, rule, lead and manage and those whose lowly standing in society brought expectations of subservience. Unsurprisingly, ideas about leadership at the time reflected a similar world view of authority and obedience. By the end of the century, as we shall come to see, expectations had almost completely inverted and strong expectations had emerged about involvement, consent, engagement and co-leadership. This is a process we describe as the *democratisation of leadership*.

Early Twentieth Century: Scientific Management and Trait Theory

In the early twentieth century, over a century after the start of the industrial revolution, the impact of science and engineering was enormous. Its principles and applications seemed limitless and the engineer Frederick Winslow Taylor suggested a theory of the 'scientific management' of businesses. In many respects this was a theory of leadership in which people (workers) were looked upon simply as economic units who were to be selected and trained for their work, incentivised for performing well and managed professionally. Yet workers were, according to Taylor, incapable of understanding what they were doing and this was why manager/leaders had to be effective and had to enforce their decisions and approaches. Perhaps it is understandable that strikes were not uncommon when Taylor's ideas about management were introduced.

Taylor's was a theory of management behaviour. It is included here as a leadership theory because it implied attitudes and values about people and how they were to be led. It became the backbone of a pervasive industrial efficiency movement that can still be seen today in many aspects of business process re-engineering. As a leadership theory, it did not depend upon or describe attributes other than intelligence (on the part of managers) and the lack of it (on the part of workers). Taylor was no friend of unions, whom he regarded as irrelevant. He was concerned with duties and obligations, efficiency and enforcement rather than any more humanitarian or egalitarian bases of leadership. His ideas depended on compliance, either given or enforced.

Later, psychologists began to theorise that individuals were born with certain characteristics or traits. According to *Trait Theory*, particular characteristics began to be associated with effective leadership. However, in a series of influential reviews, Stogdill (1948) reported the lack of a clear and consistent relationship between individual traits and successful leadership and encouraged researchers to explore alternative theories.

Trait Theory was also criticised for being unable to agree or identify a definitive list of leadership traits and, crucially, for failing to take into account the behaviour of followers or the increasingly complex situations that leaders faced. Recently there has been renewed interest in Trait Theory (see Hogan and Kaiser, What we know about leadership; *Review of General Psychology*, 2005, 9, 169–80) due to the increasing clarity about personality that the Five Factor model of personality has brought to the subject. This will be covered in subsequent chapters 8 and 9.

Yet the early trait work stumbled and eventually stopped for various reasons. *First*, different researchers came up with different lists of the fundamental leadership traits. Some included physical characteristics and others social background factors while others ignored them. All this led to confusion and dispute. *Second*, these lists of traits/characteristics were not rank-ordered by importance and it was not clear how these traits related to each other. *Third*, it was not clear if these traits were both necessary and sufficient or just necessary. *Fourth*, the trait approach was essentially retrospective and it was unclear whether the traits somehow 'caused' a person to become a leader or were a consequence of their leadership style and experience. *Finally*, the trait approach ignored the role of all other social factors (teams, organisations, etc.) in the experience of the leader, and thus were incomplete.

Trait Theory gave rise to studies of the behaviours and styles of leaders in an attempt to define the 'best' or most effective style. However, examples where leaders were successful despite having so-called 'less-desirable' styles also emerged. The limitations of *behavioural* or *style* theories led to views that it was not the leadership style per se that led to the effectiveness of leaders, but their ability to adapt their style to the needs of followers. This in turn led to *situational* analyses of leadership, taking account not just of the followers but also of variables in the organisation's external and internal context.

The behavioural or style approach involves three steps:

1. Observe leader behaviour
2. Categorise it
3. Determine which behaviours are most (and by implication least) effective.

Perhaps the most widely known *style* approach distinguished between three styles of leadership: authoritarian, democratic and laissez-faire. This is described in Table 1.3.

However, many criticisms were made of this approach to identify the most characteristic styles of leaders. Firstly, the groupings or categories

Table 1.3 Three styles of leadership

Authoritarian	Democratic	Laissez-faire
All determination of policy is carried out by the leader	All policies are a matter of group discussion and decision, encouraged and assisted by the leader	Complete freedom for group or individual decisions, with a minimum of leader participation
Tactics dictated by the leader, one at a time, so that future steps were largely uncertain	Tactics decided during discussions. General steps to the group's goal sketched out by the leader. When technical advice was needed, the leader suggested two or more alternative procedures from which choice could be made	Various materials supplied by the leader, who made it clear that information would be supplied when requested and took no other part in work discussion
The leader usually dictated the particular work task and work companion of each member	The members were free to work with whomever they chose, and the division of tasks was left up to the group	Complete non-participation of the leader
The leader tended to be 'personal' in the praise and criticism of the work of each member, remained aloof from active group participation	The leader was 'objective' or 'fact-minded' in praise and criticism and tried to be a regular group member in spirit without doing too much of the work	Few spontaneous comments on member activities unless questioned and no attempt to appraise or regulate the course of events

tend to be rather simplistic; not all observed leader behaviour fits neatly into them. Secondly, competing typologies exist and it is not clear which is most valid or most useful. Thirdly, although the typologies are a useful descriptive beginning, they tell us little about the full leadership process, nor which style is most effective in which situations, and why.

Later Twentieth Century: Situations and Contexts, Needs and Interaction, Management and Leadership

Ask most informed professionals to nominate psychological thinkers in management and usually only two are mentioned, Maslow and Herzberg, who still exercise an influence over the thinking of many managers and professionals.

Psychologists such as Abraham Maslow (1959) emphasised the part played by understanding human needs and motivations. He identified a 'hierarchy of needs' starting with physiological needs such as breathing, food and sex, continuing through safety, love and belonging, and self-esteem to self-actualisation (realising one's true potential). He held that behaviour is driven by the quest to meet these needs and that each need, once met, reveals the next need in the hierarchy. Thus, in order to meet our needs for safety we must first meet our physiological needs and so on. The theory says little about leadership or how and why leaders emerge, though inference may suggest that leadership is more likely to be conferred on those who are perceived to be more able to satisfy our basic needs.

Frederick Herzberg's Dual-Factor Theory (1959) looked at job satisfaction. He divided human motivation into either intrinsic or extrinsic. The intrinsic needs came from within and were motivators such as recognition, self-esteem and growth, whereas the extrinsic or hygiene factors were such things as salary, relationships with co-workers, the work environment and status. The data suggested that dissatisfaction would be prevented if a person's hygiene or extrinsic factors were satisfied. But this did not motivate, it merely avoided *de*motivation. People also needed their intrinsic motivating factors fulfilled in order to be motivated and satisfied.

What is remembered most about Herzberg's theory were two things: first, that money is a hygiene or extrinsic factor that played only a minor part in motivation and satisfaction (though the table below demonstrates it serves both functions to an extent). Second that people need enriched jobs to be really satisfied (Fig. 1.1).

The implications of pursuing job enrichment involve several measures:

- Removing controls from a job while retaining accountability—motivates by responsibility
- Increasing the accountability of the individual for his own work—motivates by responsibility and recognition
- Giving each person a complete and natural module of work—motivates by achievement
- Granting job freedom for a person's own work—motivates by responsibility, achievement and recognition

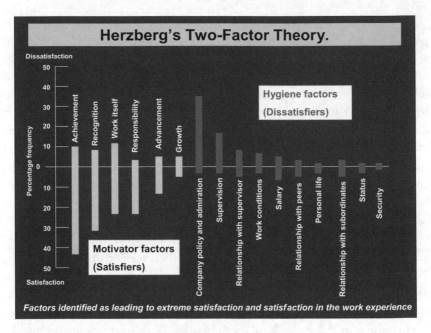

Fig. 1.1 Herzberg's two factor theory

- Making timely reports on performance available to the worker instead of to the supervisor—motivates by recognition
- Introducing new tasks not previously performed—motivates by growth and learning.
- Assigning specific tasks so the employee can develop expertise in performing them—motivates by responsibility, achievement and recognition

An understanding of human needs provides helpful insights to would-be leaders who recognise that people may be prepared to follow a leader who can meet their needs. This may even be the basis of *charismatic* leadership.

A cogent analysis of mass movements associated with specific leaders could be undertaken from the point of view of the needs that the leaders and the movements met. Thus the rise of the Nazis and the impact of Adolf Hitler met the needs of a failing nation to believe that the failure was not their own. Hitler argued in the 1930s that the German nation was failing because of a conspiracy that needed to be dealt with. Hitler offered an external attribution of failure to protect the national self-esteem. He was, of course, entirely wrong but the leadership he offered met a temporary but powerful need of a nation that has been seeking to live down the gullibility of those times ever since.

On an organisational scale, Douglas McGregor (1960) attempted to bring together the organisational *context* (situation) and the leadership found within it. He described two types of organisations and leadership styles. Theory X organisations were typified by repressive, authoritarian leadership where decisions were only taken at the top. In these organisations, workers were viewed as avoiding work where possible, needing to be coerced to meet company objectives, preferring to be directed and avoiding responsibility. Theory X organisations demand compliance and have their roots in the attitudes, values and practices of Taylor's scientific management. In theory Y organisations, by contrast, the attitudes, values and practices are dramatically different. The emphasis is on achievement and continuous improvement. By enabling staff, it is suggested, the staff will seek responsibility, apply self-control, exercise self-direction and use a high degree of creativity and ingenuity. The assumptions about human nature in the two types of organisation and the two leadership styles are diametrically opposed.

For a significant time in the twentieth century, the terms management and leadership were, if not synonymous, used interchangeably. Several authors in the latter part of the twentieth century, however, highlighted critical differences between these two activities. Henry Mintzberg (1973) described what managers do in their day-to-day lives: ten activities or roles grouped into three categories. These were:

- *Interpersonal roles*: Figurehead, Leader, Liaison
- *Informational roles*: Monitor, Disseminator, Spokesman
- *Decision-making roles*: Entrepreneur, Disturbance Handler, Resource Allocator, Negotiator

Mintzberg saw the role of leader as being the most influential of all for a manager. He considered it as essentially an interpersonal issue.

James MacGregor Burns, a historian, shifted the focus away from studying the traits of great men and transactional management to the interaction of leaders and led, as collaborators working towards mutual benefit. In his 1978 book *Leadership*, he coined the term 'Transformational' to describe the leadership in which both leaders and followers raise one another to higher levels of motivation, morality and performance in pursuit of shared goals. The idea gained acceptance rapidly and there was a great deal of interest in differentiating 'mere' managers from 'great' leaders (Table 1.4).

Unsurprisingly, given the contemporaneous interest in situational leadership, the situations calling for transactional and transformational leadership were also hypothesised and could be summarised as shown in Fig. 1.2.

Complex organisations in need of significant change were thus in need of both transactional and transformational change (management and leadership). Stable and simple organisations needed little leadership: they could be administered or managed, and so on.

Table 1.4 A comparison between transactional and transformational leadership

	Transactional ('Management')	Transformational ('Leadership')
Creating agenda	Planning and budgeting	Establishing direction
Developing HR	Organising and staffing	Aligning people
Execution	Collecting and solving problems	Motivating and inspiring
Outcomes	Produces a degree of predictability	Produces change—often dramatic

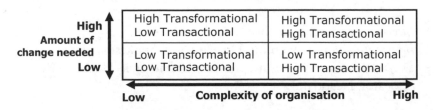

Fig. 1.2 Amount of change and organisational complexity

Table 1.5 Features of transformational leaders

Kouzes and Posner's 'Five leadership practices'	Bennis and Nanus' 'Leadership strategies'	Sashkin's 'Transformational leadership behaviours'
Challenging the process	Management of risk	Risk leadership
Inspiring a shared vision	Management of attention	Focused leadership
Enabling others to act	Management of communication	Communication leadership
Modelling the way	Management of trust	Trust leadership
Encouraging the heart	Management of respect	Respectful leadership

Subsequent writers on leadership tried to identify the most important and fundamental features of the *transformational leader*. Not surprisingly their ideas were very similar among themselves as Table 1.5 indicates.

John Kotter (1990) was credited with articulating how the concept of 'leadership' overlaps with that of 'management' and where the two are distinct. According to Kotter's definition, management copes with *complexity* by seeking to establish order and consistency within an organisation, while leadership involves producing organisational *change* and movement. He showed that it is possible to be a manager without being a leader and vice versa. He conceived of management as an active process, leadership as an interactive one. According to Kotter, management is a science and leadership is an art.

Kotter considered Leadership to comprise:

- Inspiration and motivation
- Establishment of strategic direction
- Alignment of people and organisation

Management, on the other hand, was thought to comprise:

- Controlling and problem solving
- Planning and budgeting
- Organisation and staffing

Yet it is easy to see that organisations require both these activities, leadership and management, to synchronise in order to move the organisation forward. Later in this volume (chapter 3) we will describe Pendleton's primary colours model which demonstrates the interaction between these activities and how they might be related to each other.

In the 1980s, the concept of 'vision' pervaded the leadership vocabulary, when competition forced organisations to adapt more speedily to market and technological changes. Forced to restructure or downsize, organisations found these changes struck at the heart of long-term psychological contracts with employees about job security. To help maintain employee motivation, leaders had to develop and communicate a vision of a realistic, credible and attractive future. An organisational vision needs to give a sense of uniqueness to the organisation, set a path or direction and encapsulate a set of values or ideals. While a leader's role may be to shape and communicate the vision, they rarely create it by themselves. A well-articulated vision works at all levels of an organisation, providing *meaning* that is not necessarily provided by business or strategic plans alone. Vision defines a grand purpose on the basis of which people will be prepared to make sacrifices, give of their best, de-emphasise their own needs and seek a greater good.

> While a leader's role may be to shape and communicate the vision, they rarely create it by themselves.

Transformational leaders focus on the vision they are pursuing and invite people to join them on the journey: a tactic that has spawned mass allegiance throughout history from Moses' journey to the promised land to Mao's Long March. The journey is also a powerful metaphor and a means of understanding organisational evolution. Vision sustains the effort when times get tough and transformational leaders sustain its freshness and relevance. Bass and Alvolio (1990) showed how this might be done by citing four necessary traits for the transformational leader: charisma, the ability to inspire, consideration for individuals, and providing intellectual stimulation to followers. Such characteristics ensure that the leader is able to engage with followers, appeal to their imagination, show care and compassion and also describe a credible and desirable future for them.

Continuing the theme of leadership being essentially interactive, Daniel Goleman (1995) defined emotional intelligence as the capacity to understand our emotions, manage them effectively, and to understand and manage the emotions of others. Since then, he and others have accumulated evidence to suggest that emotional competences are more crucial than intellectual capabilities as differentiating factors in job performance and leadership success. He has asserted that the higher one progresses in an organisation, the more important emotional intelligence becomes.

The Turn of the Twenty-First Century

Keith Grint (2000) proposed that leadership is more of an art than a science. He proposed four different kinds of arts that described fundamental leadership contributions addressing the who, what, how and why questions leaders have to answer:

- The Philosophical Arts answer questions of identity (key question: who are we?)
- The Fine Arts answer questions to do with strategic vision and are dubbed fine arts because, according to Grint, this has more to do with imagination than scientific enquiry (key question: what does the organisation want to achieve?)
- The Martial Arts provide clues about the organisational tactics that will lead to success against competition (key question: how will we win?)
- The Performing Arts provide the persuasive communication that induces the audience to believe in the world the leader describes (key question: why should we want to do these things?)

Having examined these four arts in a range of leaders, Grint's conclusions point to the fallibility of leaders and leadership if it resides in a single individual. Indeed he states:

the trick of leadership … is to develop followers who privately resolve the problems leaders have caused or cannot resolve, but publicly deny their interventions. (p. 420)

Yet there were those who still focused on leaders and the possibility that they can morph into new leadership forms. Rooke and Torbert (2005) apply the journey metaphor to the development of individual leaders as well as organisations. They de-emphasise cultural trends in leadership and suggest that leaders have their own inner action logics: a set of perceptions and actions that determine both their reactions to situations and their tendencies to lead in a particular way. Once a leader identifies his or her action logic, they can begin a journey of maturation and growth, progressing from earlier forms of leadership to higher forms for them and their organisations. In this way, they address the key question posed at the start of this chapter: are leaders born or made? Their answer is—both. They identify seven different action logics:

- The *opportunist*: who is essentially mistrustful and manipulative rejecting feedback and internalising blame. They focus on winning personally.
- The *diplomat*: who has a more benign view of the world and seeks to please those of higher status. They cooperate and attend to the needs of others: a tendency that can bind organisations together in middle-level roles but is disastrous at senior levels because diplomats avoid tackling difficult issues.
- The *expert*: whose goal is to perfect their own knowledge and to convince people with data and logic. Experts are hierarchical and often rigid once they have come to a conclusion, rejecting alternative suggestions from those they regard as less expert than themselves.
- The *achiever*: who is focused on deliverables. They are open to both positive and negative feedback, face ambiguity and conflict positively and balance short- and longer-term objectives. They are essentially pragmatic.
- The *individualist*: who relate to all other action logics, understanding and appreciating them while putting them into perspective. They tend to follow their own rules, ignoring those they regard as irrelevant, and can be branded as mavericks. They do not last long in bureaucratic organisations.
- The *strategist*: who believe in transformational change and strive for it by creating shared visions. They regard change as iterative, requiring close leadership attention and deal directly with resistance. They attend to relationships and seek to understand the broader context in which the organisation is working.

- The *alchemist*: who is very rare. These leaders are able to renew themselves and their organisations, dealing simultaneously with many different issues without appearing rushed, and can deal with immediate and longer-term matters. They are self-aware, charismatic and possess high moral standards.

Rooke and Torbert argued that openness to feedback is a principal means of progressing as a leader between lower- and higher-action logics. Progress can also be accelerated by seeking personal change and by experimentation. In the process of seeking to develop as a leader, however, there is a risk of seeming to be inconsistent. We raise the possibility that a simpler means of providing these different action logics may be through different leaders whose 'natural' approaches to leadership differ.

Goffee and Jones (2000) present evidence that, above all, followers want their leaders to be *authentic*. Authentic leaders tend to be regarded as trustworthy, genuine and consistent. They practice what they preach, have the confidence to reveal their true selves and admit they don't have all the answers. This stands in direct contrast to the notion of the Greek mask and Machiavelli's advice about appearance.

In the financial crisis of 2008–9, the cynicism expressed towards bankers and politicians was at a high level and shrill criticisms were levelled at those who were regarded as inauthentic and untrustworthy. Yet most surveys of longer-term social trends reveal that we are finding it increasingly hard to trust our leaders in organisations and in government. The requirement for a leader to be authentic is certainly a manifestation of current times but is also likely to be a permanent requirement if followership requires effort, self-sacrifice or inconvenience of any kind. At these times, hypocritical individuals are hardly likely to be held up as role models and faith in individuals is likely to be short lived.

The interactive nature of leadership and followership is captured by Avery (2004) who describe four leadership paradigms. They also describe four eras, each typified by a dominant leadership approach:

- *Classical* leadership was said to typify the leadership before the 1970s and stretching back to antiquity. The authors describe this in rather parental terms in which the basis of leadership was fear or respect and the leader essentially dominated his (usually *his*) followers. This was command and control leadership.

- *Transactional* leadership was said to dominate the period from the mid-1970s to the mid-1980s. In this style, leaders and followers negotiated rewards and expectations. Vision was seldom mentioned.
- *Visionary* leadership was said to typify the leadership from the mid-1980s to the end of the twentieth century. It was based on the capacity of the leader to inspire his or her followers. They cite the visionary leader as one capable of capturing hearts and minds using the image of the future communicated by the leader but which may have been co-created with the followers.
- Beyond 2000 Avery and colleagues consider the dominant approach to leadership to be '*organic*'. It is leadership based on buy-in and mutual sense-making and the vision is cultural: owned by all.

This analysis could be summed up in a power-shift model in which leadership moved from domination through negotiation to inspiration and co-creation. The role of vision changes in this analysis. In the first two approaches, vision is irrelevant since inspiration was not required. In classical leadership, 'followership' is expected due to the position of the leader. In transactional leadership followership is bought and negotiated. In true visionary leadership vision has to be more compelling, appealing and exciting than the present, and one in which followers can play a significant part. Followers identify with this vision which becomes a motivational driver as they seek to achieve what the leader has communicated. Powerful as these leaders are, it is a moot point as to whether or not they enable their followers in the longer term or create dependency on the leader's vision and purpose. In organic leadership, however, vision and sense emerge cooperatively from the group and both belong to all.

Whether or not Avery's is an accurate *historical* record is debatable and the notion that all leadership from the dawn of time to 1970 is unitary seems inconceivable, but the four styles of leadership she proposes are helpful and all of them may be seen in organisations today. Avery and colleagues have described a long history of the changing relationship between leaders and followers as the latter gain in power and influence and as leadership becomes a gift bestowed by those who consent to being led.

Democratisation

It is not just the role of vision that changes over time, however, in the power-shift we have described. There is also a shift in decision-making. Indeed, we argue that through the twentieth century, a power-shift in decision-making has occurred that we dubbed the democratisation of leadership. Here, we see three distinct phases of twentieth-century leadership that are still discernible today. The first fits into the authoritarian world view, the second corresponds with the emergence of vision and cooperation in leadership and the third institutionalises the expectation of delegation and participation in leadership. This is consistent with a study by James Spillane and colleagues from 2007. They conducted a four-year study in 15 Chicago area schools and found that the principals led alone roughly one-third of the time, they shared leadership with others roughly one-third of the time and they allowed others to lead roughly one-third of the time. We conceive of these as the three middle stages of a five-step progression from domination to abdication as shown in Fig. 1.3.

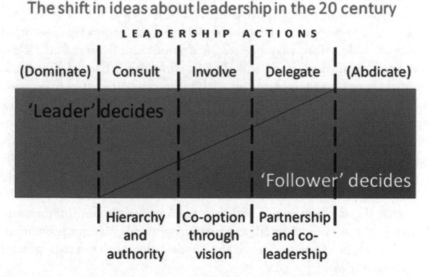

Fig. 1.3   The shift in ideas about leadership in the twentieth century

The five steps we describe are:

- Dominate: an approach to leadership in which the leader decides everything, unconcerned with the views or reactions of others.
- Consult: an approach in which the leader reserves the right to make the final decision but seeks first to understand the views and opinions of others in order to take them into account.
- Involve: in which the 'leader' and followers decide together.
- Delegate: in which the 'leader' sets the parameters and goals to be achieved (the what and why) and leaves the 'how' decisions to the delegate and authority is largely handed over.
- Abdicate: an approach in which the 'leader' relinquishes all claim to leadership and authority.

These approaches to leadership are not exclusively anchored in history but dominant at times through the twentieth century. However, they are still visible in most organisations most of the time today. Their use is often selected according to the issue in hand. The purpose of an organisation is frequently a matter of a kind of *domination*. British Airways is an airline and there will be little debate about that. By contrast, the purpose of the National Health Service (NHS) in the UK is a matter of national debate and leadership is a moot point. A wide group may be *consulted* about the livery of an airline but usually the top team will decide. *Involvement* (co-deciding) is frequently practised in teams on such matters as office use, dress code or working hours. Most significant tasks are typically *delegated* in the usual round of performance management in most successful organisations, though expectations of what this comprises differ greatly with those (wrongly) expecting no further participation from the boss resenting perceived micromanagement. And no manager would do anything but *abdicate* on the matter of comfort breaks, despite the fact that there were times when this was a matter of domination and control. Yet as the twentieth century progressed, distinct movement was discernible from left to right in the diagram: towards greater democratisation.

The View through the Windshield: The Future

The biggest megatrend through the twentieth century was to do with democratisation and the greatest developments in understanding leaders and leadership came through the new trait based approaches based on the Big-5 personality factors. The current and emerging preoccupations in leadership are concerned with followers and post-heroic, plural leadership.

Followers and Followership

Whilst it is self-evident that without followers there is no leadership, it is only relatively recently that followership has been deeply studied as a part of the study of leadership. In an excellent article in the *Leadership Quarterly* in 2014, Mary Uhl-Bien and colleagues reviewed studies relevant to a 'Followership theory', and proposed a research agenda. They identified two different frameworks for the study of followership: role-based and constructionist. In the former, followers are still regarded as subordinates, whereas in the latter they are co-constructors of leadership. Some ideas in this new tradition focus on the leaders, some on the followers and some on the relationship between them.

Many of the studies reviewed so far in this chapter have been leader-centric. The work on scientific management, the trait and contingency theorists, transformational and transformational notions and concepts of charisma are almost exclusively leader-centric. But when the research is follower-centric, the lens can be reversed so that these phenomena can be seen from the followers' points of view. Thus, the perception of leadership effectiveness can be seen as a leader conforming to the followers' beliefs about what constitutes good and bad leadership. Followers may also be regarded as falling into the fundamental attribution error of overly attributing causality of group outcomes to the leader (Meindl et al. 1985). Similarly, in the tradition of social identity theory, leaders and followers derive a great deal of their self-concept from the groups to which they belong. Thus, those whose conformance to group norms is strongest may be rewarded with leadership positions.

When the *relationship* between leaders and followers is placed centre-stage, there emerges a much less unidirectional pattern of influence. As far back as 1949, the active and dynamic reciprocal influence process between leaders and followers was said to be essential to team success, not the leader's ability to dominate followers (Follett 1949). This early emphasis was not strongly picked up for several decades but Mary Uhl-Bien and her colleagues in 2000 described Leader-Member Exchange (LMX) in which high-quality relationships between leaders and followers help to produce positive outcomes. Even here, however, it is still up to the leader to drive the relationship-building process.

Two other works in the relational tradition are noticeable not least for their graphic impact. In 1995, Klein and House described the leader's charisma as a fire that ignites followers' energy and commitment. In 'Charisma on Fire' they suggested three elements were required. A leader with charismatic qualities constituted the spark. Susceptible followers were the flammable material. A conducive environment constituted the oxygen required for combustion. This metaphor is memorable and seems to capture one form of leadership impact. Similarly tripartite and impactful but much less positive is Padilla, Hogan and Kaiser's 'toxic triangle' (2007) with a focus on the role of followers in destructive leadership behaviour. Their analysis is almost the reverse of the positive impact described by Klein and House. For Padilla and colleagues, the three elements are destructive leaders, susceptible followers and a conducive environment. Susceptible followers might be conformers (compliers) who may be operating out of fear, or colluders operating for reasons of personal gain. Nevertheless, the conducive environment was still required and this might be instability in the organisation, perceived threat, destructive values or (a culture of) negative behaviour.

Thus, whether the leadership impact is positive or negative, any analysis is likely to be incomplete unless it takes account of leader, followers and environment, and how they interact to form a benign or malign system. Not only is there no leadership without followers but there is also no leadership without a context in which the leadership operates. Typically, a status quo may well be administered quite efficiently but leadership is called for when change is needed: when the aphorism applies that what brought us to here won't get us to there and the journey requires a change of course.

The debate on transactional and transformational leadership is still alive over 30 years after it was started by Burns. Clearly a transformational style generates higher levels of engagement in a way that can produce better results over time. The downside of this can be that followers suffer from unreasonable expectations or become dependent on their leaders. Such leaders expect unity of purpose and that those who do not fit will leave, with a consequent limiting effect on diversity.

Avery et al. (2004) argue that the future of leadership is organic—a development away from a single leader of any persuasion and that networked organisations might not need a single leader. Leadership will arise in multiple forms, adaptive, multi-talented and problem-solving. Organisations could be structured into cross-functional groups, each self-managing and optimising, based on reciprocal actions and sense-making, engaging in partnerships with customers, suppliers, competitors and contractors. The organic model has its appeal in the twenty-first century in which hierarchies are increasingly mistrusted.

We agree that leadership can be, or even needs to be, a co-operative activity, but ownership and shareholding is still likely to create hierarchy in order to promote sound governance and accountability. In this book, we deliberately blur the distinction between leadership and management, especially at higher levels in organisations since both are required for organisations to thrive. Indeed, we argue that leadership and management are interdependent. We recognise that leadership requires sensitivity to, and appreciation of, context: both internal and external. We recognise the centrality of direction and purpose in leadership. Visionary leadership creates movement towards a shared view of a bright future. Focused leadership creates order. Ethically responsible leadership tends to generate trust and respect. We understand that leadership can seldom be imposed: to some extent, it is in the gift of those who are led. We recognise that leadership may be inclusive and certainly needs to be engaging since it can seldom be enforced. We shall come to see the force of involvement in building commitment and broader engagement with the aims and goals of organisations.

> Leadership can seldom be imposed: to some extent, it is in the gift of those who are led.

We further argue that all the attributes that tend to be associated with these leadership styles are seldom held by one person. In subsequent chapters 5 we shall see why this is so, but pragmatically we can already observe that it is easier to find the complete repertoire in several people acting together. So the issue we now need to understand is how to create effective leadership that is greater than the contribution of a single individual: not so much how to lead teams, but how to get teams to lead? Gayle Avery and colleagues put it this way:

'Intellectually, it is evident that the heroic leader cannot continue to exist in today's complex, dynamic organisations, no matter how talented and gifted ... Leadership is a distributed phenomenon, occurring in various parts of an organisation, not just emanating from the top.' (Avery et al. 2004)

Plural Forms of Leadership

Contemporaneous with the publication of the first edition of this book (2012), Jean-Louis Denis, Ann Langley and Viviane Sergi published a review of what they called 'Leadership in the Plural' in the *Annals of the Academy of Management*. They brought together a wealth of evidence suggesting that plural forms of leadership are becoming more common in the twenty-first century. They noted that words used to describe these forms of leadership are 'shared, distributed, collective, collaborative, integrative, relational and post-heroic' (p. 213). Thus the last words of this chapter in the first edition of our book seemed entirely consistent when we said: *For the reasons set out in this chapter, we therefore assert that 'We don't need another hero'*.

It might be expected that certain forms of corporate structure, such as partnerships, educational institutions and medical practices, would suit plural leadership but the evidence suggests that it is becoming more widely distributed than that. Denis and colleagues point out four types of plural leadership. There are teams who share leadership roles and responsibilities; top teams who pool leadership functions; leadership that, like a relay, is spread across boundaries over time; and finally leadership that is non-hierarchical and appears to be more like a web of decision-making in complex tasks.

Denis and colleagues note that most of the studies of these plural forms of leadership took place in the two decades around the turn of the twenty-first century, but that the seeds for such a focus were sown in the 1950s when C. A. Gibb (1954), an Australian psychologist, suggested that leadership 'is best conceived as a group quality, as a set of functions which must be carried out by the group' (p. 884). Robert Bales also argued in 1955 (Bales and Slater 1955) the importance of instrumental and expressive leadership functions in the context of team working, emphasising the rarity of their coexistence in an individual. Yet it took around 40 more years for this theme to be picked up vigorously.

Research reviews support the idea that shared leadership increases motivation and shared mental models facilitate the coordination of action (Burke et al. 2003; Solansky 2008). Thus, shared leadership in teams such as Boards of Directors and selling teams improves team effectiveness and performance. Denis and colleagues suggest that there is a growing assertion that shared leadership is increasingly common in knowledge-based organisations characterised by task complexity and highly qualified employees.

The examples of top teams pooling leadership functions is further exemplified by those who create co-CEOs who share authority. Google, until 2015, had co-CEOs and then announced in August 2015 that they were splitting their organisation into Alphabet and Google, appointing various top jobs. So at Alphabet, the parent company, Larry Page would be CEO, Sergei Brin would be its President, and Eric Schmidt would be the Executive Chairman.

This pooling or sharing of leadership functions was a radical response to complexity but others have been more common. In healthcare, for example, there are two hierarchies (management and medicine) and in arts organisations likewise (managerial and artistic). Each usually has its own leader who is required to collaborate with the other in a sharing of leadership functions. Such an arrangement was regarded as inherently unstable and inadvisable a century ago when 'unity of command' was considered a basic principle of management (Fayol 1917). Now, a study in the creative industries has suggested that duos and trios at the top are better at handling the external, strategic matters and internal managerial issues, despite the difficulties that confused accountabilities can cause (Alvarez and Svejenova 2005).

To illustrate the notion of a leadership relay, Denis and colleagues further cite a study in the UK NHS in which a breakthrough was created in cancer care (Buchanan et al. 2007) by four key individuals who were not in a hierarchical relationship with each other but who coordinated their efforts flexibly. They handed leadership of the initiative around the key players over time in a process which the authors dubbed 'nobody in charge'. The lack of formal authority required the individuals to be collaborative and mutually influential. It must also have required them to subjugate their egos to the needs of the project much as jazz musicians do when playing together. When the commitment to the entire enterprise outweighs individual needs, collaboration is more likely.

Finally, not all plural leadership is comfortable. It can arise out of conflict as well as cooperation. It can be taken rather than given and can emerge rather than being structured a priori. But in an increasingly complex world, the likelihood of any individual being competent across all required aspects of leadership is minimal. As Denis and colleagues put it: 'no single individual alone could conceivably bridge the sources of influence, expertise and legitimacy needed to move a complex social system forward constructively' (p. 272).

The last study cited here began with no a priori assumptions or theory to test and nor was it quantitative in nature. It simply set out to describe leadership practices deployed in six major organisations. In 2010, the Work Foundation in the UK published their empirical study based on qualitative methods (Tamkin et al. 2010). Entitled 'Exceeding Expectations: the principles of outstanding leadership', the report was based on 262 interviews of leaders who were asked to reflect on their leadership philosophy and their leadership activity. The interviews gave rise to eight broad themes which were then used to distinguish between good leadership and outstanding leadership (rather than good leadership contrasted with poor leadership). Their conclusions were threefold:

- Outstanding leaders think and act systemically. In contrast to good leaders, the outstanding leaders see wholes, move fluidly from element to element and join up their thinking and the organisation's activity. Central to this is a keen sense of purpose and their understanding of how different aspects of organisations interconnect. Purpose drives performance and the outstanding leaders both understand this and refuse to allow anything to stand in the way. They combine management and leadership into a seamless whole.

- Outstanding leaders perceive relationships as the route to performance. They give huge amounts of their time and focus to people and the climate of the organisation. For good leaders, people are one element of achievement among many. For outstanding leaders, human beings are the group that really matters, so they attend to those for whom they are directly responsible but also attend to the needs of customers, suppliers, partners, peers.

- Outstanding leaders are self-confidently humble. They realise that they cannot personally achieve any of the outcomes they strive for, so they need to achieve through their impact on people. They can only hit the target through influencing the hand on the trigger.

Many of the conclusions we can draw about leadership from the evidence seem counter-intuitive, but perhaps none more so than the power of humble and focused leadership in direct contrast to the place of charisma in the twentieth century.

Individuals: Leadership beyond Organisations

The vast majority of the literature on leadership is devoted to the leadership of groups, organisations and nations. Yet there is leadership that is shown by exceptional individuals whether within or beyond an organisation. Whistle-blowers are examples of exceptional individuals who seem hell-bent on undermining organisations when their motives are typically far more loyal than that.

Margaret Heffernan in her 2011 book *Willful Blindness* describes the intense loyalty she encountered towards the organisations that the whistle-blowers she interviewed described. Their actions were not devoted to causing mayhem but to provoking organisations to be all they could and should be. She describes the actions of many individuals in compelling vignettes: stories of everyday courage and determination. The actions of those whose high-profile cases stay in the news can cause frustration and confusion since the issues seem to be far from straightforward. Yet there are large numbers of whistle-blowers whose actions are simply laudable and brave. Heffernan's TED talk is well worth watching to remind us all of the need to speak up bravely when we see that something is wrong (https://www.ted.com/talks/margaret_heffernan_the_dangers_of_will-ful_blindness?language=en). These are stories of exceptional leadership that creates change.

There is also the story of Carol Jennings. Carol was an primary school teacher. She was born in the 1950s and raised in Nottingham in the UK. She was the only daughter of devoted parents Joyce and Walter. One day, when Carol was a young woman, she was driving while listening to the car radio when she heard the radio doctor state that Alzheimer's disease does not run in families. Now Walter, Carol's father, was one of 13 children and at least five of them, Walter included, had Alzheimer's disease.

At that point, long before the internet, Carol decided to act. Convinced that there *had* to be a form of Alzheimer's that *did* run in families, she wrote to as many neurologists whose addresses she could find, inviting them to come to Nottingham to investigate her extended family. One neurologist at St Mary's Hospital in London accepted her invitation and investigated Walter's siblings and extended family network.

As a result, he discovered that there was indeed a version of Alzheimer's that runs in families and, since then, a genetic screening test has been devised to identify the faulty gene that leads to the development of the disease. The Hollywood movie *Still Alice* depicts the situation today in which diagnosis can be specific about these matters and children can know whether or not they will contract the disease. These developments were facilitated by Carol, whose leadership was mandated by no-one and whose educational background was neither in medicine nor research. Her leadership was led by the conviction that something was wrong and that she needed to fix it.

Carol should be enormously proud of her leadership, her initiative, her powers of persuasion and the discoveries she has made possible. Yet it is not her modesty that prevents such feelings. She simply cannot remember them because she was right: Walter's form of Alzheimer's disease does run in families.

Summary and Conclusion

1. There has been a shift in the nature of leadership as societies have changed. This is best conceived as a power-shift from domination to negotiation, to inspiration, to co-creation. Followers are no longer prepared to be compliant but seek engagement and involvement.
2. Management and leadership have been distinguished on several grounds. The former deals with complexity, the latter with change. Despite the distinction, both are usually required and the distinction may be ultimately unhelpful.
3. Purpose and vision have become important. Leaders need increasingly to align their teams around a compelling view of the future and the place they seek in it for their organisations. These factors release the energy and dynamism of the people in the organisation.
4. In the twenty-first century, democratised, plural leadership is emerging as the best response to complexity, the growth of the knowledge economy and the increasing expectations of able workers for participation.

2

Leadership's Impact on the Performance of Organisations

In chapter 1, we argued that leadership has a pervasive effect on organisations. Yet this is far from universally accepted. There are still those who take the view that leadership is vastly over-emphasised when explaining the performance of organisations. In this chapter, we will consider these arguments.

Do leaders really matter? Judging by the money they are paid and the publicity they seek and receive, one would imagine the fate of great organisations lies squarely in the hands of their leaders. The inspirational vision, the motivational charm, the brilliant strategy that leaders bring must surely be the key factor to organisational success? But of course there are contrarian voices derived from many of the approaches outlined in chapter 1.

There are three significant alternative explanations for organisational success. The first is *situational* or *contingent*. Certainly the most obvious situational difference is between different sectors in which the organisation is located and differences between sectors accounts for a significant proportion of the variance in firms' performance.

Yet the situational argument is usually expressed rather differently. The argument is 'it all depends on the situation'. Churchill was a war leader; Thatcher a turnaround leader; Gorbachev a leader for the end of the Cold

© The Editor(s) (if applicable) and The Author(s) 2016
D. Pendleton, A. Furnham, *Leadership: All You Need To Know*
2nd edition, DOI 10.1057/978-1-137-55436-9_2

War; Mandela a statesman leader to move South Africa from Apartheid to universal suffrage. Examples like these are cited to illustrate the point that the characteristics of these leaders just happened to coincide with the needs of the times. They are, in short, limited to specific situations and might well be disasters in others. Thus the key to understanding their effectiveness as leaders is not to be found in the people but in the serendipitous alignment of the individual and the situation. The same is said to be true for the leaders of organisations and the best that can be done is not to appoint a great leader per se but a great leader for *now*. Not so much 'A Man for All Seasons' as a man or woman for one.

The second approach is *fatalistic*. Leadership, power, influence is really illusory. World events determine organisational outcomes. Socio-political and economic events shape company success much more than one person's charisma. A rise in the oil price, a change in EU regulations, militant unions or sudden customer disaffection can seal a company's fate irrespective of what leaders do. In this sense their power is no more than a chimera. The great leader is thus the lucky leader who simply happened to be in the top job when the happiest of circumstances emerged.

Third, it is argued that the *followers* make all the difference. It is their drive and determination which really turn the wheels, not the person at the top. A fine conductor can do little with a weak orchestra. This argument has now been explored carefully in chapter 1.

> Whether the measure is of morale, productivity or profit, leaders *can* make a positive difference.

There is even a cynical view that leaders do have real power and influence as individuals, but only to make things worse. It's a sort of one-side-of-the-coin argument that suggests that bad leaders can cause chaos and mayhem but good leaders can't (on their own) transform organisations for the better. But the data are not on the side of these doubters of leadership effectiveness. There are some excellent empirically verified case studies which show that new leaders can positively transform institutions. Whether the measure is of morale, productivity or profit, leaders *can* make a positive difference. This chapter describes the evidence for this assertion but first considers the case against.

Examples of the Case Against

In a sporting example, Keith Grint, in *The Arts of Leadership* (2000) cited the example of the management of Everton Football Club in the UK and the contribution of Howard Kendall, one of its most lauded managers. Tracking his effect during three stints as manager of the club, it is clear to see that the club's fortunes waned during these periods. In four seasons of his leadership in the mid-1980s, the club ended 1st, 2nd, 1st and 4th in the top flight of English football. In a second stint in charge, the club finished 9th, 12th and 13th. His third tenure was in the late 1990s to save the club from relegation, which he did. Kendall was welcomed back as a saviour and the club ended 18th, one place above the relegation zone. Keith Grint raises the question: how are we to evaluate his leadership? Is the performance to be attributed to the coach or the team? And how are we to take account of the fact that the team's performance also fluctuated *between* Kendall's stints in charge?

In the context of organisational performance, Stanley Lieberson and James O'Connor conducted a study of the performance of large US organisations over 20 years. They published their findings in the early 1970s. Their research examined the performance of 167 large corporations and compared the effect of leadership with other possible sources of fluctuations in performance such as yearly differences in the market, industry differences and differences between companies. They were able to estimate the size of these various influences statistically and observed that industry and company differences were far more powerful than leadership in explaining differences in sales and earnings, though leadership explained more of the differences in profit margins. They concluded that leaders have little impact on organisational performance because they are constrained by situational factors, though they admitted that there may be an interaction between the specific industry and leadership impact. In other words, they were suggesting that leaders may have an impact in some industries, but that their impact was not universal.

Typical of organisational research, there were many criticisms of Lieberson and O'Connor's research methods and almost two decades later, Alan Berkeley Thomas published a similar study correcting—as he saw it—many of the methodological criticisms of the earlier study.

He examined the performance of large retail firms in the UK between the mid-1960s and the mid-1980s. He concluded that CEOs can make a real difference to corporate performance. In a similar tradition, Jim Collins identified so-called 'Level 5 Leadership' as a particularly effective leadership style adopted by CEOs who have transformed the performance of organisations whose performance had been unremarkable for years. This was far from charismatic leadership but rather the effect of modest individuals who brought a relentless focus to the organisation.

So does leadership make a difference? And if so, how? In answer to the first question, Barrick and colleagues (Barrick, Day, Lord and Alexander 1991) demonstrated that, compared with average performing executives, high performers added a further $25 M in value to an organisation during their tenure. Nevertheless, the question of *when* leadership makes a difference is the key issue.

A more sophisticated analysis informs this debate more helpfully. Three professors at Harvard Business School: Noam Wasserman, Bharat Anand and Nitin Nohria (2010) asked 'When does leadership matter?' Using analytical techniques like those of Lieberson and O'Connor, they examined data from over 10,000 observations (from 531 companies over 19 years) and concluded that the CEO effect was significant, accounting for around 14 % of the variance in company performance. However, they also noted that this effect varied between different types of business. In some types of business, the CEO effect accounted for just 2 % of the variance (e.g., meat products and commercial banks) whereas in others it accounted for 21 % of the variance (e.g., communications equipment). They concluded that 'focussing on *the contexts where leadership matters* appears to be perhaps a more productive line of enquiry than simply asking *whether* leadership matters' (p. 56). The difference seems to be accounted for, in part, by situational issues such as the availability of opportunities and the resources by which they can be pursued. Their argument supports the notion that the difference between good and poor leadership shows up most starkly in tough times, even though the seeds of an organisation's demise might be sown in good times.

Various suggestions have been put forward to explain *how* leaders and leadership make a difference. Lord and Maher argued in the mid-1990s that the impact of leadership was potentially both direct (through feedback and instruction) and indirect (through culture and strategy). We shall see both impacts in the studies we describe later in this chapter. Hambrick and Mason, in the context of studying the development of specific organisations, proposed that the characteristics of top teams matter much more than the characteristics of individual CEOs. In our view this is a key idea, but the effect of leaders is not to be judged through the performance of the organisation alone. There is also the matter of meaning and morality, as Joel Podolny and colleagues (2010) assert. Leadership has an impact on how people in the organisation feel about and understand themselves and their lives. This is also a positive outcome and may even contribute to the motivation with which people approach their work, making a better performance more likely.

We are supportive of the indirect impact of leadership as argued by Richard Hackman: that leaders fashion and influence the context in which people work (Hackman 2010). We too argue that leadership has an effect on the bottom line—not directly, but by shaping the *culture* within which an organisation operates, its *climate* and through its influence on *employee engagement*. A great deal has been written about organisation culture but perhaps the most straightforward understanding of the culture of an organisation is 'the way we do things'. According to Edgar Schein, culture can be understood by observing the behaviour, artefacts and shared assumptions of an organisation. Job applicants judge an organisation's culture from the moment they see an advertisement for a job, even if the ad comes from a third party. Further impressions are gained from the induction process, and subsequently throughout the employee's time with an organisation. It is subject to the enduring power of first impressions and needs to be looked after by the management team with the care extended to any other asset.

Climate is 'the way it feels'—the subjective response of those who work in the culture. The climate of an organisation cannot be measured objectively. It is the product of an interaction between individuals and groups on the one hand, and the dominant culture on the other. Climate surveys can provide a guide to the climate by asking for the subjective impressions of those answering the survey. Accordingly, it can be understood and managed but it cannot be observed: it has to be experienced.

Fig. 2.1 The service-profit chain at Sears

Research into the experiences of staff in a major chain of department stores in the USA sheds light on this. In 1993, researchers at the Harvard Business School attempted to discover the reasons for variations in store profitability. Their findings are summarised in Fig. 2.1.

Good leadership is inextricably linked with the internal quality of the organisation (its culture and climate), which is then closely associated with staff satisfaction and loyalty. This is unsurprising. Similarly, it is unsurprising that customer satisfaction and loyalty are associated with greater profitability. But the interesting part is in the middle—as staff satisfaction and loyalty increased, so did productivity and therefore the value offered to customers. Thus, however else productivity may be improved, some aspects of productivity were in the gift of the people working in the stores and offices. Productivity is the gift that loyal staff give back to an employer that treats them well and creates for them a great place to work. Thus, so-called 'soft' issues, such as how people are treated, have a clear impact on the ultimate 'hard' issue: the bottom line.

> Good leadership is inextricably linked with the internal quality of the organisation.

On average, the researchers found that for every 5 % improvement in staff satisfaction, there was an increase of 1.2 % in customer satisfaction and ultimately profits went up by 0.5 %. So the impact of great leadership on the staff who experienced it led to a clear improvement in the bottom line. The sequence of cause and effect was also clear: leadership led to improved staff satisfaction and the staff improved their productivity. This in turn led to greater value perceived by customers and their satisfaction and loyalty to the stores increased, thus swelling profits.

The specific sequence here is crucial to understand. Unlike transactional processes in which the employee doing well is rewarded for his or her efforts *after the fact*, here leaders take the initiative. They first create the conditions in which people love to work and then gain the benefit of increased employee effort that is the reciprocal response to a great place to work—thus bringing out the best in people.

The Gallup organisation proposes a similar model: the Gallup Path illustrated in Fig. 2.2. Their argument states that it is fundamental in business that good managers are appointed and their strengths identified and built upon. There needs to be a fit: the right person in the right job, because good managers can (and must) engage their employees who in turn engage their customers. It is engaged customers who are happy and loyal which leads to the real goals of all organisations: sustained growth, real profits and stock increases. The *entry point* is leaders who find, nurture and develop good managers, creating the conditions that bring out the best in them.

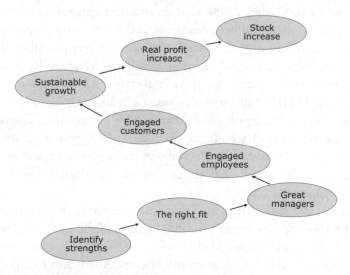

Fig. 2.2 The Gallup Path

The model has been influenced by positive psychology and the key concept *is engagement* which is as much about 'heart' as 'head'. Engagement is easy to measure but not always easy to achieve. There are many different factors that lead to employee engagement:

- A corporate culture that values outstanding and sustained work;
- Clear, consistent and relevant job expectations;
- Access to coaching, development and mentoring;
- Reward, recognition and incentive systems that are felt to be fair and appropriate

Not only is the model conceptually appealing and 'intuitively right', it has been tested and found to be robust. Thus Gelade and Young (2006) tested the model in the retail banking sector and showed that team climate leads to staff commitment which leads to customer satisfaction and which leads to sales achievement.

More broadly, the Gallup organisation in 2006 published two reports about the power of employee engagement. The first, Harter et al. (2006) entitled 'Gallup Q12 meta-analysis', examined 23,910 business units and compared top-quartile and bottom-quartile financial performance and engagement scores. They found that those with engagement scores in the bottom quartile averaged between 31 % and 51 % more employee turnover, 51 % more industry shrinkage (often used as a euphemism for theft among other things) and 62 % more accidents. Meanwhile, those with engagement scores in the top quartile averaged 12 % higher customer advocacy, 18 % higher productivity and 12 % higher profitability.

The second Gallup report published in 2006 was entitled 'Engagement predicts earnings per share'. It considered the EPS growth of 89 organisations and demonstrated that those with engagement scores in the top quartile had EPS growth 2.6 times that of organisations with below-average engagement scores.

These two and many other studies are summarised in the report commissioned by the UK Government in 2008 and published in 2009 by David MacLeod and Nita Clarke. Their brief, at the start of a major recession, was to 'take an in-depth look at employee engagement and to report on its potential benefits for companies, organisations and individual employees'

(p. 3). The report was entitled 'Engaging for success: enhancing performance through employee engagement'. In his introduction, the then Secretary of State argued that the report 'underpins what we all know intuitively … That only organisations that truly engage and inspire their employees produce world class levels of innovation, productivity and performance' (p. 1).

The report's methodology included reviewing large published studies as well as taking evidence from organisations about their own internal data and soliciting the views of academics and researchers who had made such matters their research topics. The evidence was consistent and clear.

Many of the studies were very large in scale and international in their scope. Towers-Perrin-ISR reported a 2006 study conducted globally that included opinion survey data from 664,000 employees from over 50 companies around the world: larger and smaller companies were included from a range of different industries. They compared the performance over 12 months of those companies with more and less engaged employees. They report many findings, but several of the financial differences were most striking. Among these, there was a near 52 % gap in the performance improvement in operating income over the year comparing the two groups. This comprised an improvement in operating income in the highly engaged companies of 19.2 % and a decline of 32.7 % for those with low-engagement. Thus, not only is high engagement a benefit, but low engagement is a risk.

The same impact is to be found in the public sector. The MacLeod and Clarke report took evidence from the UK Civil Service in which it was reported that departments with high engagement levels as measured through staff surveys tend to perform well in capability reviews, a key metric of departmental performance.

More powerfully, Beverly Alimo-Metcalfe and colleagues (2008) conducted a longitudinal study for three years in 80 teams in the UK NHS. They demonstrated that engaging leadership predicted productivity, morale and even the health of the team members and more powerfully than competencies. Their engagement model included, at the heart of engagement: acting with integrity and being honest and consistent. The other elements were:

- *engaging individuals* by being accessible, showing genuine concern, enabling and encouraging questioning

- *engaging the organisation* by supporting a developmental culture, inspiring others, focusing team effort and being decisive
- *moving forward together* by building shared vision, networking, resolving complex problems and facilitating change sensitively

Naturally, two questions remain. The first is this: does engagement lead to improved performance or is it the other way around (where organisations that are doing well produce higher engagement)? Evidence submitted to the MacLeod and Clarke report summarising various longitudinal studies suggests that the engagement comes first: it is a lead indicator and engagement levels tend to rise in advance of superior performance or performance increases. The second question is: does engagement improvement cause performance improvement or merely accompany it? The report answered this question as follows: '... while each of the studies indicated above, together with individual company studies, are all open to some degree of challenge, taken together they offer a very compelling case' (p. 13).

The report offers other evidence suggesting that engagement has a major impact on sickness absence, customer service, employee retention and the likelihood that an employee would recommend their organisation's products or services. The differences, comparing high versus low engagement, show effects on these crucial indices of performance that are not merely statistically significant but large. For example only 13 % of disengaged employees would recommend their organisation's products and services, whereas the figure for engaged employees is 67 % (Gallup 2003).

It was the stability of the effect that satisfied and engaged employees can have on organisational performance that influenced Bill Catlette and Richard Hadden back in the 1990s. The authors of *Contented Cows Give Better Milk* suggested a wager to financial intermediaries: that the authors would compete with the intermediaries to pick superior stock performance based on different indicators. The authors would pick stocks based on the data of staff satisfaction, and the intermediaries would pick them based on whatever other data they usually used. The problem was that the authors could not persuade any financial intermediaries to take part.

So Catlette and Hadden compared their a priori stock choice with the average increase in the market and confirmed that more satisfied employees did indeed outperform the market. They found that companies that make employees happy outgrow competitors by a 4:1 margin and out-earn them by more than 2:1. Their 1998 book summarises their thinking and their 2007 book, *Contented Cows MOOve Faster*, suggests leadership actions that can bring about the effects they describe. Consistent with the Harvard research, it bears repetition here that the sequence is significant: leaders act first by creating the conditions in which people want to work and the reciprocal gift is greater discretionary effort.

Yet there are still critics of the entire body of research on employee engagement. Principal among them in the UK is Rob Briner, Professor of Organisational Psychology at Bath University. In an article in 2014 he sets out his criticisms. He argues that definitions of engagement are poor or inconsistent, that the topic is nothing new and that the measures are neither reliable nor valid. More importantly, he is critical of the quality of the evidence cited in its favour. He describes a hierarchy of evidence from anecdotes, through commercial reports to meta-analyses and systematic reviews. He suggests that the vast majority of the evidence cited in favour of engagement's power comes from those evidence sources at the bottom of the hierarchy rather than the top: the least reliable.

Briner argues that we cannot know whether increases in engagement *cause* increases in performance, nor can we know whether interventions increase engagement and produce better performance. He argues that the proponents in this field are guilty of misclaiming and over-claiming because we tend to favour getting things done over doing things in an evidence-based way. He is right empirically, moreover, because the definitive studies have yet to be done but neither he nor anyone else is arguing that low engagement is good: that it is good to disappoint, frustrate or alienate employees and reduce their commitment. While the world of employment awaits the definitive study, action does indeed need to be taken and the balance of evidence we have, such as it is, is in favour of engagement being key to motivation and commitment.

So how does leadership make a difference to the *climate* of an organisation? Steven Brown and colleagues conducted research into the management of sales teams in a medical equipment sales company. Their 1996 research paper showed that there were six aspects of leadership that made a difference: three concerning psychological safety and three with mean-ingfulness. These were:

- Supportive management
- Clarity of expectations
- Feeling free to speak up
- Having work to do that made a contribution to worthwhile goals
- Feeling recognised for work that is well done
- Having challenging work to do

The more these feelings were experienced by the sales teams, the more involved they felt in their work. This led to greater effort—the team members put in more time and worked harder. The consequence was improved performance—these teams not only increased their sales but also their knowledge of their products and their administration. In short, everyone benefited: staff, customers and shareholders.

Now, this could lead some to conclude that the team members who put in more time and effort were increasing their stress and therefore reducing their ability to sustain such levels of work. According to the psychologist Donald Broadbent, empowering people to take control is also key. Many years ago, he conducted a study on a production line in which he first showed that stress was proportionate to the speed of the line: the faster the line was made to go, the more stress experienced by those working on it. But in the second phase of the study, he allowed the production line workers to control the speed of the belt themselves. The speed went up and the stress came down. It seemed that it was not the speed of the belt that was causing stress but rather the lack of control over the speed of the belt.

More recent research was conducted by Charles O'Reilly and Jeffrey Pfeffer in 2000 on how to get extraordinary results from ordinary people. They compared ten *pairs* of companies where products and market segments were matched, but performance and profitability varied greatly. For example, Levis and Wranglers were both dealing in denim and selling to the stylish and young (or young at heart), but one was much more successful at the time than the other.

The factor accounting for the significant difference in performance between the matched pairs of companies surprised the investigators. The better-performing company in each pair had a clear set of values, widely understood and shared by staff, and a management team dedicated to ensuring that all aspects of the company reflected the company's values. The more profitable of the pair had relentlessly aligned their managerial and human resources practices to their values. Senior management reckoned their primary role was not to make money but to maintain these values so that the making of profits was a by-product.

How Do Leaders Create this Climate?

Our reading of the research suggests that a key element is to build *trust*. This is built by consistency and contributes hugely to a feeling of psychological safety.

To build trust, it is vital that what leaders *do* aligns with what they *say*. This internal or personal congruence is one form of alignment, but not the only form. There is the alignment of the top team. The most effective top teams have learned how to disagree over issues but, once the matter has been decided, to align with each other behind the decision, trusting their collective wisdom more than their individual insights. Alignment also has to extend to the organisation's practices (and hence its culture) which need to be aligned with its declared values. As O'Reilly and Pfeffer put it:

> Partial alignment does not result in partial credit. The payoff function is not linear but exponential … there has to be alignment among all of these levers if the levers are to be real and effective.

In other words, leaders have to be consistent in what they do. To achieve trust, management must pay relentless attention to drive out any inconsistency between what they say is important and what they do, or allow to be done in their name.

The Danaher Corporation has built a huge organisation which might even be dubbed an unfashionable conglomerate, but nevertheless surely one of the most successful organisations to be found anywhere. When they take over a company they 'Danaherise' it by focusing on the relentless attention to process and getting the details right. The power of such an approach is to be seen in the spectacular growth of that company. Creating alignment is analogous to the pursuit of cleanliness in health-care. Imagine a surgeon 'reassuring' a patient by stating that the operating theatre is 85 % clean! Even small degrees of misalignment causes damage analogous to the contamination of a clean operating theatre.

O'Reilly and Pfeffer's research looked closely at ten pairs of companies. By contrast, a major piece of research by Huselid and Becker used data from four US national surveys and more than 2,800 companies,[1] to mea-sure the effect of good management practices on people's performance and therefore on profits. Examples of good practice might include involv-ing people in decisions and promoting personal development.

To produce a macro measure of productivity, the market capitalisa-tion of the companies was divided by the number of their employees. The firms were then divided into one of five groups according to how they treated their people. This was measured by the extent to which their 'HR' actions matched best practice (described a priori), although this was not merely the actions of the HR department. They were examining the broader ways in which the employees were managed and led.

The resulting graph of HR practice related to market value per employee showed an interesting profile (Fig. 2.3). Once an organisa-tion rose above those who were worst at leading and managing people, there was an instant uplift in productivity. However, to improve from this point required a great deal more effort. Leaders, it would seem, need to be relentless in their drive to improve standards and drive out incon-sistencies in the culture of their organisation. This is the Danaher effect.

What Impact Do Different Leadership Styles Have on Climate?

Daniel Goleman aimed to answer this in research published in the *Harvard Business Review* of 2000. He used data from Hay McBer on 3,871 managers drawn at random from a sample of over 20,000 for

---

[1] In fact this was 700 companies studied four times.

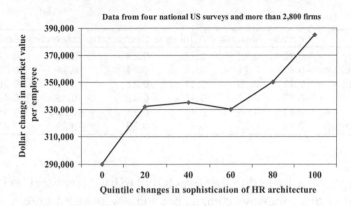

Fig. 2.3   'HR' as a source of value creation

whom they had data on both their leadership styles and the climate in their teams. He found six distinct leadership styles which he defined as:

- *Coercive*—demanding immediate compliance
- *Authoritative/visionary*—mobilising people towards a common vision
- *Affiliative*—creating emotional bonds and harmony
- *Democratic*—building consensus through participation
- *Pacesetting*—expecting excellence and self-direction (a style commonly practised in professional service firms where each partner has his or her own clients as is expected to contribute roughly the same as other partners)
- *Coaching*—developing people for the future

The researchers also defined six elements in an organisation's climate:

- *Flexibility*—feeling free to innovate
- *Responsibility*—feeling a sense of responsibility to the organisation
- *Standards*—feeling committed to high standards
- *Rewards*—feeling the rewards and feedback received are appropriate
- *Clarity*—feeling clear about the company's mission and values
- *Commitment*—feeling a sense of commitment to a common purpose

Table 2.1 The impact of leadership on climate

	Coercive	Visionary	Affiliative	Democratic	Pacesetting	Coaching
Flexibility	−0.28	0.32	0.27	0.28	−0.07	0.17
Responsibility	−0.37	0.21	0.16	0.23	0.04	0.08
Standards	0.02	0.38	0.31	0.22	−0.27	0.39
Rewards	−0.18	0.54	0.48	0.42	−0.29	0.43
Clarity	−0.11	0.44	0.37	0.35	−0.28	0.38
Commitment	−0.13	0.35	0.34	0.26	−0.20	0.27

Each of the six leadership styles was found to have a measurable effect on each aspect of a company's climate, but some were found to have a more powerful overall effect. The two styles found to have the most negative effect on climate were pacesetting and coercive, as Table 2.1 illustrates.

The other four leadership styles were all positively correlated—that is, the more a leader emphasised relationships at work, or an interest in training and developing the team, or gave them a chance to participate in decision-making, the better the climate became. The leadership style most consistently associated with positive climate was the leadership that emphasised a compelling vision towards which everyone was invited to contribute.

Naturally, leaders show more than one style of leadership, even among the six described here, but usually a leader has a core style and occasionally an alternate, but, as we shall come to see, leaders are not infinitely flexible or even as flexible as they imagine they are. Similarly, an organisation's culture tends to have a distinct or dominant flavour. Leadership style has also been found to have an impact on discretionary effort or the amount of extra effort employees choose to put in.

The debate about the impact of leaders on organisational performance can be resolved from the evidence we have seen. Avery and her colleagues concluded: '… after years of debate, the popular view that leaders impact organisations has received general research support'. We concur. The debate has now to shift to matters of how this works and what can be done to enhance the effect.

Laurie Bassi and Daniel McMurrer, writing in the *Harvard Business Review* of 2007, cite evidence of a variety of positive effects brought about by improvements in leadership and other drivers of human capital management. They were able to demonstrate improvements in sales and safety in a manufacturing organisation, and even improvement in educational test performance in relatively disadvantaged South Carolina Schools in Beaufort County. Their measures included the leadership practices described in Table 2.2.

Helpfully, their study was prospective. They measured the extent of the practices one year and the effects the next: a higher research standard than merely correlating at the same point in time. They demonstrated

Table 2.2 The contents of leadership practices

Practice	Comprises
Leadership practices	• Open and effective management communication • Collaborative management that seeks employee input • Managers and Executives who remove obstacles, provide feedback and inspire confidence • Leadership development that is structured and systematic
Employee engagement practices	• Work that is well organised and utilises employees' skills well • Jobs that are secure, and in which employees are recognised and advanced through the organisation • Workload that allows employees to do jobs well and enables good balance between work and home • The continual monitoring and evaluation of employee engagement
Knowledge accessibility practices	• Ready availability of job-related information and training • Encouragement and enablement of teamwork • Sharing of best practice • Systems that make information easily available
Workforce optimisation practices	• Well-defined work practices and effective training • High performance is expected, rewarded and supported by appropriate working conditions • Employees are chosen on the basis of skill; new hires complete a thorough orientation • Effective employee performance management systems
Learning capacity practices	• New ideas are welcome • Training is practical and supports organisational goals • Employees have formal career development plans • Leaders demonstrate that learning is valued • Various aspects of training are automated through a learning management system

Is There a Place for Coercive Leadership?

There certainly is: in a crisis. In order to land a jumbo jet at some major airports, airlines have to show that they can get all the 400+ passengers out of the plane in 90 seconds. No airline will do this in a participative way: you'll never hear 'Who'd like to go first?' Orders are given and everyone follows them willingly.

Similarly, when working with the top 300 officers in the Hong Kong Police, we asked how they handle this. They were clear about two matters: first, the norm has to be non-coercive and officers have to be recruited who are not naturally coercive. Second, teach the officers how to handle a crisis. So, there is real clarity in their minds. It is not at all easy to persuade a natural bully to change his or her ways.

Crises demand directive leadership in the short term. The rest of the time, a different approach is required.

that not only did those who scored well in the various practices do well in the dependent measure (sales, safety, school performance, etc.) but also that those who improved in the practices between two occasions also improved in the dependent measure. The differences were major: for example 60–130 % greater improvement in sales compared to the groups whose practice scores increased the least and 10–30 % in safety.

The Impact of Leadership on Employee Engagement

We have seen how leadership has an impact both on the organisation's culture, and on its climate, and through these effects, on the productivity of the organisation. Several of these effects are very straightforward: people choose to work longer and harder. Other straightforward effects are that engaged people simply turn up to work more often and tend to stay in their jobs. Evidence from a major review by Gallup (published in the *Gallup Management Journal* 2006) makes this crystal clear. They summarised data from 1.7 million employees. Their findings are presented in Table 2.3. Woody Allen's argument that 90 % of success comes from just turning up would find some support here!

Table 2.3 Employee engagement and productivity

	% of workforce	Absenteeism (days per year)	Annual staff turnover costs (£M)
Engaged			
Loyal and productive	17	4.67	6.97
Non-engaged			
May be productive but not bonded to the organisation	63	5.95	11.48
Disengaged			
Unproductive/destructive influence	20	10.68	31.00

Gallup: From the *Gallup Management Journal* 2006. *n* = 1.7M employees.

The effects are easy to understand. There are real costs and opportunity costs in finding new employees, training them and allowing them time to get up to speed. Employees who have been around for a while are better networked, quicker to find the answer to their questions, know who to call for information and so on. On balance, the longer employees stay around, the better it is for everyone.

More recently, IBM, citing their big-data database of around 4.5 million employees surveyed each year from 2008–12, assert that fully 70 % of employees are engaged and only 12 % disengaged. In their report, authored by Jeffrey Jolton and Brian Hayes (IBM 2014), entitled 'Big data helps bust the top three myths of employee engagement and leadership', the IBM Smarter Workforce Institute claim that engagement is holding steady at these high levels. Yet the very discrepancy between these two studies suggests that Briner's argument may be right that engagement studies frequently work with different definitions. Yet the IBM report also pointed to the effect a leader or manager can have on engagement. They pointed out that a toxic manager can do positive harm to engagement and that 'leaders' ability to focus energy on an inspiring mission is key to driving organizational success via the alignment of employees to this vision' (p. 6).

However, there are two types of engagement of an employee with an organisation—emotional and rational. The more favourably employees feel about an organisation, the more likely they are to stay with it. Research from the Corporate Leadership Council (CLC) in 2004 found this to be a sizeable effect. Their study showed that employees who felt strongly engaged with an organisation were 87 % less likely to want to leave than disengaged employees. So what are employees looking for from leaders in their organisations? The rewards that motivate them—and thus encourage greater engagement and discretionary effort—are less connected to money than an employer might think.

The CLC report claims that, for employees, the most important aspect of their working life is the impact of their immediate line manager and his or her leadership style. The IBM big-data report (IBM 2014) disagrees. It claims that the effect of the immediate manager on engagement has been overemphasised and that the biggest impact on engagement is the leadership's future vision, though the CLC report spoke of the direct manager characteristics and the IBM report addressed the manager's effectiveness. These are different issues and this difference may account for the different findings.

The full range of impacts on discretionary effort, estimated statistically from their pooled data by the CLC in 2004 were as illustrated in Fig. 2.4. Organisation culture, the areas of induction focus and the perceived qualities of the senior team, all had their impacts. The characteristics of the work itself and opportunities for learning and development were also significant, and all these effects dwarfed even the combined effects of compensation and benefits, though these financial effects were not irrelevant. It may be that, from the moment of induction—when the organisation's values are first conveyed—everyone notices the degree of consistency

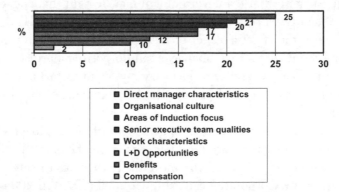

Fig. 2.4 Estimated impact on discretionary effort

Table 2.4 Ranked drivers of employee engagement

Leadership future vision	1	1	1	1	1
Recognition	4	3	2	3	2
Quality and customer focus	4	6	5	5	2
Diversity and inclusion	2	5	5	3	4
Growth and development	3	3	2	5	4
Collaboration involvement	4	2	2	2	4
Ethics and corporate governance	4	6	8	10	7
Performance management	9	10	7	7	7
Creating change	4	6	8	7	9
Open communication	9	6	8	10	9
Leadership living values	11	10	8	7	11
Manager effectiveness	11	10	8	10	11

between the promise and the reality. Dissatisfaction, or disengagement breeds in the gap between the rhetoric and reality. The more congruent an organisation is with what it states it believes in, the more an employee will trust the organisation. The same is true of individuals.

For IBM, the ranked drivers of employee engagement are as shown in Table 2.4. They recommend a shift away from the immediate manager's impact to the impact of the senior managers who need to lead by example, create and communicate a powerful vision of the future of the organisation and the employee and seek to focus everyone's energy on it.

According to the Gallup book *Strengths Based Leadership*, what employees expect from their leaders are: trust, compassion/care, stability and hope for the future. These are qualities employees look for irrespective of a leader's style. These are the elements that underpin employees' commitment to an organisation, and if employees commit to an organisation, the benefits in terms of lower costs and improved productivity are clear to see.

In contrast to the studies that aggregate data, straightforward examples of engaging leadership and the effect of engagement on performance can be observed directly. One such example, at the Fairmont Lake Louise hotel in Western Canada, occurred in September 2015. At breakfast in the Gold Lounge, an elderly gentleman said quietly to his wife that he was disappointed that there was no bacon on the buffet that day. Andrews, a waiter,

(continued)

overheard this and immediately beamed a big smile and offered to get the gentleman some freshly cooked bacon, even though it was not on the buffet menu. The man was delighted and, five minutes later, the bacon appeared without charge since the buffet was free to Gold members.

One of us (DP) observed all this directly and sent a congratulatory note to David Roberts, the Regional VP for Fairmont in Western Canada, and this triggered a sequence of events such that, within a few hours, David Roberts had congratulated the GM of the hotel who had congratulated and thanked the Gold Lounge manager and all of them had thanked and recognised Andrews. In addition, they took the decision to have bacon on the buffet every day. No-one *had* to do any of this. The gentleman was not complaining. Subsequent investigation discovered that Fairmont in Western Canada take service *leadership* so seriously that they train everyone in it and have a leadership coach at the Lake Louise hotel, Sonya Flood, who is passionate about her role and purpose.

Service leadership of this kind is a role, not a position, and the guests benefit. Neither is it left to chance: a great deal of time and effort is invested in ensuring that service priorities are clear and developmental investment is made in the people who serve the guests, their supervisors and managers.

Summary and Conclusion

1. The evidence is now overwhelming that leaders and leadership have significant impacts on organisations—on culture, climate, employee engagement, productivity, customer satisfaction and ultimately on profitability.
2. The power of employee engagement is large and pervasive, though there is considerable room for improvement in the evidence base. Yet, if leaders can get engagement right, many virtuous consequences are likely to follow for all stakeholders.
3. The evidence suggests we should take leadership and its development seriously if we want our organisations and people to thrive.

Understanding the impact is just the beginning, however. Chapter 3 shows what leaders can do to engender trust, exhibit care or compassion, provide stability and offer a sense of hope to those they lead.

3

The Primary Colours of Leadership

In chapter 2, the part played by culture and climate in the success of an organisation and the impact of the leader on these and other organisational features were explored and supported from research. This chapter switches from an emphasis on previous research and thinking and starts to outline more of our own ideas and propositions.

Here, we develop the Primary Colours Approach to leadership, exploring further the three domains of an organisation in which the leader's influence is felt and illustrates how specific leaders have functioned in the three domains during the course of their leadership.

There are four propositions in the Primary Colours Approach:

- The first concerns the *territory* of leadership which we describe by reference to the Primary Colours Model of Leadership
- The second asserts that most leaders are *incomplete* so that it is extremely unlikely that any individual leader will become excellent in all aspects of leadership
- The third describes two different kinds of strengths and limitations so that any leader wanting to develop needs to *choose carefully* and realistically where development effort is most likely to yield results

© The Editor(s) (if applicable) and The Author(s) 2016
D. Pendleton, A. Furnham, *Leadership: All You Need To Know*
2nd edition, DOI 10.1057/978-1-137-55436-9_3

- The fourth suggests that leaders need to work in teams made up of colleagues whose differences are *complementary* to his/her own.

In this way, we illustrate how incomplete individuals have been able to provide complete leadership by putting teams with complementary leadership talents around themselves. We shall also see how dangerous it can be for leaders either to try to be complete in themselves or to put around them only similar, rather than contrasting, contributions.

Deborah Ancona at MIT and her colleagues have described a similar idea in their February 2007 *Harvard Business Review* article 'In praise of the incomplete leader'. They suggest that effective leadership comprises four capabilities:

- *Sense-making*—understanding the context in which a company and its people operate, identifying the complexities and explaining them to others.
- *Relating*—building trusting relationships with others.
- *Visioning*—coming up with a compelling image of the future by collaboratively articulating what the members of an organisation want to create.
- *Inventing*—developing new ways to bring that vision to life.

Ancona and her colleagues argue that:

> Rarely will a single person be skilled in all four areas. That's why it's critical that leaders find others who can offset their limitations and complement their strengths. Those who don't will not only bear the burden of leadership alone but will find themselves at the helm of an unbalanced ship.

The idea of using broader domains to understand leadership is not new. Hogan and Warrenfeltz (2003) maintain that every existing competency model can be captured within the four domains described by Warrenfeltz. These are:

- the *Intrapersonal Domain*, which comprises internalised standards of performance and contains such personal qualities as courage and integrity
- the *Interpersonal Domain*, which is essentially about social skills and hence contains listening and negotiating, communication and political savoir faire

- the *Business Domain*, which comprises the technical knowledge to plan and monitor and coordinate organisation activity
- the *Leadership Domain*, which is essentially about influence and team building and so contains such competencies as communicating vision and setting direction.

In contrast, we want to provide a framework which is different in content but follows the idea of domains in which other descriptions can be placed. We do not want to include the intrapersonal domain at all, since we believe this is of a different nature entirely. We do not deny its importance or relevance but we suggest that it is of a different nature: a precondition for many elements of effective leadership but not essentially what leadership comprises. We believe that the framework we are proposing is conceptually clearer and shows the extent of the overlap between the domains. It is based on understanding what leaders have to *do*: the TASKS of leadership.

The Primary Colours Model of Leadership

Our research and consulting experience of working with leaders over many years leads us to argue that there are three domains in which leadership operates: the strategic, operational and interpersonal domains.[1] Visualise these domains by reference to a human being:

- The *strategic* domain acts like the head: it makes sense of what is going on, envisages the organisation's future and creates plans to take it forward. Its principal capability is a creative intelligence.
- The *operational* domain represents the hands and legs: it gets things done, achieves results and drives the organisation forward. Its principal capabilities are determination or will power and puzzle solving intelligence.

---

[1] The notion of primary colours is a metaphor that works best in this context with reference to the additive primaries of light rather than the subtractive primary colours of pigments. The idea is that, as the three colours are added, pure white light is created and we contend that, as the three domains are added, leadership becomes complete.

Fig. 3.1 The Primary Colours of Leadership

- The *interpersonal* domain is like the heart: it is where feelings reside and relationships are maintained. Its principal attribute is the ability to form and sustain relationships: occasionally called emotional intelligence.

David Pendleton has dubbed this model the Primary Colours of Leadership, since we propose that most leadership competencies are made up from these three underlying capabilities.

It is illustrated in Fig. 3.1. This image provides a way of visualising these three areas or domains in terms of overlapping circles of influence, each of which represents a different primary colour. The domains we describe are similar to the idea developed by Steve Radcliffe (2008) which he described as 'Future, Engage, Deliver'.

The Strategic Domain

In the strategic domain (or the head), *sense has to be made* of the context in which the organisation resides. The key task in the strategic domain is what we have called *Setting Strategic Direction*. The external environment can be understood in many different ways but a PEST analysis illustrates how this might be done formally: by understanding the political, economic, social and technical environment. Based on careful understanding of the external environment, forceful features may be identified that exercise a particularly powerful effect or demand on the organisation. These are the compelling influences to which an organisation must respond in order to be successful.

The task here can be likened to constructing the emerging story of the environment in which the organisation is working. The task is part deductive and part inductive: seeing the world change and spotting the emerging trends. It involves being clear about how the world is changing and showing that picture to the organisation so that the future, which is inherently unpredictable, can be anticipated *to some extent* so that it does not seem so bewildering or overwhelming. The aim is to reduce some of the uncertainty for most people in the organisation, even for short periods of time, so that effort can be focused.

In a study in 2014 of more than 150 CEOs from all over the world, Oxford University's Saïd Business School teamed up with Heidrick and Struggles to consider the challenges facing those charged with leading the world's businesses. One of their findings they dubbed 'ripple intelligence': the ability to sense complex and changing factors in their environments and attribute to them the appropriate significance so that their organisations can anticipate their impact and get ahead of the game. This is a key element in the strategic domain to do with *Setting Strategic Direction*. It is a kind of contextual intelligence on the basis of which responses can be formulated. They also argue that developing this ability might require letting go of the operational orientation that characterised and enabled the CEO's rise to the top. This is a scary prospect: a journey into the critically important but largely unknown new world of strategic thinking.

The Case of Innocent

Innocent is an ethically oriented food and drinks company known for its smoothies. It was founded by Richard Reed, Jon Wright and Adam Balon, who identified a need among fellow workers for an easy way to make each day a bit healthier. The simple idea was to create food and beverages in which every product contains 100 % pure, fresh ingredients. They set out self-consciously to be different and have demonstrated that with a non-corporate attitude, a sincere commitment to the cause and creative thinking, it is possible to create a successful company that acts responsibly.

(continued)

Innocent takes uniqueness into fresh territory (if you will forgive the pun). They cover their delivery vans with AstroTurf to illustrate their green aspirations and have as a logo an apple with a halo. Their HQ is called Fruit Towers and in it they use wooden furniture because it is sustainable. They seek to live their values at all times: Responsible, Entrepreneurial, Generous, Commercial, Natural. They sit together irrespective of job titles so that hierarchy seems irrelevant and organise social events for everyone in the company who are encouraged to bring their families along to have fun together.

They give 10 % of their profits to charity. They make a virtue of informality and yet in the early twenty-first century they have become the UK's fastest-growing food and drink company and have won many outstanding business awards. Perhaps the most impressive fact about Innocent is that their values and ethical credibility has largely survived a major buy-in by Coca Cola who acquired 18 % in 2009 and 58 % in 2010.

Consider the airlines. Every few years, or so it seems, the economic and political environment, for example, requires airlines to consider the parlous state of the economy and their paper-thin operating margins, the massive cost of aircraft replacement, the need for consolidation in the industry, the impact of the green lobby on the acceptability of aircraft pollution, the demand for inexpensive and plentiful international travel, the volatility of the cost of airline fuel and many other influences. The leaders of airlines have to make sense of this in order to create a strategy to take them forward. This takes place in the strategic domain. One airline with which we have worked recently has determined that the operating conditions occasionally favour a full-service business class which can be sold at a high profit, but at other times in the economic cycle, the pressure is created to trim out all superfluous elements of service and offer rock-bottom prices. This is making sense of the operating context and market conditions. Having done so, a strategic response can be fashioned.

Determining the *purpose* for which the organisation exists is also part of *Setting Strategic Direction*. Walmart's purpose has always been to make it possible for less-well-off people to buy the same things as wealthier people. That is the idea around which the organisation was created. Just after the Second World War, Sony set about working to a different purpose: to change forever the world's perceptions of Japanese goods being of poor quality. Looking back from the twenty-first century standpoint, it is hard to believe that this was ever a problem because Sony, and many other Japanese companies, have successfully achieved this purpose. Occasionally, product recalls such as those of Toyota cause a temporary re-evaluation, but the perception of Japanese goods is of their being high quality.

Vision is also created in the strategic domain. Vision is a compelling view of the future and the place the organisation wants to occupy in that future. However it is derived, it has to be powerful in its effect if it is to be worthy of the name 'vision'. Few organisations have a really powerful vision: they seem to have become lost in straplines and lip service. For many, a powerful vision is no more than a plaque on a wall or a marketing device, but for others it is their very lifeblood. For many years, the Johnson & Johnson Commitment (called the J & J Credo) was so important that their CEO made regular visits to their plants and offices worldwide to run 'Credo challenge meetings' in which anyone was allowed to challenge the extent to which the company was living and operating consistently with the credo. The credo was a mix of vision and values.

> For many, a powerful vision is no more than a plaque on a wall or a marketing device, but for others it is their very lifeblood.

Other visions have been pithy statements of audacious goals. Few will forget the vision for NASA given to them by John F. Kennedy at the start of the 1960s: to put a man on the moon and return him safely to earth by the end of the decade. A decade earlier, Boeing had given themselves a visionary task of becoming the dominant player in commercial aircraft and of bringing the world into the jet age.

The point about visions is that they paint pictures. They appeal to the imagination like the chorus at the start of Shakespeare's *Henry V*. They are seldom data rich or logical but aspirational and inspiring. They seldom involve numbers, since numbers are seldom inspiring although the drive to be Number One is sometimes deployed as a vision. William Van Dusen Wishard put it like this: 'Vision is seeing what life could be like while dealing with life as it is. Vision deals with those deeper human intangibles that alone give ultimate purpose to life. In the end, vision must always deal with life's qualities, not with its quantities.'

Mission is related to vision. The word derives from the Latin verb 'to send' and missionaries have always been sent with a clear purpose to achieve a goal. An organisation's mission is its medium-term agenda. It is the focus for its activities over several years in support of its vision. Occasionally, these mission statements are simple, straightforward and aggressive, defining a common enemy. 'Crush Adidas' motivated Nike in the 1960s. 'We will destroy Yamaha' was the battle cry of Honda in the 1970s, for Canon in the 1980s it was 'Beat Xerox', while 'Kill Kodak' worked for Fuji.

Other organisations deal with the matter of purpose, vision or mission differently and very originally. For Harley-Davidson, one executive famously defined the purpose of the organisation as to provide the opportunity for a 43-year-old accountant to wear black leathers, drive through midwestern American towns and have people be afraid of him! Virgin Atlantic have at times stated that their purpose is to allow their customers to have fun at 37,000ft. And Starbucks have defined their purpose as to provide a third place (after home and work). All these statements are located in the strategic domain and are part of *Setting Strategic Direction*.

The organisation's *values* also live in the strategic domain. They are the guiding principles and ethical standards that will help the organisation solve problems and navigate a sustained course in good times and bad. Cynics might argue that values are the indulgence of organisations going through easy times but they are best observed when the organisation is in difficulty. The story of Enron confirms that they are as relevant in good times as bad and such stories as BP's handling of the oil leaks in the Gulf of Mexico and the response of the big banks to paying bonuses during the major financial troubles of the 'noughties' bring these issues into the twenty-first century.

The acid test of whether values matter to an organisation is to be found in the organisation's reactions to tough challenges. The reaction of Nestlé to concerns over the marketing of baby milk and the reaction of Johnson & Johnson to the contamination of its products were bold, values-based responses. A cynical counter-argument can be made that these reactions were really commercially driven but the leadership challenges implicit in dealing with multi-stakeholder organisations are considerable. No undiluted focus on any single group of stakeholders will last in the longer term. Even a belief that the customer is king is simplistic. Leaders have to recognise that any significant group of stakeholders (customers, shareholders, employees or the communities in which the businesses are located) can do harm to an organisation if their interests are not served. An organisation's values have to reflect these realities and be credible to all. Headquartered in The Netherlands, Ahold is a major force in retailing on both sides of the Atlantic. It maintains a triple focus on stakeholders at all times in order to get better every day. It aims to be a better place to shop, a better place to work and a better neighbour.

> Leaders have to recognise that any significant group of stakeholders (customers, shareholders, employees or the communities in which the businesses are located) can do harm to an organisation if their interests are not served.

Indeed, values and purpose ideally come together. Those organisations which for years have placed the creation of shareholder value at their core have more recently had to turn to efforts under the heading of corporate social responsibility (CSR) to create a countervailing force to the relentless drive to increase margins. Some have done this for entirely laudable reasons. Others have been driven by more cynical motives: *we may exploit our customers and staff but we'll do something nice so that our PR people can have a good story to tell about us*. Certainly, companies involved in CSR have carried out worthy projects and many do considerable good in areas unrelated to their main work.

Recently, Harvard Professor Michael Porter and his colleague Mark Kramer have argued for the creation of shared value, rather than just shareholder value (*Harvard Business Review* 2011). The idea here is that businesses are beginning to move in a different direction: towards more ethical practice and sustainability. They are seeking a business model that does actual good for *all* its stakeholders in the longer term. This is the creation of truly shared value rather than favouring one stakeholder group over the others. It is a choice about a new way of thinking and operating in all aspects of the business and is reminiscent of the distinction between dieting (episodic and temporary) and a genuine and permanent lifestyle change. This debate is at the heart of *Setting Strategic Direction*.

Naturally, the strategic domain is also where strategy itself is decided. *Strategy* is, as defined by the *Oxford English Dictionary*, 'a plan designed to achieve a particular long-term aim'. The strategic domain is where a leader or leaders prepare and plan for the future, define its journey and set its course. In the days of the cattle drives, a simple strategy might have been to keep the herd moving west, thus defining north and south as irrelevant and east as counter-productive. In organisations, strategies integrate the organisation's various functions and divisions, stretch over longer periods of time and identify the key priorities that enable important choices to be made.

Once set, the purpose, vision, mission and values become the rallying cry of the organisation, and the strategy its high-level plan. They give its existence both a meaning and a mandate. They become the broad aims to which other people can subscribe: the reason to join, stay with or leave an organisation. The process of building commitment to the organisation's aims is what we have called *Creating Alignment*. Alignment is the shared basis of engagement with the organisation: specifically the act of lining up together behind a common purpose or goal. It is based on rational communication and logical persuasion on the one hand, and on passion on the other: a matter of hearts and minds. It is aided by imagination and excitement about what could be. Creating interpersonal alignment is a matter of involvement, influence and persuasion and, once achieved, liberates the energies and enthusiasm of the entire working group in addition to that of the leaders. Other forms of alignment are more technical, such as alignment of investment, systems and processes with purpose and strategy, but alignment is always crucial. In the model, we refer to the alignment of the people in the organisation with the strategic direction, values and plans it is pursuing.

When the *Guardian* newspaper in the UK wrote in their business section about Nike in 2003 they said this: 'Nike is the real deal. These guys are jocks. They are the happiest in the locker room. Phil Knight is driven by a love of sport but not necessarily a love of business. Anyone who has visited the Nike corporate campus knows immediately – these guys are real jocks!' They were describing an organisation that had created alignment to release and realise the power of their collective efforts. They had everyone facing the same way and working towards their goal.

In physics, the difference between a 40-Wwatt light bulb that can barely light a small closet and a 40-Watt laser that can punch holes in metal is the alignment of the electrons. When they are aligned, their effect becomes amplified. When they move at random in a myriad of directions, they function inefficiently and their effect is small. Our view is that the alignment of people with purpose and with each other has a similar amplificatory effect.

As strategy is broken down into its linear steps, and timelines are created around its tasks, it becomes the first element of *Planning and Organising*, which keep the organisation on track. They embody the focus around which the work is arranged and help everyone understand the size and nature of the tasks that have to be achieved. Planning is the first element of performance management as plans become objectives, targets and tasks. Organisation is its twin: ensuring that structures, processes and procedures are created that support the achievement of the plan. There is no such thing as good organisation in its own right: the quality of organisation is determined entirely by its appropriateness for the plan it serves.

The Operational Domain

The operational domain represents the 'hands and legs' of an organisation. Its goal is to achieve results. Indeed, it could be argued that the goal of the entire organisation is to achieve results, but not just any results: those that serve and advance the organisation's purpose. *Planning and Organising* belong as much to the operational domain as the strategic domain. The higher-level the plans, the more they are a part of the strategic domain. The more plans are broken down into objectives and tasks, and as timescales shorten, the more they reside in the operational domain. There is no strict dividing line between the two, merely a matter of degree as two colours in the spectrum cannot be strictly divided; yet there is a point in the spectrum where the colour is clearly blue and another clearly green.

Delivering Results represents the ability to drive work through to completion. It is hard edged and determined. Its skills are tempered in steel and its methods robust. It is a challenging and forceful aspect of leadership that asserts, drives, completes. It also acknowledges that motivation has to be sustained and so it may celebrate success and deal with performance shortfalls, but it is not soft. It is the most transactional part of leadership and is embodied in the performance management process.

Team Working acknowledges that organisational life is seldom made up of solitary contributions. Team working holds out the possibility of synergy: that the team may become so adept at working together that the whole becomes greater than the sum of the parts. Leaders who value team working have first to keep their own egos under control and have to model the cooperation they want to see in others. It is an irritating cliché that 'there is no I in team'; there is no I in ego either, but it is still a problem that has to be eliminated! Many great leaders have learned this through team sports in their formative years.[2]

The emphasis on team working is twofold: team and work. Team membership carries considerable advantages as Michael West and colleagues have demonstrated at Aston University (Borrill and West and colleagues 2002). They have been able to show that there are significant gains in employee satisfaction, innovation and even in the mental health of team members to be gained from effective team working. But the emphasis is clearly on getting work done and realising significant gains in productivity.

The Interpersonal Domain

The interpersonal domain encompasses the 'heart' of an organisation: the way it feels to work in an organisation is its climate and it is set by the actions of the leaders. When *Creating Alignment*, the effective leadership team will appeal to hearts and minds creating both rational and emotional commitment to the organisation and its journey. This is why creating alignment sits at the intersection of the strategic (head) and interpersonal (heart) domains. *Creating Alignment* recreates the power of the true amateur who loves his or her enterprise (from the Latin 'amat' meaning he/she loves).

Team Working is also at a point of intersection between domains: the operational (hands and legs) and interpersonal (heart) domains. The matter of discretionary effort illustrates why. Discretionary effort is the effort

---

[2] See the descriptions of Sir Rod Eddington and John Rishton in chapter 6.

that does not have to be given, but is given because the individual chooses to do so. Whenever we lecture about this in classes of executives at the Saïd Business School at Oxford University or elsewhere, we ask them to imagine that the minimum acceptable level of work represents 100 on a hypothetical scale of unknown length, and then ask how much more could someone put in if they were totally committed? The answer on this hypothetical scale usually varies between 150 and 300. It is through creating alignment (engagement) and team working that the commitment builds and discretionary effort increases. Napoleon considered one motivated soldier was worth three unmotivated soldiers (hence 300 on our scale). Notoriously, he would shoot a few to encourage the others, but these days HR might have something to say about that!

Building and Sustaining Relationships is the epitome of the interpersonal domain. Leadership is as much to do with who we are as what we do. It is hard to trust an organisation or a cause, but we may trust people when we get to know them. Relationships may be with colleagues, customers, suppliers, shareholders or the community in which the organisation resides. Relationships with all stakeholders need to be built and sustained over time. They will work best if they are also perfused with the same values, standards and behaviours. Indeed, shared values may even be a condition of entry into an organisation or team.

Leading

Where all three domains in the primary colours model overlap, they form a central zone where the essence of leadership can truly be said to reside. The Primary Colours Model is all about leadership and leadership in general is the fulcrum that sits at the core of the organisation and around which the organisation turns. At the core of leadership is the act we have dubbed leading. To follow the anthropomorphic analogy—if the strategic domain is the head, the operational domain is the hands and feet and the interpersonal domain is the heart, then leading is the nervous system: it senses, provides balance and coordinates the other functions.

Leading balances the other leadership contributions in response to the demands of the situation. As the orchestra conductor may encourage the strings to play louder in some passages and the woodwind to stop playing for a while, so *leading* may call for a great deal more short-term results being delivered at one time, and rather more investment in developing people at other times; it may push a decision through rapidly to facilitate action at one time and insist on taking time to build commitment at another; it may call for more and more thorough planning at one time and greater strategic clarity at another. This is a matter of judgement based on further sense-making and as these various phases are implemented, leading may pass the baton to different leaders to take advantage of their respective leadership strengths.

We propose that, in this central zone are five core *enablers* of leadership which facilitate all the other activities. These are to inspire, focus, enable, reinforce and learn. We will describe these in detail in chapter 4. However, as we shall also go on to see later in the book, it is hard for any individual person to excel in all these enablers. The reasons are essentially psychological, and Gallup, in their 2008 review of more than 20,000 interviews with senior leaders, more than a million work teams, 50 years of polls about the world's most admired leaders and a study of more than 10,000 followers, concluded that the most effective leaders surround themselves with the right people since, 'while the best leaders are not well rounded, the best teams are.'

The same applies to the three domains in general. Some people are good at strategy and at discerning the big picture. They tend to be massively bright and expansive in their thinking. Some are good at operations. This calls for a different mindset—one that is concerned with practicalities, knows what to do, when and how much. They tend to be sequential thinkers and highly focused and determined. Some are good at dealing with people—they know instinctively what matters, how to treat people, and how to put themselves in other peoples' shoes. They have high levels of interpersonal insight: awareness and sensitivity mixed with good judgement and social skills.

We shall argue in chapter 5 that people who become expert in these different domains have often developed by taking rather different journeys in life. Finding one person who is expert in all three domains is rare indeed, as the following case studies illustrate. The first is a fictionalised figure from history but the rest are leaders we have known.

Case Study 1: An Emperor of Ancient Rome: S+, O+, I–

Julius Caesar, described by Shakespeare as a flawed military and political genius, demonstrated great strategic skill and military operational excellence. However, he allowed his ego to grow to the point where he no longer listened to those who really cared about him. He was warned about the ides of March, was warned by his own wife not to go to the Senate on that fateful day and alienated many who had recognised his achievements. In our terms he could have been described as S+, O+, I–; recognising his strategic and operational excellence whilst acknowledging his interpersonal flaws. Julius Caesar illustrated beautifully Peter Drucker's aphorism: strong people always have strong weaknesses.

Case Study 2: A CEO of a Mobile Phone Company: S–, O+, I+

When, in 2001, British Telecom sold its mobile communications arm, BT Cellnet, the market believed that the company was unlikely to survive, let alone thrive. The CEO was Peter Erskine and he and his team renamed the company O_2, rebranding the organisation as cool, blue, fluid, life-affirming. Four years later, in 2005/6, O_2 was one of the most successful organisations in the UK, and was bought for £18B by Telefónica of Spain.

How was this extraordinary turnaround brought about? Peter Erskine himself, in an open lecture delivered at Oxford's Saïd Business School, put it down to the team he had assembled around him. This was more than the usual public modesty expected of successful people: Erskine was much more specific. He listed his own skills: in marketing, in forming effective relationships, in communicating and inspiring faith in the organisation, and in driving performance. He asserted, to put it in terms of our model, that while he was very good at the operational domain, and possessed excellent interpersonal skills, he was not so gifted at strategy, though marketing *was* an area of competence for him. His mantra, often repeated, was operational: deliver, deliver, deliver.

As a result, he described how he made sure he employed someone as strategy director who did possess those strategic skills. And importantly, he ensured that the person with the strategic skills (that he recognised were not so strong in himself), was enabled and given opportunities to make his voice heard. In fact, he put around himself a team of strategy and finance professionals who complemented his own skill set. He acknowledged both his strengths and his limitations and he took account of both. Peter Erskine was, in our terms, describing his own profile as S–, O+, I+ (not great strategically, but good operationally and interpersonally). He was also modelling the general principle of leadership excellence: a frank and honest self-appraisal followed by deliberate action to create a complementary team.

Case Study 3: A Technology Start-Up: S+, O–, I+

A new technology company, spawned out of discoveries in materials science at Imperial College London, was created to realise the potential of combined heat and power. This new company, Ceres Power, appointed a hugely bright CEO, Peter Bance, who understood the potential in the science and became a powerful advocate and champion of the dream behind the organisation. He was greatly skilled in strategic thinking and in communicating the possibilities inherent in the science. In order to create the company, the dream had to be sold long before there was product on the shelves. Bance's talent was essentially strategic and interpersonal. He was much less skilled operationally but made it his job to assemble around him those who were. He identified technologists, operations experts and finance professionals who would complement his own ability to build and sell the dream. Bance's talents would be described as S+, O–, I+, but the team as a whole had all the complementary talents required to make the organisation successful although the technology simply could not be made to work commercially. Consistent with his talents, however, Peter has gone on to form another new technology start-up having spotted a gap in the energy market and is assembling his team of complementary colleagues to help him lead it. This time, however, original discovery is not on the critical path to success.

Case Study 4: A Team in Trouble: Too Many S–, O+, I–

An engineering-based company had experienced difficulties in its top team. Its MD was due to retire within a year and it had three dominant members of the top team who frequently clashed. Each was an expert in his or her field and each was greatly valued. The difficulty was that each had a similar profile: S–, O+, I–. There was no complementariness among these three, rather, there was great duplication of their leadership contribution and they were locked in a Darwinian competition for the hard-driving results deliverer niche in the ecology. They were not separated by their differences but by their similarities. The issue was temporarily resolved when one left the organisation and the other team members together reached a facilitated agreement to observe a code of conduct. This, according to the MD, made a huge difference but the problem was finally and permanently solved only when one of the remaining two became the new MD and the other disputant left to join another company as FD where he is thriving.

Case Study 5: A Multinational: S+, O+, I+ Together

One of us (DP), heading a team of psychologists in a programme of leadership development for a large multinational organisation, has conducted in-depth analyses of the leadership skills of the top 50 executives in Europe and North America. The executives, from some ten countries, were assessed as leaders against the seven areas of competence described by the Primary Colours Model, plus their ability to cope with pressure. The executives were scored by the team of business psychologists on a scale of 1–5, ranging from poor to excellent, with three representing the level required by an executive at their level to be considered fully competent in a world-class organisation.

Each of the 50 executives was given eight scores in all, and each score was verified and calibrated by at least two further psychologists on the consulting team. This process of quality assurance and peer review represents best practice in our field. The overall mean score among the 400 scores given was greater than 3, indicating that this group was of a high standard as leaders. However, of these 50 people, only ten received an outstanding rating of 5 in any of the eight areas measured. And of these ten people, despite their excellence in some areas, seven of them scored 3 in one or more area, meaning they were no higher than one might expect in those aspects, and three were below the required standard of competence—scoring less than 3—in one area.

We also considered each division's leadership team as a whole using the same criteria. Again, this showed clear evidence of areas of excellence in all the teams, but this was not evenly distributed across all team members. In leadership teams where some of the individuals had low scores for certain criteria, the overall performance of the team could still reach above the standard required, provided there were others in the team whose skills could compensate. The leadership teams needed each other's skills for their leadership to be complete.

This is the value of complementarity—for leadership teams to perform well as a whole, it is much more effective for their members to excel in one or two areas, to recognise this, and to work with others who are excellent in different areas. Indeed, it is our view that it is better for top teams to comprise people who are excellent in one or two areas, who recognise where they are not strong, and who seek out colleagues in their team who compensate with different areas of excellence. The key is a degree of modesty, maturity and mutual respect to make such an approach effective.

The Heptathlete and the Duck

The alternative is to fail to learn from the heptathlete. Heptathletes have to run, jump and throw in seven events and their training causes them to compromise their running for their jumping, their jumping for their throwing and so on. The consequence is that seldom is a world record held in any one of the seven events by a heptathlete. The exceptions are the long jump and hurdles, but each is already the fusion of two of the seven events (running and jumping). To put it more memorably: consider the duck. According to an Argentinian saying, ducks can walk, fly and swim, but none very well. We urge leaders not to emulate the duck but to push for excellence in a more realistic range of leadership contributions!

Summary and Conclusion

1. Leadership may be conceived as comprising three domains described by the Primary Colours Model: the strategic domain, the operational domain and the interpersonal domain. The domains are not independent: they overlap, and at the heart of this model is the function of balancing and coordinating the other leadership contributions. We have dubbed this core Leading.
2. Many other competency models of leadership can be subsumed within the Primary Colours Model. We suggest it represents the deep structure of leadership whereas typical competency models represent alternative surface structures. Such a deep structure makes other models comparable by reference to a common root.
3. Fulfilling all the requirements of leadership at a high standard calls for an almost impossible combination of skills and attributes from one individual, though it is entirely possible for a *team* of leaders operating together.

In the next chapter we will find out in more detail about the five core enablers of leadership. In chapter 5 we will describe and explore ways of creating and maintaining complementarity in leadership teams.

4

Five Enablers of Leading

In chapter 3, we described and defined the Primary Colours Model of Leadership. The model describes the three domains in which leaders operate—the strategic, the operational and the interpersonal domains. We also looked briefly at five enablers of leadership that lie at the centre of the model: the area we have called leading. These are each described by a single verb—*inspire*, *focus*, *enable*, *reinforce* and *learn*. This chapter explores in more detail how the enablers are translated into leadership behaviours.

Inspire

Inspiration has an intellectual component and an emotional component. A leader has to be able to show that he or she understands the business context, can read trends and knows how to direct an organisation. Intellect orientates an organisation and shows it the direction in which it needs to go. Inspiration will not happen if data are thin or if arguments weak and lacking in substance. The more capable and better educated the senior team members, the stronger their demand for intellectual rigour.

© The Editor(s) (if applicable) and The Author(s) 2016
D. Pendleton, A. Furnham, *Leadership: All You Need To Know*
2nd edition, DOI 10.1057/978-1-137-55436-9_4

In certain types of organisation, cultures are created with intellectual rigour at their heart. The British Standards Institution (BSi) is such an organisation: it contains many scientists and technologists at the fore-front of their professions whose task is to help define quality standards in a broad range of technical specialist fields such as medical devices. Rolls-Royce (RR) is another organisation in which their proud heritage and reputation for cutting-edge technology in aerospace, marine and power systems has attracted the best in their fields. The National Institute for Health and Care Excellence (NICE) is a third such organisation, setting standards for healthcare in the UK. All organisations in the knowledge economy are alike in this respect.

Inspiration has an intellectual component and an emotional component.

Inspiration also contains a powerful emotional component. Leaders will not be able to galvanise and inspire people unless they are to some extent inspired themselves. The leader has to connect with the feelings of the workforce, and be able to appeal to those feelings if people are to become motivated to buy in to change. Inspiration demands passion as well as thought in order to win hearts and minds. It demands authentic-ity. This is also true at BSi, RR and NICE, where passion is expressed not in gushing emotions but in fierce determination and commitment to their causes where only the best will do. No-one could seem less emo-tional on the surface, for example, than Dr. Colin Smith, Engineering Director at Rolls-Royce, but it is impossible not to sense the passion with which he speaks about and leads the team of scientists and engi-neers he has assembled. His is a passion backed by fierce intellect, as illustrated by the clutch of honorary doctorates he has received includ-ing an Oxford DSc.

In order to inspire, leaders also have to be trusted. Leaders cannot buy trust, and neither can people be trained in it. If leaders are to inspire, they must be sufficiently credible, confident and trustworthy in order to inspire confidence, trust and commitment in others. These responses have to be genuine: leaders have to show people that they are worthy of it. It is a matter of authenticity since most people detect insincerity or inauthenticity rapidly.

In Box

Exercise: Thinking About the Things That Inspire You

Who inspires you? What inspires you? Is there an image that stands out for you? Is it an act of courage, compassion, brilliance? Is it a piece of music, a play or a visual scene? It is important to know where our inspiration comes from so that we can reconnect with it when we need to do so.

Sharing our sources of inspiration in a team can build understanding between team members. Try it in your team.

Finally, how will you inspire your team, department or organisation? It is unlikely to be by pursuing a number, even if it is a stretch. We tend to be inspired by life's qualities rather than its quantities. Winning or being the best can inspire, but they are getting rather tired. An excellent civil servant with whom we have worked, Robert Footman, coined the term 'serving the community' and used it to inspire a generation of civil servants in Hong Kong in the 1990s. BAE Systems claim that their aim is to protect those who protect us. Disney has as its aim to make people happy. So how will you inspire your people?

What inspires trust? We believe there are four constituent parts. The first is *competence*: it is hard to trust anyone who is not competent. Competence is not sufficient but it is necessary especially in the workplace. The second is *care*: we have to believe that the leaders care for something more than themselves—ideally the organisation and its vision and people. Competence without care can be harsh and breeds cynicism. The third is *consistency*: we need to believe that the leaders will not change radically from day to day or from event to event. We need to know that their behaviour yesterday was a reasonable guide to their behaviour tomorrow. Finally, there is *courage*: leaders have to be prepared to stand for something firmly and not be put off by difficulties or opposition. Together, these qualities make up the integrity and coherence that inspires trust.

It is acceptable to set out on a difficult journey so long as we can show that there is some reason to believe that it is worthwhile, that we might complete the journey successfully and that we will lead it with integrity. In this way, leaders engage their followers and build commitment to the journey. Empirical support for these contentions comes from research conducted by the CLC in 2004 which, having analysed pooled data from a number of companies' surveys, concluded that there were two kinds of engagement—rational and emotional—and these factors played different roles. Rational engagement was associated with the intention to stay in an organisation; emotional commitment was associated with contributing more discretionary effort. Hearts *and* minds needed to be engaged in order to gain the maximum benefit: to get good people to stay and also to strive to contribute to the best of their ability. So, inspiration stands on two feet: intellect and passion. Intellect orientates. Passion motivates.

Jim Collins, in his 'Level 5 Leadership' article in the *Harvard Business Review* of 2001 explained that his research had led him to conclude that 'breakthroughs require a simple understanding of … what a company can be the best in the world at, how its economics work best, and what best ignites the passion of its people." Intellectual understanding makes clear what a company can be best at and how its economics work best. Passions are matters of the heart.

Focus

It is not enough for a leader to be inspirational—employees also need to know where to place their effort for maximum effect. Leaders have to have the ability to focus their organisation's work. A leader has to transform enthusiasm and passion in their workforce into results.

Providing focus has an impact on a wide range of activities from building strategy and developing plans and objectives, through to daily operations and attending to priorities. This task requires sometimes mundane but critical attention to objectives, priorities, plans and schedules. Those who are best able to help people focus tend to be detail-orientated, methodical and disciplined. They value clarity and pursue it. Their contributions may seem anodyne, but they are essential. Without focus, effort is dissipated, efficiency falls and people become exhausted from unproductive activity. They lose confidence and trust in their leaders and in themselves as they see the unproductive consequences of unfocused effort. They become like the powerful car that cannot get traction on the road, spinning its wheels, burning rubber and fuel but failing to create movement.

Focus has not only to be established but also maintained over time. There are many external factors that can reduce focus: competing priorities, the tyranny of the urgent, emergencies and disasters all play their part for reasons that are understandable and may be defensible. Other factors are within us: our enthusiasm for new projects, our need for variety, our intolerance of repetition or routine, our distaste for bureaucracy. Yet leaders who maintain their focus are more effective than those who do not. Jim Collins' 'Level 5 Leaders' (cited above) epitomised focus and created spectacular success after years of mediocre performance. This is also characteristic of the Danaher Corporation in the USA where their Danaher Business System (DBS) establishes and maintains a relentless focus on the vital priorities.

Our own research (Pendleton 2010)[1] suggests that people who focus tend to be good at planning and organising. This requires problem solving, sequential thinking, and breaking complex challenges into bite-sized pieces. More than that, they are conscientious and disciplined. They keep their eyes on the distant goal while maintaining their sense of priorities in the shorter term. The danger for them is that they become rigid: unable to change a plan or shift their focus as situations change significantly. Yet their great strength is that they embody the principle that a mediocre strategy brilliantly executed is likely to be more successful than a brilliant strategy poorly executed. Focusers execute well.

We agree with Heifetz and Laurie (*Harvard Business Review* 2001) that:

> a leader must sequence and pace the work. Too often, senior managers convey that everything is important. They overwhelm and disorient the very people who need to take responsibility for the work.

Enable

Leaders who have inspired their organisations and provided clear focus need also to ensure that their people are *able* to do what is required. Enabled people have the mandate, resources and skills they need to act. Enabling people allows leaders to focus on processes and attend to such

---

[1] Internal research validating a Primary Colours-based 360-degree feedback questionnaire showed that ratings of how well a leader was able to focus loaded highly on a factor comprising questions on planning and organising (Edgecumbe Consulting Group, January 2010).

matters as delegated authority, budgets, training, employee numbers, skill mixes, talent management and succession. It also prevents micro-management. In this way, leaders ensure that their people can deliver what is required of them, now and in the foreseeable future. So focus ensures that people are clear about what they need to do and when, and enablement ensures it is possible.

> focus ensures that people are clear about what they need to do and when, and enablement ensures it is possible.

Empowerment was a mantra for delegation in the 1990s and became both a source of enthusiasm and frustration. Enthusiasm was created when previously highly controlled and able people were allowed more say in how their work was done. Customer service gurus recommended putting discretion into the hands of those who were closest to the cus-tomer. Yet frustration resulted when those who were poorly trained and who had a loose grasp of the organisation's goals made poor decisions and gave away profits needlessly. When considering how empowerment should be done, it is clear that there should be no empowerment without enablement.

But should there be empowerment at all? And, if so, how are we to take enablement sufficiently seriously? The answer lies in the strategy, structure and values of the organisation. In retail organisations, a no-quibble return policy may work well. It was one source of Nordstrom's reputation in the USA and store employees were empowered always to use their best judgement to serve the customer. Yet British Airways' CEO from 2000 to 2005, Sir Rod Eddington, had to curtail empowerment because the airline was a networked carrier where decisions needed to be optimised centrally. On a rainy afternoon in London, he explained this to the top 300 managers in the organisation and related the explanation to the successes and failures of the airline over the preceding ten years. The rapprochement between these two extremes is in the nature and structure of the organisations. Both tactics were right for their organisa-tions at the time.

The best example of empowerment that is both appropriate and enabled is Tony and Barbara Laithwaite's Bordeaux Direct: founded in the UK and now trading in many other countries. Bordeaux Direct was the pioneer of selling wine remotely (by mail order, internet and telephone). They have become the model for many other 'Direct' businesses. They empower their front line call centre staff to please their customers and will exchange wine with which customers are dissatisfied courteously and without any fuss. Their customers are delighted by this as the authors can testify through personal experience. Yet they are also enabled by technology and systems. The customer who has had such discretion offered by the staff member also has his or her account marked in case a pattern should emerge that needs to be dealt with differently. Everyone wins: the staff are empowered and enabled, the customer is happy and the business is not troubled by anyone repeatedly acting selfishly. To make this work, the company also ensures it employs wine enthusiasts and then trains them well.

It makes sense that leaders who empower and enable their people do so in a manner that suits and is consistent with their purpose, vision, mission, strategy and values. They equip their people to handle the discretion they are given and support their actions with guidance, encouragement, technology and systems. The exception here is leaders themselves. Leaders tend to be self-empowering. They are prepared to do what they consider to be right for the organisation and take the consequences. Leaders who complain they are not being empowered need to redefine themselves as followers! Empowerment is ultimately a matter of alignment with the purpose and strategy the organisation is pursuing and yet it will not work at all without enablement.

Mary Gledhill, writing in the *Times* newspaper in 2008 put it well:

> In a large company, being in charge means taking responsibility for the performance of the business as a whole, not micromanaging at project level ... Leadership is about enabling a company to achieve more than one individual, however talented, ever can.

Reinforce

Employees who do what is required for an organisation can reasonably expect their leaders to appreciate and reward their efforts appropriately. They can also expect that if colleagues do not contribute anywhere near as much as others, or fail to contribute at all, those colleagues will be dealt with appropriately. In this way a leader creates a 'moral' organisation in which the consequences for different contributions are defensible. In this way, good performance is rewarded, people who are struggling are helped and persistent poor performers are removed. This convinces the workforce that a leader can be trusted. Leaders who do this well tend to be disciplined and organised, warm and positive, firm and decisive. They are attentive to individual differences in performance, keen to give praise and recognition and to celebrate successes. They are also generous, giving praise where it is due rather than finding a way to claim credit themselves.

Reinforcement is not solely to do with remuneration but is a part of performance management in general. There is considerable evidence (Sachau 2007) that, once someone reaches an average salary level, offering them more money is no longer a motivator. Instead, a leader can add to rewards in other ways, by giving opportunities, awards, praise and thanks. It is still likely that Herzberg's (1975) suggestion is true: that money and other hygiene factors may be more powerful in explaining dissatisfaction than satisfaction, at least for those who are not impoverished.

Yet employees often underestimate the effect of money on their motivation (Rynes et al. 2004). So what is a leader or leadership team to do? The answer is: create a system of recognition and reward that is appropriate to the business they are in. Reward as a whole has usually to match the market, but using pay and bonuses alone as motivators soon runs out of steam—the money ceases to motivate and an inevitable escalation takes over. The psychological principle supporting these thoughts is the principle of satiation in which an overused reinforcement ceases to be effective. The salutary implication is: if money is the only reward, there has to be a great deal of it.

The 2004 report from the CLC estimated the size of various effects on discretionary effort. Salary and benefits had significant effects but, combined, their effects were no greater than the opportunities the organisation provided for learning and development. By far the largest impact, however, was the relationship with the immediate line manager (see chapter 2 in this volume).

Of course, work can be its own reward. For many professionals and enthusiasts, the satisfactions are intrinsic, just as having to compromise standards is a stressor and a disincentive. But extrinsic reward is also powerful for most people and leaders need to understand these matters and apply them consistently: rewarding successes, taking on difficult issues rather than shirking them and using disciplinary procedures where necessary.

Finally, leaders are not just responsible for doing these things themselves, but for creating systems that embed such actions in an organisation's culture. The appeal of working for an organisation that understands individual motivation and applies its standards and reinforcements consistently is considerable. Failure to create and deploy these reinforcements fairly depletes trust, and those who have a choice tend to leave such organisations or such managers.

Case Study 1: The Hong Kong Police

In a leadership seminar for the Commissioner of the Hong Kong Police and his top 300 officers in 2006, we discussed the recent World Trade Organization talks which had been marked by protests from Korean farmers on the streets of Hong Kong. At the seminar, we spotted an officer with his arm in plaster. The man had been commanding a unit during riot control operations and had put his safety at risk in the line of duty. I asked him what his leader could do to make it worthwhile for people like him to take such risks. The officer replied that his superior had simply put a hand on his shoulder and said 'Thank you very much'. The leader's gesture demonstrated to the officer that the leader had noticed the officer's actions and appreciated them. The officer offered his superior's actions as a great example of doing exactly the right thing to reinforce and reward him. He neither wanted nor expected any more.

Case Study 2: Renaissance Man

Physician John Horder was a former President of the Royal College of General Practitioners in the UK. He was also an excellent organist and talented watercolourist. When one of us worked with this gifted man at the King's Fund College in the 1980s, he noticed that John wrote small cards to recognise people for points well made in meetings or speeches delivered well. This simple, sincere action could have taken John no more than 30 seconds, but was always hugely appreciated by the recipient.

Learn

The idea of a learning organisation has a great deal to commend it. In some ways, it is impossible for an organisation NOT to learn, since organisations are staffed by intelligent people who notice the consequences of actions taken. But some organisations go out of their way to ensure that learning takes place at all levels as frequently as possible. Other organisations and teams seem to create norms by which people rush from task to task with hardly a backward glance and make a virtue of their action orientation. Yet a learning organisation, team or individual sets aside time for review and reflection before embarking on a new task. Michael West and colleagues at Aston University Business School have demonstrated that this 'reflexivity' pays off in increased performance in teams (West 1994).

In many safety-critical organisations, the leaders seek to create a no-blame culture to encourage people to own up to their mistakes and share information about them so that people may learn from them. For many years, the *British Medical Journal* carried an occasional column called '*Mea Culpa*', in which doctors who had made mistakes were encouraged to write anonymously so that others may learn from their errors and prevent *maxima culpa*. Yet all organisations experience both successes and failures and it is possible to learn from both. Even when performance is reviewed, the process tends to focus on learning from mistakes when it is usually much more helpful to focus on successes and to understand how they occurred so that those steps can be repeated. Learning from successes is also positively motivating as well as insight building.

Leaders serve their organisations well by building the organisation's capability to learn. They ensure the growth of insight and intelligence as their experience grows and the market changes. How better can they equip the organisation to deal with new challenges? Yet modelling is also a powerful learning mechanism and leaders who want to create learning organisations have to show their personal commitment to their own continued learning and development. Such leaders tend to have a relentless dissatisfaction with the status quo and challenge everyone at all times to raise their game, including themselves. In The CEO Report (2015), the Oxford University and Heidrick and Struggles researchers noted of their 150 CEOs: 'To maintain their edge in times of complexity and change,

CEOs commit to sustained renewal, continuously seeking ways to reignite their own development in "life-cycles" of personal growth.'

Charles Handy argued in 1991 that 'the learning organisation can mean two things: it can mean an organisation which learns, and which wants its people to learn. It should mean both ... Learning organisations want everyone to learn always and bend over backwards to make that obvious.' We agree.

> **Case Study 3**
>
> Warren Bennis and Burt Nanus, in their outstanding 1985 book *Leaders: The Strategies for Taking Charge*, recount an old story of when James Watson was CEO of IBM. The story goes that Watson, who took a personal interest in the graduates he recruited, was about to brief an intern about his next project, despite the fact that the intern had lost the company $10M in his last project. The intern interrupted Watson to confirm that he was not being fired. Watson, an inveterate champion of learning, replied 'Fire you? I've just spent $10M educating you!'
>
> The story does not go on to explain how Watson handled matters of accountability, or how well he tolerated second mistakes, but the point was still well made. The resonance of such a story is still powerful after several decades.

Five Leadership Enablers Taken to Extremes

Enablers are meant to be facilitative but is it possible, as popular wisdom asserts, to have too much of a good thing? There are many reasons to believe that it is. Two examples of this thinking come to mind: one from the arts and the other from psychological science.

Richard Olivier is the famous son of a famous mother (Joan Plowright) and father (Laurence Olivier). He has created a business educating twenty-first-century leaders about leadership by teaching the stories of William Shakespeare and other great wisdom stories. Improbable as that sounds, the effect and the process are hugely successful. His theme of 'Inspirational Leadership' is taught through the story of *Henry V*. In it, he outlines four different leadership archetypes demonstrated by Henry through the play. There is the Warrior (dynamic and masculine), the Good King (static and masculine), the Great Mother (static and feminine) and the Medicine Woman (dynamic and feminine). The Warrior challenges everything and creates action, the Good King creates order, the Great Mother nurtures and the Medicine Woman is visionary and creates change. Each of these different personae had to be adopted by Henry at different stages of his leadership journey because of the forceful features in the current situation.

Olivier (2001) suggests that there is also the potential for each archetype to go wrong. Each leadership style, overplayed, becomes counter-productive and obstructive. The Warrior can create conflict and become a tyrant. The Good King can become a bitter and obsessed with detail, bureaucratic, rigid and cynical. The Great Mother can encourage ego-centrism and become a Devouring Mother. The Medicine Woman can become addicted to change, causing confusion: a Mad Woman.

We have also mentioned *Why CEOs Fail*, an excellent book by Dotlich and Cairo (2003) and based on the Hogan Development Survey. The research underpinning this work suggests that, under pressure, or in unguarded moments, we may all be prone to various over-reactions that transform a good characteristic such as imaginativeness, into an unhelpful characteristic such as eccentricity. Olivier's contentions derived from studying Shakespeare and Jung are supported by academic research into personality disorders embodied in the Hogan Development Survey. The latter is based on the descriptions of personality disorders listed in the *Diagnostic and Statistical Manual* of the American Psychological Association (DSM4). In all cases, the contention is the same: too much of a good thing is bad. In the same way, the five leadership enablers—*inspire, focus, enable, reinforce* and *learn*—can become counter-productive if driven to extremes as illustrated in Fig. 4.1.

'Inspire' Overplayed

Inspiration creates excitement, idealism and confidence about what is possible. But on a bad day, the inspirer, pushing inspiration to extremes, simply overwhelms people. They disorient their colleagues and cause confusion. So much seems possible and important that no-one knows quite what to do, or certainly what to do first; and this can be as harmful to

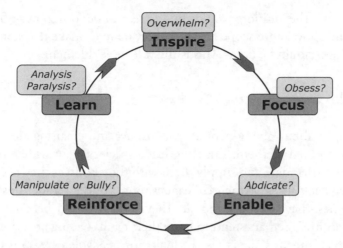

Fig. 4.1 The enablers taken to extremes

people in an organisation as not having any inspiration at all. Everything can be made to seem so important that no-one knows quite how to prioritise.

To reiterate Ronald Heifetz and Donald Laurie cited earlier: 'A leader must sequence and pace the work. Too often, senior managers convey that everything is important. They overwhelm and disorient the very people who need to take responsibility for the work.' Heifetz and Lawrie were implying that the antidote to unconstrained inspiration is a healthy dose of focus: but not too much, as we shall see next.

'Focus' Overplayed

Focusing is all about sequencing and prioritising. It is about getting things done, planning in detail, making the steps clear and doing what is required. But when pushed to an extreme, focus can become rigidity, inflexibility and obsessionality. Caught in the grip of extreme focus, leaders will assert that there is only one way of doing things and the plan has to be followed even when the circumstances change. They will obsess over detail and lose sight of their objectives. If leadership at its best is about doing the right things, an overly focused leader descends into micromanagement and supervision. The antidote would thus appear to be to step back from the detail and allow more scope for the subordinate to make decisions about how things should be done. This is the role of enablement.

'Enable' Overplayed

Enabling is about giving people scope to act and ensuring they can do what is required of them. Enabling leaders delegate, provide employees with a clear mandate and supply them with the resources they need. They then step back and give their colleagues room. But if a leader pushes that to extremes, they step back too far. They abdicate. They become remote, appear uninterested and tend to leave their teams feeling abandoned and vulnerable. This mistake is easy to make for benevolent reasons to avoid interfering. The desire to help people grow by giving them stretching challenges and letting them stand on their own feet is where it starts. There are several antidotes to this particular excess but one powerful example is to stay sufficiently close to colleagues to welcome updates and to help them celebrate successes. This is the role of reinforcement.

'Reinforce' Overplayed

Reinforcement is the creation of appropriate consequences. Successes need to be celebrated and underperformance diagnosed so that wilful failure can be disciplined and difficulties helped, but if a leader pushes reinforcement too hard, he or she can turn people into cynics. They appear to operate with the assumption that colleagues will only do what is required because they receive rewards. Many colleagues will work hard out of a genuine enjoyment for the work: so-called intrinsic motivation. In this circumstance, reward from elsewhere is at best irrelevant and, at worst, patronising. There are many conscientious folk who work hard merely because they have a strong sense of responsibility or do not want to let their colleagues down. In these cases, it is the person that needs to be appreciated rather than the behaviour.

Extreme positive reinforcement can also become manipulative, hoodwinking people into doing what they believe to be inappropriate.

The banks immediately before the 2008 financial crisis had become overly reinforcing. They had created such huge bonuses that they tempted their employees to abandon common sense and their values in order not to miss the gravy train. Being overly severe on underperformance, on the other hand, can turn the leader into a bully. They can become so dictatorial that they create a culture of fear and obedience. Thus, there are dangers in over-reinforcement of either kind: positive or negative. One powerful antidote is to engage people in reviewing their *own* work in order to learn.

'Learn' Overplayed

Learning and reflection are at the core of continuous improvement. Whether by formal reviews, informal reflection, or the meticulous analysis of data, learning needs to be systematic and time needs to be set aside for it. But if a leader pushes analysis and reflection too hard and too far, it prevents, delays or otherwise hinders action and becomes paralysis by analysis. Under these circumstances there develops an unhelpful norm and no-one is prepared to do anything unless they have clear evidence that this is the right thing to do.

Learning and reflection are at the core of continuous improvement.

Empirical evidence is a powerful ally but its absence is not necessarily an enemy. Hunches need to be tested and originality encouraged. If an action is unprecedented or genuinely innovative, there will be little evidence to support it. Pilot studies may be initiated and experiments created to test an entirely new idea: an idea that may have come from innovative flair or inspiration.

Summary and Conclusion

1. We propose that five leadership enablers sit at the centre of the Primary Colours Model. These are: inspire, focus, enable, reinforce, learn. It is unlikely that any individual will be able to perform at the highest level in all these aspects of leadership.

2. The enablers can be overworked to harmful effects. The antidote to overplaying any of them is usually to move on to the next.
3. The elements of leadership we are proposing cannot be cherry-picked. They have to be practised together if they are to be effective. This requires complete leadership: the collective leadership of a true leadership team acting in concert.

Organisations need complete leadership. The challenge is not how to lead teams, but how to help teams to lead. In the next chapters, we will examine how leaders become better suited to certain leadership contributions, how they can recognise their own strengths and limitations and how they might ensure complementarity in their leadership teams.

5

The Improbability of Being a Complete Leader

This chapter is in two parts. The first part describes three arguments why logically, empirically and psychologically it is improbable that an individual leader will be extremely good at all aspects of leadership. Not only does common sense suggest the improbability of this; in addition, awareness of the facets that make up personality and the evidence from many thousands of interviews we have conducted with top executives support this view. The second part describes three different types of jobs and three journeys that lead people to them. It provides further support for the contention that the various elements of leadership require different skills and are likely to appeal to different sorts of people. If we are right, the implications are profound.

Part One: Three Arguments

Logically

People do not usually excel in a wide range of tasks that require skills diametrically opposed to each other. We would not expect a rugby prop forward or a nose tackle in American football to excel at ballet or even

© The Editor(s) (if applicable) and The Author(s) 2016
D. Pendleton, A. Furnham, *Leadership: All You Need To Know*
2nd edition, DOI 10.1057/978-1-137-55436-9_5

the high jump. As we mentioned in chapter 3, heptathletes do not hold world records in their single events. The world records in the single events go to specialists. We pointed out that heptathletes have to run, jump and throw: each type of event requires a specific musculature and skills and yet the skills and abilities required for running tend to compromise the throwing ability and likewise with the jumping events. The world records go to specialists because they have not had to compromise in any way.

We have described the three domains in which leaders have to operate: the strategic, the operational and the interpersonal and seven leadership tasks defined by the three domains. There are specific capabilities required in each domain and task and these are quite different from each other as we have described in chapter 3. Similarly, we have described five leadership enablers which do not appeal to the same people and nor do they easily coexist. Let us take as examples to *inspire* and to *focus*.

Inspire

People who are inspirational tend to be big-picture people: forward looking, optimistic, imaginative. They often think in pictures and speak in metaphors. They may be imprecise but they will outline what may be possible and enthuse about where organisations could go. Their call to the imagination is not just a matter of communication: inspirational communicators seek to connect with the imaginations of their audiences so that the audiences' creativities might be awakened by the same possibilities. Inspirers want to take their listeners imaginatively to the place they are describing long before the listeners can experience it in reality. Inspirers generally recognise the power of imagination in the same way that radio broadcasters taunt those on TV: on radio the pictures are better. Inspirers want people to see in their mind's eye first.

Inspiration is typified by the speech on the eve of battle in Shakespeare's *Henry V* as described and explained by Richard Olivier in *Inspirational Leadership* (Olivier 2001). Henry knows that his army is in peril. They are on foot, surrounded and hopelessly outnumbered by fresh and mounted French troops and Swiss mercenaries. The English army is exhausted and depleted. Henry paints a picture for his soldiers of the war stories they will tell their grandchildren, friends and neighbours on future eves of St. Crispin's Day, recounting their tales of derring-do. He does not reassure them or tell them they will be victorious, but asks them to imagine themselves there. In order for them to tell their tales, they must have survived and must have been victorious. He, like other visionary leaders, wants people to close their eyes and see the possibilities. Nobody can know if this is how Henry addressed his troops but this approach was clear in Shakespeare's mind and this 400-year-old interpretation of the 600-year-old story still speaks to audiences today since it captures a crucial element of truth: the persuasive power of the call to imagination. This is inspiration, eschewing the facts and emphasising the possibilities. Imagine.

Activities that inspirational leaders engage in include:

- Delineating an imaginary future
- Drawing pictures with words
- Suggesting possibilities

They speak as if unconcerned with practicalities. They are happy taking a leap of faith, and comfortable with the sort of 'discontinuous thinking' Charles Handy describes:

> Discontinuous change requires discontinuous thinking. If the new way of things is going to be different from the old, not just an improvement on it, then we shall need to look at everything in a new way.

Having painted the picture of a better future state, inspirational leaders ask, 'Wouldn't it be great if we could get there?' Their concern is not with journeys but destinations. They work back from where they want to be. Their speeches move between the present and future frequently: back and forth until the future is clear and seems impossibly appealing, despite there being no plan in place to get there. On YouTube, Nancy Duarte illustrates this beautifully with respect to arguably the greatest modern inspirational speech: 'I have a dream'. The mindset being expressed is pictorial, emotional, fervent and irrepressible. It approaches the future through imaginative leaps.

Inspirational leaders ask, 'Wouldn't it be great if we could get there?'

Tony Tyler, the Director General of the International Air Transport Association (IATA) headquartered in Geneva understands this principle well. The former CEO of Cathay Pacific Airways, he arrived at IATA in 2011 to discover that the organisation had urgent need of a new strategy to galvanise its people and align their efforts. He had spent almost his entire career in the airline industry and knew the marketplace and its requirements from personal experience. The industry was relatively safe and secure but needed to become much more sustainable: more profitable. He posed this conundrum to IATA in a vision statement which proposed that IATA had to become a source of innovation and change in the industry to serve their clear and shared goal of helping create an industry that was safe, secure and profitable. This became the start of a strategy defining process that involved a large number of people in the organisation and which still guides their activities today.

Focus

Contrast the inspirational personality with people who are skilled at focusing and getting other people to focus. They think sequentially, taking one step at a time. They work forward systematically from the present to where they want to be. They are concerned not with what is possible but what is practical and able to be achieved. They deal in reality. Leaders who are good at focus do not want to leave people excited and yet unclear. On the contrary, they tend to use language that is anodyne, orderly and pragmatic. They are concerned with facts, details and deliverables. Their language is logical, their planning incremental and their attitude determined rather than fanciful.

> Leaders who are good at focus do not want to leave people excited and yet unclear.

These are two completely different mindsets and it is extremely difficult at the same time to be both focused and inspirational. Whereas inspirers are evangelical and passionate; focusers are systematic and disciplined.

Inspirers approach the future in imaginative and radical leaps, where focusers approach the future in small and incremental, systematic steps. Neither is better, but they are different: different and complementary.

Empirically

When assessing executives in major organisations around the world, we have sought to understand and describe their strengths and limitations as leaders. We have also attempted to describe how they work best: how their personalities interact with their experience to provide skills for leading their organisations.

Over a period of more than 25 years, we and our colleagues have assessed thousands of executives and we have yet to discover a single executive, however successful, who is outstanding in all aspects of leadership. We find people who are *competent* across the board, but big organisations require leadership that is above average, even world-class, in order to compete with other multinationals.

To become *excellent* in some areas, leaders have generally left other capabilities relatively undeveloped. Indeed, we have noticed that CEOs and their team members are seldom rounded people. Gallup have also observed that, while the best leaders are seldom well rounded, the best teams are (Gallup 2008) and that the best leaders surround themselves with the right people and build on each person's strengths. Our experience echoes that of Oxford University's CEO report that those who have achieved the ability to think strategically have frequently had to leave behind the operational orientation that brought them to their senior roles.

The journey from the most junior levels to the middle of most organisations is frequently made by eliminating errors and shortfalls in performance. But the journey to the top is made by developing one or two capabilities to the highest standard. In terms of the Primary Colours Model, by the time most senior managers have made it to the top of their organisations, they usually excel in one domain, are competent in a second domain and struggle in the third. But this is fine so long as they can work alongside others whose capabilities are complementary.

Table 5.1 A new approach to leadership at the top

The old deal	The new deal
Individual responsibility for unit performance	Collective responsibility for corporate performance
Independent units pursue separate business strategies	Interdependent unit heads integrate corporate strategy and value creation
Financial managements and controls; delegation of strategic choices	Transparent measurements demonstrating how interdependencies improve performance; substantive strategic dialogue by the top team
Functional and unit-specific expertise	Overlapping experience and responsibility
Results-oriented: emphasis on outcome control	Values-oriented: emphasis on normative control (promoting internalised rules for behaviour)

In an important study published in 2007 in the *Harvard Business Review*, Yves Doz and Mikko Kosonen lent weight to this argument. They researched a dozen large companies around the world to discover what made a large company strategically agile: able to change its strategies rapidly and repeatedly in response to changes in the marketplace but without major trauma. What they discovered was that such companies had created a new approach to leadership at the top. They described the different elements of the new leadership that add up to fostering mutual dependence as in Table 5.1.

Case Study

During 2008–9, the Edgecumbe Group conducted executive assessments of the top teams of three very different organisations, on the basis of which we can offer several empirical observations. The groups comprised the top teams of an international airline, a retail multinational and an engineering organisation. In these three groups, around 100 executives in all were assessed against the Primary Colours Model's eight capabilities: the seven in the model plus Coping with Pressure. We deployed a five-point scale to grade their capabilities where 3 was defined as 'fully competent for a senior manager at your level in a world-class organisation'; a 2 represented a shortfall, a 1 a significant shortfall; 4 represented a clear strength and a 5 implied outstanding performance. The scores of each assessor were calibrated and quality assured by two further psychologists. All five scale points were used

(continued)

to grade the executives, all of whom were successful and valued by their organisations. The following was also observed:

None of the executives scored a 5 in all areas.

The highest mean score was 4.14, the lowest was 2.57.

The individual with the highest scores received two 5 s but also scored two 3 s.

Of those who scored a 5 in any of the eight capabilities (around one in ten of the population), they also scored as low as 1 in other areas.

The empirical data from our recent assessments thus support our contention that it is extremely rare for anyone to be competent in all areas and none has yet scored full marks in all areas. Our wider assessment population, comprising thousands of assessments, provides further supportive evidence.

Psychologically

Scholars have been attempting to describe differences between people systematically for generations, and certainly since the ancient Greeks described the four humours: melancholic, sanguine, phlegmatic and choleric. Scientific psychology began in the late nineteenth century and has created many descriptions of personality but the very term 'personality' came from the masks worn by actors in Greek dramas, as we mentioned in chapter 1. Two widely used twentieth-century approaches to individual differences are the Myers-Briggs Type Indicator (MBTI) and the Big 5 Model of personality, best typified by the NEO personality inventory or Hogan Personality Inventory.

The theory of personality 'types' described by Carl Jung in the 1920s suggested that much seemingly random variation in people's behaviour is actually quite orderly and consistent, and is due to basic differences in the ways individuals prefer to use their perception and judgement. Though these are described as preferences, they were thought to be constant throughout life. They did not cause behaviour but they predisposed people to act in consistent ways more often than not, and required effort to break the patterns established.

The MBTI identifies four basic preferences:

- Do you draw your energy from the outer world or your own inner world? This is called Extroversion (E) or Introversion (I)

- Do you prefer to focus on facts or do on possibilities? This is called Sensing (S) or Intuition (N)
- When making decisions, do you prefer to use dispassionate, logical analysis to come to conclusions or do you prefer to concentrate on your feelings and values? This is called Thinking (T) or Feeling (F).
- In dealing with the outside world, do you prefer to get things decided and live a more ordered existence or do you prefer to stay open to new information and options and to live a more spontaneous existence? This is called Judging (J) or Perceiving (P).

To find out your personality type, decide on your preference in each category. There are 16 personality types, expressed as a four-letter code of combinations of these preferences: hence INTP or ESFJ, and so on.

For more information on finding out your Myers-Briggs personality type visit http://www.myersbriggs.org/

Certain types seem better suited to inspiring and others to focusing, although all types can learn to do both. Similarly, certain types may seek to inspire in some ways, other types in other ways, with varying degrees of success. Inspirers need to feel comfortable with people and keen to communicate. Extroverts find this somewhat easier than introverts. Inspirers need to work easily with concepts and possibilities in the future. This is a natural focus for Intuitives (N) rather than Sensing types (S). They may deploy either logic or passion in their arguments, so either T or F will be equally helpful. Inspirers will be unconcerned with resolving issues but are likely to prefer to challenge the status quo and propose new options. So a P preference may be slightly more helpful than a J preference. Hence ENTP or ENFP preferences may be particularly appropriate for inspiration. They are consultant or leader types and studies show that people in such professions as consultancy are disproportionately ENTPs, as are the authors of this book.

Inspirers need to feel comfortable with people and keen to communicate.

By contrast, a focuser is concerned with the present and with facts and details (S). Focusers are logical and dispassionate decision makers (T). They prefer to resolve matters rather than leave them hanging (J).

Hence ISTJ or ESTJ types are well suited to focusing. They are the managerial types as studies also confirm.

To validate such claims, type psychologists study the probability that certain types of people opt for, and succeed in, in different walks of life. For example people who prefer ST are practical and analytical and find scope for their interests in applied science, engineering or administration. People who prefer SF want to offer practical help to people and tend to go into teaching, community care or nursing. Those who prefer NF are insightful and enthusiastic and with their interest in understanding people go into human resources, the arts or politics. Those who prefer NT are interested in theoretical and technical frameworks and might be suited to management, law or consultancy.

David Winsborough and Vithany Sambath (2013) studied New Zealand CEOs and described three different CEO types in terms of their behaviour and style. They identified 'Alphas' who were dominant and hard-driving, 'Pragmatics' who were diligent and rule-following and 'Mavericks' who had some characteristics of the Alphas but were more mercurial, had a greater risk appetite than most and were less interested in rules and structure. Unsurprisingly, the personality characteristics of these three different types varied considerably as measured by the three Hogan psychometric scales: HPI, MVPI and HDS. Ambition characterised them all but in other respects their personality, values and derailers were different between CEO types (see chapters 8 and 9).

It follows that the type-based preferences and personality characteristics that suit certain aspects of leadership are hindrances to other aspects of leadership (see Fig. 5.1). Personality does not make us good or bad at things but it sets up a pattern of helps and hindrances. The same is true of the effects implied by the Big 5 Model of personality.

The Big 5 and the NEO

Another inventory of personality types is known as the Big 5 personality factors. These are five broad factors or dimensions of personality initially developed through lexical analysis and subsequently confirmed by factor analysis.

	LIMITATION	STRENGTH
PERSONALITY HELPS	***Potential Strength*** Work ON: Become competent	***Natural Strength*** Work WITH: Develop to world class
PERSONALITY HINDERS	***Resistant Limitation*** Work AROUND: Find a different solution	***Fragile Strength*** Work ON: Maintain competence

Fig. 5.1 Personality and competence

The Big 5 enables are:

- Neuroticism—a tendency to experience unpleasant emotions easily, such as anger, anxiety, depression or vulnerability—sometimes called emotional reactivity. Low scorers on this trait are called emotionally stable or resilient.
- Extroversion—energy, positive emotions, assertiveness, and the tendency to seek stimulation and the company of others. High scorers are gregarious, low scorers more reserved.
- Openness—appreciation for art, emotion, adventure, unusual ideas, imagination, curiosity and variety of experience. High scorers are exploratory. Low scorers tend to be more pragmatic and conservative.
- Agreeableness—a tendency to be compassionate and cooperative rather than suspicious and antagonistic towards others. High scorers tend to adapt to other people. Low scorers are more challenging and abrasive.
- Conscientiousness—a tendency to show self-discipline, act dutifully and aim for achievement. High scorers tend to be organised and to plan. Low scorers are more flexible and spontaneous.

Research conducted in the 1990s (Hogan and Kaiser 2005) suggests that leaders tend to be more emotionally stable (i.e., low neuroticism, or N–). They tend to be more extroverted (E+) and more open-minded (O+). There is a slight tendency for leaders to be more challenging (A–) and they are much more conscientious (C+).

If we consider our five leadership enables, it is clear that the characteristics that help with some of them can get in the way with others. So, for example, inspiring people tend to be more extroverted and more open-minded (E+, O+); those who are better at focusing are certainly more conscientious (C+) but they are often more introverted (E–) and more pragmatic (O–). Since we cannot change our personality quickly, those with a very distinct profile are likely to be well suited to certain aspects of leadership and not others. This is the psychological argument for incomplete leadership. This argument is developed further in chapter 8.

Summary of Part One

In this chapter we have looked at the improbability of being a complete leader. We have looked at ways of defining personality types and how different types can help or hinder with leadership tasks such as inspiring and focusing. A leader can learn to be good at things their personality type does not naturally lead them to do, but it makes it harder for them.

Activities like marketing deal principally in possibilities whereas engineering and operations deal principally with sequences and processes. They also need quite different sorts of people with different personality characteristics. In the same way, certain aspects of leadership are facilitated by the characteristics that hinder other leadership contributions.

As Deborah Ancona argues in her article 'In praise of the incomplete' (Ancona et al. 2007), once leaders diagnose their own capabilities, identifying their unique set of strengths and weaknesses, they must search for others who can provide the things they are missing.

Part Two: Jobs and Journeys

The Primary Colours Model suggests there are three domains in which leaders have to operate. It has also been suggested by others that there are essentially only three types of jobs: technical, supervisory and strategic. These frameworks, though not identical, map onto each other reasonably well. Each framework contains a strategic dimension. Our operational domain is somewhat related to technical jobs and our interpersonal domain to supervisory jobs.

The path to positions of leadership is usually a *journey through* these three types of jobs. Not everyone continues the journey: some get stuck for a variety of reasons; others choose not to continue. It is a journey from specialist education and training to corporate leader. It is about a person's career or vocation. It is the stuff of biography and autobiography. It is also beautifully parodied, though with serious intent, in the *Peter Principle*, a 1969 book by Lawrence Peter and Raymond Hull who contended that people tend to rise in a hierarchy until they reach their level of incompetence. Their corollary is equally tragi-comic: that all jobs eventually become occupied by someone incompetent, leaving work to be done by those who have not yet reached their level of incompetence! In this part of the chapter, we contend that the Peter principle may be avoided by more careful attention to the kinds of work and leadership to which people are suited.

The Technical Job

The word 'technical' is often used pejoratively. Technical education is seen to be inferior to academic education; the polytechnic to the university; the trade to the profession. However we use the word here to mean mastery of techniques which inevitably involves knowledge and skills.

Most people are selected on their technical knowledge and skills. These may be relatively easy or difficult to acquire. They may take years of apprenticeship, training or experience; or they may be achieved in a matter of weeks. Either way, brain surgeons and fighter pilots just as much as tree surgeons or bus drivers have technical jobs.

Over time, if the recruit is good at the job, he or she may be offered promotion. There are *essentially two types of promotion*. The first is to be made a senior 'X' such as a senior train conductor, a senior account executive, a senior lecturer. Technical people are recognised for their ability, skills and knowledge and through experience, are asked to do more complex, difficult and demanding tasks within the same area.

Some technical people thrive at their tasks. Because of their aptitudes, temperament and values they discover they are 'the right peg in the right hole' and are able to exploit their talents. Most are extremely happy to do so and opinion or satisfaction surveys frequently find craftspeople among the most contented staff. They do every day what they like doing most, are often extremely good at it and highly effective.

The Supervisory Job

There is, however, a second, very different type of promotion. This involves *supervision*. It means doing less of the task oneself and more delegating and monitoring of others. While supervisors may also do a great deal of 'the task' themselves, their newly promoted role is intended to be supervisory. In essence, other people report to them who require guidance and instruction.

It is the job of supervisors to get the best out of those who work with and for them. They need the ability to plan, organise and control but, more than that, they need the ability to *engage* staff. Job satisfaction, commitment and engagement are, to a large extent, determined by the immediate supervisor.

>Supervisory jobs are much less 'hands on' and more 'hearts on'.

For many the problem is 'letting go'. What supervisors have to relinquish is the temptation to do the job themselves: the very job they loved and at which they were extremely good. Supervisory jobs are much less 'hands on' and more 'hearts on'. They are about helping, supporting, co-ordinating and inspiring. The purpose of supervisory or managerial roles is to achieve *through others*: hence the importance of interpersonal skills.

The Strategic Job

The third type of job is *strategic*. Usually at a senior level, some people are asked to provide direction for the organisation as a whole or at least to take part in high-level strategic planning: turning broad direction and policy into specific goals and plans. At this stage a person, often a senior manager or a general manager, largely relinquishes the job of supervising the operation. The task moves on to dealing with the future.

People at the strategic level have to learn to 'read the signals' from the context in which the organisation is operating and the trends to which they seem to be responding. What is coming down the line? What are the opportunities or threats to the company? How should the organisation react to them? Global competition soon puts paid to organisations without insight, planning or strategy. 'Third-level' top, strategic jobs are about the future and the organisation's place in it.

Those in planning/strategic jobs have to 'let go' of the remnants of task execution and play down supervision and management, both of which they have been good at. They need to refocus more *outwardly* than inwardly. Strategists need to look to the future as well as the present and they need to look around them at competition. Changes in technology, in customer expectations and in demography have to find their place alongside shifts in the legal, economic and political spheres to form a clear view of the forceful features to which the organisation must respond moving forward.

> Those in planning/strategic jobs have to 'let go' of the remnants of task execution and play down supervision and management, both of which they have been good at.

The strategist plots the journey to the future. That is what we mean by strategy: a high-level destination or goal and a means of achieving it, but a brilliant strategy that no-one understands or believes in is essentially a failed strategy. Thus, along with planning, the strategist also has to be persuasive in order to *sell* his/her vision, strategy or plan. (This is why we have placed creating direction, planning and creating alignment all in the strategic domain in the Primary Colours Model.)

Careers and Vocational Choice

The journey to the role of leader starts when people make vocational choices. Many people struggle to decide what they are going to do with their careers. Many experience 'false starts' and discover what they like doing and are good at only later in life. Some discover their 'true vocation' in middle age. Others, because of early life circumstances or choices they have made, are condemned to explore and exploit their abilities and their passions only in their leisure pursuits and hobbies.

Vocational guidance is about helping people discover the ideal or optimal job for them which makes them both productive and happy. Job choice is a function of many things:

Abilities: Many technical jobs require very particular abilities or talents. This may involve capabilities as diverse as computational/mathematical ability and musical ability. Overall cognitive ability is a marker or a cap on certain highly analytic jobs. Skills can be learnt, but natural ability in certain areas may be a distinct advantage.

Personality/Preferences: It is very apparent that people have strong preferences for particular tasks. What one person is enchanted and captivated by, another hates. Some seek to maximise people-contact, others to minimise it. Some enjoy working with their head, others their hands and still others their hearts. Much of vocational guidance is based on assessing preferences and fitting them to particular jobs.

Values: People learn to value some job outputs more than others. The output or processes involved in performing many jobs may be at variance with a person's values. This often brings a moral-ethical dimension to job choice and creates the militant union leader, priest or social worker from the same raw material as a potential senior manager.

Luck: Early experience and exposure due to 'accident of birth' influence both a person's hopes and aspirations. People are 'born into' a medical family; others inherit a family business; some come from backgrounds that seem to condemn them to menial work with little chance of leadership.

However a diversion into vocational psychology may be very instructive. It partly explains why some people find the journey to leadership so difficult while others find it so easy and why certain types of leadership contribution are made by some people rather than others.

We all have an ability and preference profile, and the stronger the preferences, often the more inflexible the approach of the individual. In personality psychology there is the *spectrum hypothesis*. The idea is that extremes of 'normality' may indicate abnormality. Most people are in the middle of all dimensions: neither brilliant nor dull; neither obese nor anorexic; neither extremely introvert nor extrovert. There is a bell curve: a normal distribution for all attributes. But there are inevitably, and by definition, people at the extremes.

People at the edge are unbalanced because they show very strong preferences. Those people (the majority) who are in the middle can adapt and change, 'crossing the line', whereas people with a very strong 'things' orientation may find it very difficult to become 'people' orientated and vice versa. In essence the nearer to the centre you are, the greater the possibility of change.

A Two-Dimensional Model

In Fig. 5.2 we have plotted the three domains/jobs. It is a simple expression of a complex insight. Note that the epicentre of the three jobs are some distance from each other.

Vocational psychology espouses the concept of 'fit': the right person in the right job. This very simple, two-dimensional model comes from vocational psychology which strives to fit the person to the job by trying to define their nature, aptitudes and values (see Fig. 5.2). One dimension is *people-things*. Some individuals show an early interest in *people*: their emotions, idiosyncrasies and foibles. They are drawn to people as a source of stimulation and support. They are more likely to be extroverts than introverts, females rather than males; more tolerant of ambiguity and uncertainty.

Others are interested in *things*, be they animal, vegetable, mineral or mechanical. They become fascinated by how things work, become obsessed with collecting things or constructing them. They become interested in categorisation and function.

The other dimension is *ideas-data* and is expressed in several personality models. In MBTI terms, it is expressed in the intuition-sensing

Fig. 5.2 Two dimensions from vocational psychology

dimension; in terms of the Big 5 personality model it corresponds to Openness. Some people love possibilities, theories or new ideas. They enjoy 'what if' questions and they tend to be divergent thinkers. They may be thought of as creative or impractical dreamers. They enjoy discussions, debate, mind games. Their polar opposites are the practical, hard-headed, data analytic types. Their concern is with facts: the here and now; what the numbers say. They are persuaded not by ideas but by the logical analysis of what is known.

It is possible to plot a person on these two dimensions. They may be moderate or extreme on both or either. However Fig. 5.2 shows clearly the amount of movement or change required to take on the three different jobs. It suggests that the nearer a person is to the centre on both dimensions, the less the distance to be travelled in switching roles but also the less ideally well suited to each role they may be than are other people.

Another way to think of a similar idea has been proposed by Jon Cowell at Edgecumbe Group (Fig. 5.3). He reminds us that the Primary Colours Model implies two slightly different dimensions: the first is to do with scope, the other with focus. Scope may be generic (broad) and its time-frame is the future; or it may be anchored in the present and much more specific. Focus may be on people or tasks. The four quadrants thus defined in relation to the Primary Colours Model are illustrated in Fig. 5.3.

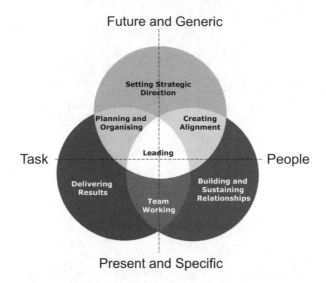

Fig. 5.3   Two dimensions underlying the Primary Colours Model: future and generic

More recently, we have specified how these four quadrants describe rather different orientations to leadership. Those with a Future and Task orientation are likely to be strategists. Those with a Future and People orientation are likely to be Influencers. Those with a Present and Task orientation are implementers and those with a Present and People orientation are relationship builders. And these orientations echo the ancient Greek notions of the elements: earth, air, fire and water as illustrated in Fig. 5.4, which leads us to speculate on whether we may have described something a little more substantial in the Primary Colours Model than another of Richard Pascale's fads. Could it somehow describe the deep structure of leadership?

A Hexagon Model

Arguably the most important theory in vocational psychology is that of John Holland (1973) who, wisely and uniquely, tried to *categorise jobs and people according to the same terminology*. Thus you have artistic people and

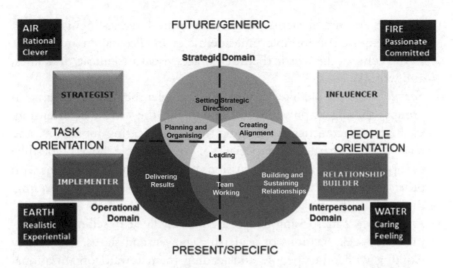

Fig. 5.4 The deep structure of leadership?

artistic jobs; conventional people and conventional jobs. Holland's view was that vocational choice is an expression of personality (1997). He argued that there were only six kinds of jobs which suit people to varying degrees:

- *Realistic.* Realistic people like activities, jobs, and co-workers whose interests are similar: mechanical, construction, and repair: nature and the outdoors; and who like adventurous, physical activities. They enjoy working with tools, machines, and equipment. They are interested in action rather than thought and prefer concrete problems to ambiguous, abstract problems. They are nature's pragmatists.
- *Investigative.* Investigative people have a strong scientific, inquiring orientation. They enjoy gathering information, uncovering new facts or theories, and analyzing and interpreting data. They are most comfortable in academic or research environments and enjoy pursuing advanced degrees. They prefer to rely on themselves in their work rather on others. They dislike selling and repetitive activities.
- *Artistic.* Artistic people value aesthetic qualities and have a great need for self-expression. This type, more than any other, includes people who enjoy being spectators or observers (in this case, of the arts) rather than participants. Artistic types frequently express their artistic interests in leisure or recreational activities as well as in vocational

activities or environments. With their typical verbal-linguistic bent, they are quite comfortable in academic or intellectual environments. In this context, the artistic theme embraces visual arts, music/dramatics, and writing.

- *Social.* Social people like to work with people; they enjoy working in groups, sharing responsibilities, and being the centre of attention. Central characteristics are helping, nurturing, caring for others, and teaching and instructing, especially of young people. Social types like to solve problems through discussions of feelings and interactions with others. They may also enjoy working with people through leading, directing, and persuading.

- *Enterprising.* Enterprising people are verbally facile in selling and leading. They seek positions of leadership, power, and status. They enjoy working with other people and leading them toward organizational goals and economic success. Enterprising people may like to take financial and interpersonal risks and to participate in competitive activities. They dislike scientific activities and long periods of intellectual effort.

- *Conventional.* Conventional people especially like activities that require attention to organization, data systems, detail, and accuracy. They often enjoy mathematics and data management activities such as accounting and investment management. They work well in large organizations, but do not show a distinct preference for or against leadership positions.

Holland's Hexagon is illustrated in Fig. 5.5.

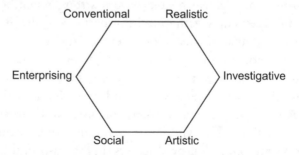

Fig. 5.5 Holland's Hexagon

Holland also noted the personality types and salient characteristics associated with each of the six types. They are described in Table 5.2.

Holland's theory and model are fecund. He suggested that, within a person or environment, some pairs of 'types' are more closely related than others. These degrees of relatedness or *consistency* affect job satisfaction and general wellbeing.

The types are ordered in a particular manner: realistic, investigative, artistic, social, enterprising and conventional. As a useful and approximate way of showing the degrees of relatedness among the six types, they are arranged at the vertices of a hexagon, such that the closest are most similar. Thus, the *investigative* and *artistic* types are similar and hence closer together, because both are concerned with intellectual pursuits, although in different ways: the investigative type is more methodological and data orientated, the artistic type more spontaneous. By contrast, the investigative type who is relatively asocial and analytical differs most from the self-confident and persuasive enterprising type. Similarly, the spontaneous, disorderly and creative artistic type contrasts sharply with the self-controlled, conforming and unimaginative conventional type.

By inference, intermediate proximities on the hexagon depict intermediate degrees of psychological similarity, although the correlated results do not totally support that particular shape. For an individual, the preferences are ranked (1–6) thus providing 720 different possibilities of types of people and types of job, though only the first three preferences tend to be used in vocational guidance. Holland has also made available a dictionary of most available jobs, each described by a three letter code drawn from the hexagon (Holland 1997) which can be used to help make career choices based on an understanding of personality preferences described in the same way. Thus, if your preference is ESC, then a career as a business manager, financial planner or retail store manager may suit you best.

A second concept is *differentiation*, which means that some people and environments are more clearly defined than others; for example, a person or environment may be dominated by a single type (well differentiated) or may resemble many types equally well (undifferentiated). The better the environment or person is differentiated, the more likely the person is to find a congruent job, and the more likely he/she will be to have high job satisfaction and good mental health as a result. Holland (1973) suggests

Table 5.2 Holland's personality characteristics

	Realistic	Investigative	Artistic	Social	Enterprising	Conventional
Enables	Hard-headed Unassuming Practical Dogmatic Natural Uninsightful	Analytical Intellectual Curious Scholarly Open Broad interests	Open Non-conforming Imaginative Sensitive Creative	Agreeable Friendly Understanding Sociable Persuasive Extroverted	Extroverted Dominant Adventurous Enthusiastic Power-seeking Energetic	Conforming Conservative Unimaginative Inhibited Practical-minded Methodical
Life Goals	Inventing apparatus/ equipment. Becoming outstanding athlete	Inventing valuable product Theoretical contribution to science	Becoming famous in performing arts Publishing stories Original Painting Musical Composition	Helping others Making sacrifices for others Competent teacher or therapist	Being community leader Expert in finance and commerce. Being well liked and well dressed	Expert in finance and commerce Producing a lot of work
Values	Freedom Intellectual Ambitious Self-controlled Docility	Intellectual Logical Ambitious Wisdom	Equality Imaginative Courageous World Beauty	Equality Self-respect Helpful Forgiving	Freedom Ambitious (–) Forgiving (–) Helpful	(–) Imaginative (–) Forgiving

Famous examples	Thomas Edison Admiral Byrd	Madame Curie Charles Darwin	T. S. Eliot Pablo Picasso	Jane Adams Albert Schweitzer	Henry Ford Andrew Carnegie	Bernard Baruch John D. Rockefeller
Aptitudes	Technical	Scientific	Arts	Social and Educational Leadership and Sales Interpersonal	Leadership and Sales Social and Educational Business and Clerical Interpersonal	Business and Clerical
Greatest skill	Mechanics	Science	Arts	Human Relations	Leadership	Business

that, for inconsistent subjects with little differentiation, an incongruent environment in which they work can become less stressful as they meet people involved in that environment and adapt to their needs and values.

The third measure is *congruence* or compatibility, referring to a person and job type that are very similar (e.g., a realistic type in a realistic environment). This measure is also derived from the hexagon model. Incongruence occurs when a type lives or works in an environment that provides opportunities and rewards foreign to a person's preferences and abilities (e.g., a realistic type in a social environment). Congruence is therefore the best measure of fit. Strictly speaking, it is only congruence and not consistency or differentiation that measures person–environment fit. Consistency is a characteristic of either a person's profile or an environment, but it says nothing about the relationship between the two; nor does differentiation.

Again, as in the two-dimensional model mentioned earlier, this model sheds further light on how certain people end up in certain jobs, how their journey is more easy or difficult and how some are better suited to certain types of leadership. Artistic types may struggle in a conventional environment or working for conventional leaders just as social types may struggle with the realists. Incompatibility of people and role, or of people and setting may seriously hamper leaders' emergence and effectiveness.

Playing to Strengths

Another approach to vocational guidance is the strengths approach. The past decades have seen the emergence of positive psychology and the strengths-based movement. Its proponents argue that authentic happiness, health and satisfaction are all about finding and playing to one's strengths. This helps people decide what they should do. The strengths have been listed and currently stand at 24 and these group under six virtues as described by Peterson and Seligman (2004). They are:

- *Wisdom and Knowledge*: creativity, curiosity, open-mindedness, love of learning, perspective, innovation
- *Courage*: bravery, persistence, integrity, vitality
- *Humanity*: love, kindness, social intelligence
- *Justice*: citizenship, fairness, leadership

- *Temperance*: forgiveness and mercy, humility, prudence, self-control
- *Transcendence*: appreciation of beauty and excellence, gratitude, hope, humour, spirituality

Seligman (2002) argues that once you find, explore and exercise your personal signature strength, you receive various specific benefits including:

- A sense of ownership and authenticity ('This is the real me')
- A feeling of excitement while displaying it, particularly at first
- A rapid learning curve as the strength is first practiced
- Continuous learning of new ways to enact the strength
- A sense of yearning to find ways to use it
- A feeling of inevitability in using the strength ('Try and stop me')
- Invigoration rather than exhaustion while using the strength
- The creation and pursuit of personal projects that revolve around it
- Joy, zest, enthusiasm, even ecstasy while using it

This approach is unashamedly upbeat and has a great deal in common with our own model in part one of this chapter describing natural strengths, potential strengths, fragile strengths and resistant limitations. It also has many common themes with Schein's concept of career anchors, which is a mixture of abilities, needs, motives and values that are areas of people's working lives that they would find very difficult to give up.

Values

Various researchers have studied values. Robert and Joyce Hogan, who developed a measure called the Motives, Values and Preferences Inventory (MVPI), believe that all individuals have core values and goals. These relate to the things they like to do and to the meaning and satisfaction they derive from them. They become an aspect of a person's identity. Further, they are drivers because people choose to work *with others* who share their values and *for causes* and *in environments* which support those values. The Hogans have grouped work values into ten areas as shown in Table 5.3.

Table 5.3 The Hogans' work values

MVPI term	Characteristics
Recognition	Desire to be known, seen, visible and famous, which leads to a lifestyle guided by a search for opportunities to be noticed and dreams of fame and high achievement, whether or not they are fulfilled
Power	Desire to succeed, make things happen, make a difference and outperform the competition
Hedonism	Pursuit of fun, excitement, pleasure and a lifestyle organised around eating, drinking and entertainment
Altruism	Desire to help others, a concern for the welfare of the less fortunate in life, and a lifestyle organised around public service and the betterment of humanity
Affiliation	Needing and enjoying frequent and varied social contact and a lifestyle organised around social interaction
Tradition	A belief in and dedication to old-fashioned virtues such as family, church, thrift, hard work, appropriate social behaviour, and a lifestyle that reflects these values
Security	A need for predictability, structure and efforts to avoid risk and uncertainty—especially in the employment area—and a lifestyle organised around minimising errors and mistakes
Commerce (Business)	Interest in earning money, realising profits, finding new business opportunities, and a lifestyle organised around investments and financial planning
Aesthetics	Need for self-expression, a dedication to quality and excellence, an interest in how things look, feel and sound and close attention to the appearance of things
Science (Rationality)	Being interested in science, comfortable with technology, preferring data-based as opposed to intuitive decisions, and spending time learning how things work

Robert and Joyce Hogan argue that values drive job choice and management and leadership style. They have an instrument which gives feedback to those that complete it and describe very different implications for leadership according to how a person's values are captured by their instrument. For example, those whose MVPI shows high scores for Commerce, Rationality and Power have a particularly hard-headed and hard-driving leadership style well suited to the business world and *Delivering Results*, while those whose greatest motives are to do with Hedonism or Altruism may not seek leadership roles at all or, if they do, will find that they thrive only in more people-oriented environments where *Building and Sustaining Relationships* is emphasised.

Summary and Conclusion

1. For reasons that are logical, empirical and psychological, it is extremely difficult for an individual to be a complete leader. It may be folly to try.
2. The journey a person takes to a major leadership role is often complicated. Yet it is seldom random. Initial choices made during education are related to our personality, values and preferences. These also determine how we choose our careers and respond with differing degrees of success and enthusiasm to our career experiences. We choose our environments and they exacerbate the initial differences that shaped our choices. Thus, by adulthood, and certainly by the middle point of our careers, we have become shaped by a multitude of factors that suit us better to certain types of roles and contributions.
3. Leadership generalists, who attempt to maintain leadership contributions equally in all three domains, all seven leadership tasks and all five leadership enablers are likely to find that they are no better than mediocre in all aspects. Leaders who want to be truly excellent may need to specialise rather more.

So we have suggested that leadership may need to be regarded as a team sport. How to put such teams together is the subject of chapter 6.

6

Building a Leadership Team

*I don't need a friend who changes when I change and who nods
when I nod; my shadow does that much better.*

Plutarch

We saw in chapter 2 how the impact of the leader is key to creating the
culture of an organisation: the common practices and beliefs its members
share. Leaders also have a disproportionate effect on the climate, or how it
feels for those working there. The culture and climate affect the degree of
employee engagement, and thereby both the amount of discretionary effort
they put in and their intention to stay. Climate and culture have an impact
on the bottom line: on the results of the organisation in terms of productivity, creativity and profits, as well as on levels of employee retention.

In this chapter, we look at ways of building teams. We offer examples
of how effective teams work together, after first describing the influences
on leaders' behaviour.

Understanding Influences

There are two major influences on a leader's behaviour: his or her behavioural repertoire and the demands of the situation or context in which he

© The Editor(s) (if applicable) and The Author(s) 2016
D. Pendleton, A. Furnham, *Leadership: All You Need To Know*
2nd edition, DOI 10.1057/978-1-137-55436-9_6

or she is operating. Leaders' behaviour is frequently the product of the interaction between both factors.

Behavioural Repertoire

By adulthood, our personality, motives, preferences and values are quite stable. It is not that they cannot change, but that they change slowly, barring any life transforming traumas. The mix of genetic inheritance and experience that has fashioned us: which was bringing about rapid learning and change in childhood, has slowed in adulthood after the turbulence of adolescence. Change in adulthood is a more sedate affair. Our *behaviour* changes constantly but common patterns are observable. Our *moods* change from hour to hour but generally within the overall framework of our temperament. We can readily acquire more knowledge and skills with effort, but our *attitudes* are relatively resistant to change and our *personality* evolves at a glacial pace.

Our *behaviour* changes constantly but common patterns are observable.

The result is our behavioural repertoire. This is the set of behaviours or common practices that we demonstrate in our approach to leadership and other challenges or tasks. Some are more people oriented, others more solitary and reflective. Some involve themselves intensely with their teams, others are more remote. Some plan meticulously, others prefer to be more flexible and spontaneous. Some celebrate success and deal firmly with poor performance, others avoid extreme reactions of all kinds. The impact of personality on leadership and the specific influences on elements of our model are covered in more detail in chapter 8.

In terms of our leadership model, as we have seen in chapter 5: by adulthood, some have settled into a more operational mindset. They notice details, think sequentially and orient with urgency towards goals and targets. They are action oriented. Others are more strategically minded. They look to the future, think in concepts and orient towards possibilities. Still others focus more on relationships. They are emotionally intelligent, give equal weight to their thoughts and feelings and orient towards the people in their environment. The same is true of the leadership enablers: some have learned to inspire quite naturally, others to focus. All tasks can be attempted by every leader but some come more naturally than others and they fit more easily into our behavioural repertoire. These are not matters of capacity but of orientation and preference, though the more we play to our preferences, the more capable we tend to become in those aspects of our lives. This is Thorndike's (1911) law of exercise, or, as it is more commonly expressed, practice makes perfect. Our repertoire is fashioned by the choices we make and in turn fashions our leadership.

Situational Demands

When a leader takes on a new job, he or she rapidly becomes aware of the demands of the new situation. There are many ways in which this happens. The job description or recruitment advertisement may have described the essential features. The new boss will probably want to explain what is required and new colleagues will have opinions they want to share. A leader's new team will also convey a sense of what is required, if asked.

The situation makes demands, both implicit and explicit and the leader needs to understand the demands in order to ensure that he or she is aware of their effects. There are many tools that can be used to appreciate a situation. One such tool, a PEST analysis, was mentioned in an earlier chapter. It encourages the exploration of the political, economic, social and technical factors in the context. Yet whatever technique is deployed, the aim is to reveal the current forceful features of the situation. Forceful features are the dominant influences or demands in the situation to which the organisation, team or leader must respond. They may include a rapidly dwindling market share, a team in turmoil or an unbroken run of successes, but they demand the leader's attention and may well be the criteria by which the organisation will judge the leader's impact.

The Leader's Repertoire

The leader's repertoire is an internal matter. The situation is external. The interplay between the two constitutes the demands and the resources at the leader's disposal to meet them. But there is a crucial difference. The repertoire is relatively stable whereas the demands of the situation are not. They can vary in ways that are unpredictable and unstable. They can stretch and challenge a leader beyond the limits of his or her repertoire. In an economic downturn following a period of growth, the emotional demands of the team increase. Whereas in busy and successful times, careful organisation and planning are the keys to success, now such matters as understanding, reassurance and empathy become critical.

The unstable nature of the situational demands can call for a broader repertoire than most leaders can muster on their own. If a team has been assembled with complementary differences in mind, the repertoire of the team is much broader than that of any individual team member. Collective complementarity is the solution to the situation's unpredictability. In Fig. 6.1, we illustrate this with reference to the Primary Colours Model.

Leaders who fail to build complementary teams are at the mercy of their own limited repertoires. Individuals can, of course, be resourceful, their repertoires may be broad relative to the repertoires of others, and they can learn. But when they are challenged by situational demands beyond their capacity, they are likely first not to notice or to deny the demands that are beyond them or, at worst, to pretend that what is required is more of their favourite contribution. Thus, the inspirer will continue to try to inspire a

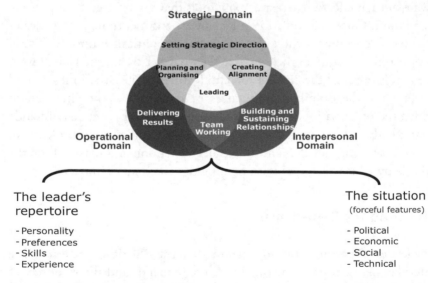

Fig. 6.1 Influences on leadership

team that is crying out for more focus and organisation. We have turned into a joke the idea of a doctor who only ever prescribes baked beans to any patient and when the patient finally succumbs to the disease claims that it just wasn't possible to get enough baked beans into him—and yet the leader who always does the same no matter what the changing situation demands is doing the same as the doctor. It has become a truism that 'if you always do what you always did then you will always get what you always got'. It was Einstein who defined insanity as doing the same thing over and over again and expecting different results!

Organisations have to thrive in constantly changing environments and Charles Darwin argued that it is not the strongest species that survive but those that adapt fastest to change. The principle here is essentially Darwinian: the greater the variability in the resource pool, the greater the range of external events that may be responded to successfully. To play with the apostrophe: the issue is not the leader's repertoire but the leaders' repertoire, and the willingness of the individual leader to embrace the possibilities that the wider team provides for responding effectively to change. Empirical validation of this proposition is easy to find. For example, Williams and O'Reilly (1998) demonstrated that a team's cognitive resources and abilities increase with increasing levels of multi-disciplinarity due to their greater breadth of knowledge, skills and attitudes and the wider social networks on which they can draw.

Looking for Complementary Differences

The clear message is that we need *different* people on a leadership team. Duplication of skills, attributes or preferences restricts the team's collective repertoire. At a conference entitled 'Leaders in London', Tom Peters was heard to suggest:

> If you find anyone in your organisation who agrees with everything you say, fire them! Why pay twice for the same opinions?

Yet working with very different people can be difficult. Relating to people who are least like us is a real challenge. As with any long-term relationship, such as marriage, the best chance of two people working effectively together is to have some elements of attitudes or personality in common (touchpoints) and some that are different. The differences should be such that they allow both parties to continue to develop by challenging one another and, at the same time, complementing one another.

Touchpoints bind people together, while differences help them to grow. If there are insufficient touchpoints, or if they are too weak, then the differences cause problems and prevent complementarity (see the box 'Teams at Work' on Julius Caesar, p. XX). The differences that complement can also tear relationships apart and need to be fostered with care. People can be separated by their differences or their similarities. Difference alone does not guarantee complementarity, nor does similarity guarantee a strong relationship, but complementary differences *do* guarantee more complete leadership. We have to work out what turns a mere difference into a complementary difference.

In leadership terms, a complementary difference is found when one leader's resistant weakness is another's natural strength Fig. 6.2. Making use of the difference is a matter of coordination and is most effective when the arrangement is explicit. Key to this is respect, but of several kinds:

- respect for one's own abilities in other areas. This helps us not to feel threatened that we are not complete on our own
- respect for the complementary difference. Immature responses to personal inadequacies can include minimising their role or importance
- respect for the task of leadership. This makes it more likely we will pursue complete leadership with others.

	David	Potential Strengths	Natural Strengths
Nathalie	Potential Strengths	Natural Strengths	Fragile Strengths
	Resistant Limitations	Fragile Strengths	

Fig. 6.2 Colleagues' complementary differences

On a personal note, the authors of this book both need highly organised colleagues to manage projects. In their absence, entropy rules and projects descend into chaos! Our saving grace is that we know this and seek out such colleagues. We also have to do as we are told, or else our colleagues' help has no effect. In the diagram, we illustrate this principle with respect to two people but the principle holds with multiple team members. The key here is to find colleagues whose natural strengths are in the areas of our resistant limitations.

In Boxes—Teams at Work

1. Characters in Julius Caesar

The conspirators in Shakespeare's *Julius Caesar* had different personalities: Brutus was an extrovert and a visionary, whereas Cassius was concerned with the details of the plot to overthrow Caesar and worked hard to get others involved. Their differences were potentially complementary: inspire and focus, but in the end they broke apart the conspiracy. Instead of replacing the dictator Julius Caesar with a more democratic system, they ended merely with the domination of Mark Antony. Their different personalities and values caused such difficulties in communication that the plot unravelled. They had too few touchpoints and the introspective Cassius, unable to keep Brutus' vision in mind, was so riven by doubts that he committed suicide in the midst of battle.

2. Jazz Musicians

The way excellent individual musicians play jazz offers a metaphor for team working. In great jazz, virtuoso instrumentalists come together to become great ensemble players when what matters most to them is their commitment to the common vision of playing great music together, not their individual playing. When this happens, they listen to each other, and are not threatened but inspired by each other. When it is time for a solo, they will communicate among themselves subtly. They seem to agree what the music demands, and are aware of the need for variety, sensitive to the instrument that has not featured in a solo recently. One of them will play less or more, saxophone or guitar, as the music requires. They are not receiving instructions but are looking out for one another. They do not all have to be playing at once—they are already achieving their bigger goal of making wonderful music together irrespective of whose instrument is more prominent at any given time. The range of instruments is, of course, complementary. Egos have to be subordinated to the love of the music: the process to the end result.

(continued)

Harald Knudsen, a business school professor from Norway, conducts sessions on leadership jazz, at Oxford's Saïd Business School. He brings together a group of jazz musicians who play together temporarily, and at other times play with others. Each member knows the tunes in the musical repertoire by heart. The difference when they play as an ensemble is that they are committed to the music, not to their individual playing. In this way, Knudsen explores the themes of rhythm, melody and harmony in the life of an organisation, and explicitly connects the melody with the strategic domain, rhythm with the operational domain and harmony with the interpersonal domain. He asserts that the Primary Colours Model of leadership also works for musicians playing together.

Team Complementarity

What does it take to create a complementary team? Allegiance to a common vision is a prerequisite. Without it, working together as a team is not easy. Recognising this is the first stage. It is a matter of alignment and engagement. It has to be real and authentic in order to be effective.

> Allegiance to a common vision is a prerequisite. Without it, working together as a team is not easy.

The power of alignment is easy to illustrate. David Pendleton and Jenny King were asked to work with a medical practice that wanted to split well: without acrimony. The doctors had decided that they were incompatible and wanted to create two practices, each with a different approach. There were six partners (doctors) at the time and they were going to create two smaller practices, each with three of the existing partners.

A workshop was convened to effect the split. David and Jenny each met with one of the two groups of three: the nuclei of the two practices that were to be formed. The two groups were asked to formulate their different visions for their practices: what they wanted to achieve together once the 'other' group had been jettisoned. When the two groups came back together, they discovered, to their great consternation, that the groups had independently written almost identical visions for their two future practices. They did not split. They stayed together and worked out their differences having realised that they satisfied the first and crucial precondition of association: they shared a dream. The rest could be worked out, and was, relatively swiftly.

Signing up to a common vision is the best chance of making teams work. But that means you have to be prepared to make a trade-off—as the jazz musicians do, when they downplay their own selfish needs for the good of the music. Ego has to be left at the door or it will get in the way.

In Jim Collins' *Harvard Business Review* article 'Level 5 leadership', he described leaders who had each achieved a remarkable turnaround of companies that had been moribund for years. The team researched data on the Fortune 1000 companies in the USA. They were looking for companies whose performance had lagged behind their sectors for 15 consecutive years and then outperformed their sectors for another 15 years. They found just 11 companies that satisfied these unusual criteria. The defining difference in the turnaround seemed to be the CEO's personality. They were each characterised by a singular lack of ego and a relentless focus on a few key priorities. They were not charismatic but modest and intensely persistent. In the research, little mention is made of the *team* at the top but modest CEOs tend to listen well and have a significant advantage over those described as charismatic: they tend to take their teams with them.

Examples of these Principles in Action

John Rishton is a clear example. John was brought in as CFO and became CEO to turn around Ahold, the Amsterdam-headquartered food retailing multinational, from a series of setbacks that had caused a collapse in the share price and had been accompanied by a fraud in one of its US subsidiaries. John's style is quiet, calm and down to earth. He is bright and sees issues clearly but he is extremely self-effacing, believing in the collective judgement of the team at the top when they work together effectively. He does not impose his will on his team but ensures that they debate issues fully and carefully until they reach a shared understanding of the issues and opportunities they are facing. They then take decisions together and commit to them. When John had achieved a successful re-establishment of credibility of the organisation and a stable and growing share price, he was asked to take over and become CEO of Rolls-Royce in the UK, from which he has now retired. Even after a remarkable turnaround at Ahold, and even in private, he simply would not accept credit for the turnaround. It was the team's success. This is a mark of great integrity and maturity. It is authentic.

John will argue seriously that many of the lessons he has learned about life and about leadership have been learned on the sports field. His background includes an almost fanatical enthusiasm for watching and playing football. Despite his success and elevated position running a €31Bn organisation, he still turned out to play football on a public park on Sunday mornings and suffer the ignominy of being dumped on his backside as a result of a rough tackle from an over-enthusiastic youth who neither knows nor cares who John is or about the 186,000 people who worked for him. John loves the game and plays for the team. That is a key part of his DNA and it shows whether he is running to collect a pass or running one of the world's leading retail organisations.

Dick Boer took over as Ahold CEO and has inevitable changed some of John Rishton's practices while holding on to others. Dick, a retailer for the majority of his career (and was even brought up in a retail environment as a child), brought great strategic clarity to the next stage of Ahold's evolution. He has continued John's huge respect for complementary differences and has christened the Primary Colours Model 'the incomplete leadership model' to convey the key tenet that we are all incomplete as leaders, needing the contributions of others to complete us. He has ensured his team complements him and even applied the same idea to organisational change, ensuring that the capabilities of the Europeans and Americans work together to create capabilities that neither possessed alone and ensuring transfer of knowledge, insights, skills and people between the two continental organisations.

Dick Boer's personal modesty and authenticity get him trusted in the organisation and foster trust in others. As Delhaize and Ahold now seek to merge in 2016, authenticity matters. Huge issues are at stake and strategic matters predominate but trust between CEOs is an essential ingredient which could scupper the deal. In this case, trust between the CEOs seems to be facilitating. Dick Boer is unthreatened by the capability of others, embracing it in the knowledge that complementary differences make people, teams and organisations stronger.

Another example of team based leadership is Sir Rod Eddington. He has been CEO of three airlines: Cathay Pacific Airways, Ansett Australia and British Airways (BA). In each of these organisations, he was deemed to have been successful. He achieved arguably the greatest of his successes at BA where from 2000 to 2005 he established the conditions for the airline to move from a position of making almost no profit at all to being the world's most profitable airline. He is an Australian but was honoured with a Knighthood by Queen Elizabeth II for his services to the aviation industry. He is now Chairman for Australia and New Zealand of JP Morgan, the global securities and banking firm and a non-executive director of other major organisations.

Eddington's success could be attributed to many things. He is extremely bright and has a near-photographic memory. He was a Rhodes Scholar to Oxford University where he gained a doctorate in nuclear physics. It may not take a rocket scientist to run an airline, but BA had one. He spent almost 30 years in the airline industry but his success probably owes as much to his sporting history as to his academic and career histories. Rod represented the Australian Universities at Australian rules football. He represented Oxford University at cricket and was also a keen rugby player. His best position was captain. Now, of course, we know that captain is not a position, strictly speaking, but his strategic nous and his ability to create the conditions for others to succeed was still probably his greatest contribution on the sports field (though he might protest and refer to his prowess with bat and ball!).

Jack Rowell, who captained the England rugby team in its amateur days and went on to coach England successfully, stated that he learned more about managing people when he was captain of the rugby team than when he was working for Procter & Gamble. In Rowell's era, as player and as coach, players were unpaid, so they had to respect his leadership—otherwise he was in trouble.

Rod Eddington will readily explain the significance of sport for business success. It is nothing to do with sponsorship or advertising but with learning about teamwork. When Rod ran BA, his team of direct reports (earlier dubbed the BA Leadership Team or BALT) functioned well.

They discussed issues vigorously—his maxim was 'play the ball and not the man' emphasising the need to respect colleagues and treat them with courtesy while focusing important disagreements on the issues in hand: on the view that was being expressed rather than the person who held it. He lived by this rule personally and demanded it of others. He also refused to overrule the team and seemed willing to live by the decisions made from the joint wisdom of the team rather than from his own view of the world. His CFO? John Rishton. Great teamwork seems to seek out and beget those who are compatible with such a dearly held ideal.

A third powerful example is David Cruickshank, Chairman of Deloitte in the UK since 2007. Deloitte is one of the world's leading professional service firms and it is a partnership. Accordingly, leadership is far from straightforward since those being led include the partners who are also co-owners of the organisation. Deloitte grew strongly in the first decade of the twenty-first century and took over the UK Andersen practice in 2002 after Andersen was derailed by Enron's collapse. David led the integration of the Andersen and Deloitte tax practices in the UK and was widely recognised as having done so successfully and without significant disruption.

Deloitte also had a larger-than-life CEO during this time—John Connolly—thus the role of Chairman was fraught with potential difficulties which David navigated effectively as witnessed by his re-election as Chairman in 2011 when John had stepped down as CEO and David Sproul was appointed CEO from the partnership. David Cruickshank has always intuitively understood the power of complementary leadership. At the top of the organisation, Connolly was frequently described as a bold bruiser and Cruickshank an entirely different character: urbane, reasonable, thoughtful and modest. The two were a highly effective pair.

Cruickshank has always operated on these principles, however. As the head of Deloitte's tax division from 1998 to 2006, he worked closely with one partner who acted as a virtual COO who handled the detailed issues in the tax operation, and another colleague who led on matters of innovation. David took care of three issues: setting strategic direction, building the team and looking after the relationship with the Regulators. It was not that David could not do the other roles at all, but rather that he took no particular satisfaction from them and recognised that his colleagues could handle them more effectively than he could himself. He ensured that each of the three freed up the other two people to do what they did best. Interviewing Cruickshank in 2011, he was clear:

> I had no problems taking the tough decisions if someone was not perform-
> ing, though that is never pleasant, it is just that I knew where my strengths
> lay and wanted to play to my strengths as well as the strengths of my col-
> leagues. We used to put potential partners through assessment centres and
> expected them to be good at everything, but now we want them to be world-
> class at something since average performers are exposed in flat markets.

It is not insignificant that David Cruickshank is modest and this shows up in his personality profile. He is prepared to trust the collective wisdom of his Board and refrains from seeking to push through decisions for which there is inadequate buy-in, recognising that this usually actually speeds up implementation despite sometimes taking a little longer to get to a decision. The trade-off is generally worth having. Similarly, he has brought in prominent Chairmen of other world-class organisations to help his own Board develop insights into their role and contributions. He has his ego well managed and yet he is hugely ambitious for the firm and his own tax practice.

In Box—Teams at Work

3. Football
Sporting examples of team success are so plentiful that it is hard for them not to seem like clichés. Contrast the fates of Real Madrid in the 1990s and 2000s with Nottingham Forest FC in the 1970s. Real Madrid twice assembled a team of 'galácticos'—the best players, irrespective of cost. Real have won many trophies but their quest has been the Champions League title, which eluded them during this time. Nottingham Forest in the 1970s may not have been the team with the best individual players but they won the European Cup two seasons running in 1978/9 and 1979/80. Great individuals often find it hard to play together, as they are used to being pre-eminent and being supported by others. The difference was, almost certainly, Brian Clough who, as manager of Nottingham Forest, blended an odd assortment of players into a championship-winning team. Yet he did it by subjugating the players' wills to his own. We are not recommending this approach because the legacy, when the despotic leader finally bows out, is that the team tends to fall apart.

Teamwork

We have argued that, in order to make a team work, there needs to be a lack of ego and a willingness to subjugate individual needs to a common good. Michael West and colleagues at Aston Business School have conducted extensive research on what makes teams effective. They have described the inputs, processes and outputs that lead to effective outcomes for teams. They have shown that effective teamwork is the result of such factors as:

- Inputs: Having a clear team task, having clear and distinct team roles in pursuit of the task, having a diverse team and ensuring that the team size is not too big
- Processes: Having and pursuing clear objectives, wide participation in the work of the team, having an emphasis on quality, supporting innovation, taking time out to reflect and, of course, effective leadership

These inputs and processes have been shown to have powerful effects. They are protective of the physical and mental health of team members, associated with vastly increased productivity in teams, increased innovation and greater commitment to stay with the team and the organisation.

Yet the issue of team effectiveness is not the point of this book. Nor even is it about how to lead teams effectively. The issue with which we are dealing is how to create *teams that lead*. We need to understand how to create complementary teams of leaders who will provide the leadership of an organisation *together*. There may be a single individual who is thought of as the boss, but the wise leader does not seek to dominate but to create the conditions in which the team around him or her leads together. This was Rod Eddington's, John Rishton's, Dick Boer's and David Cruickshank's *modus operandi* and it is likely to be their legacy unless the Boards of their respective organisations subsequently lurch between extremes.

The issue with which we are dealing is how to create *teams that lead*.

Building and Balancing the Leadership Team

When new leaders are appointed, they naturally see it as their job to find out how well equipped the team is to face the challenges ahead. In 2008, when Carl Schlicker took over as President of Stop and Shop, the Massachusetts-based retail supermarket chain and part of the Ahold Group, he understood the size of his challenge after several years of gentle decline. Around 80,000 people looked to him for leadership of their $17Bn-turnover organisation, in one of the deepest recessions in history.

He looked at his team, and the corporate strategy, to find out who he had on the team to deal with the various functions it had to perform. He knew he had people hired by his predecessor to deal with marketing, someone on merchandising, a manager for operations, people for HR, finance and so on. In other words, he went through his team auditing it against the usual corporate functions. Yet Carl knew that he worked in a particular way. He had an uncanny instinct for the business and for the changes that needed to be made. He could recognise well-run supermarkets and could inject a sense of urgency into the organisation concerning changes that needed to be made. He could plot the course ahead with skill and clarity. He saw the size of the changes required and approached them unafraid.

Yet Carl also knew that he was not a detail-oriented manager. He was an inspirer and an enabler with great credibility. Yet for many of his more recent years, he had worked with a detail-oriented executive who would put the focus into his organisation. He needed his colleague Jeff Martin to join him. It was not that Carl did not have people for each function, it was that he and Jeff were *complementary leaders*. They were not blind to each other's failings but rather they knew each other's strengths and limitations, they liked and respected each other and they cared deeply for each other and the organisation.

Carl invited Jeff to join him from the organisation they had, with others, led to 52 successive quarters of growth: Giant of Carlisle, Pennsylvania, another Ahold subsidiary. Jeff agreed and the old team set about its business of creating change and growth in their new setting. The rest of the team was assembled around this central pair: new team members to head finance and HR, blended with established team members leading operations and legal. As we write, there has been a major turnaround in the sales at Stop and Shop, and the team goes from strength to strength.

The first step in this journey was for Carl to understand what he brought to the task personally, his natural strengths, what he could work on to improve in himself and what he needed from others to complement his personal contributions. He then had to ensure he put these people and capabilities around him. He did not need functional complementarity: he had that already—an Executive Vice President (EVP) for each organisational function. He needed leadership and managerial complementarity: complementarity of style and orientation. When Carl retired in 2013, it was not long before Jeff also left the company.

When working with a senior executive—one who is familiar with the usual vocabulary about functions—we tend to ask, 'What's missing when you are not at the team meeting?' and they often reply along the lines, 'I'm the CFO, so what the team lacks in my absence is a deep knowledge of finance.' Yet we want to encourage him or her to consider the question differently. What this new leader lacks is an alternative vocabulary or framework for thinking about contributions in a different way. It makes sense that, in the absence of the CFO, the team may lack a deep knowledge of finance, but beyond that, *what else is missing* if they are absent? We are seeking such comments as: 'I'm the one who defuses the tension', or 'I'm the one who injects a sense of humour', or 'I give the team confidence' or 'I'm the one who challenges'. Once having embarked upon this journey of discovery, we can introduce the frameworks from this book: the Primary Colours tasks and enablers. We may also conduct formal psychological assessments of the teams to provide a more objective view about these matters.

Then we can get to an analysis that might suggest that a team has a predominance of operational types but not many who take care of the interpersonal domain. Such a team is task oriented but can seem relentless in its style. Perhaps a team might have a great number of operational and interpersonal skills but little sense of strategy. A team may be made up of focusers, but not inspirers. Or it may have a tendency to lead through focus and reinforcement (a common, achievement-oriented leadership style) but with little concern for enablement or learning: no capacity or appetite for reflection and development.

An Alternative Leadership Audit

When taking over the leadership of a team, in any kind of business or organisation, a leader should ask questions like, 'Who looks after strategy? Who is going to drive the delivery of results? Who are the people who are in touch with, and sensitive to, the needs of employees in our division or our department?' These are the first questions to emerge from the Primary Colours Model. At a finer level of detail, the leader needs to ensure there are people who are strategic thinkers, who take the values of the organisation seriously and have a keen sense of the direction the organisation needs to take. Frequently, the CEO considers this to be his or her task, but it does not need to be so: so long as there is at least one senior team member who has this as a key strength.

Then the leader needs to know how strong the planning and organisation is. If the top team have little feel for this, then who is attending to the detail that usually distinguishes between success and failure? A COO or operations director might be looked to for such a contribution but it would be a serious error to assume this is so without confirming it in fact. We have known the senior teams of large project-based organisations whose planning and organisation is less than strong, confounding all expectations. Next, we need to know who is the inspirer: who has the capacity to align the organisation. This contribution is likely to be made at a senior level by someone who is known to care, *and* to be a clear thinker and a powerful communicator. Remember that inspiration has an intellectual component and an emotional component. Just one or the other will seldom be sufficient (see chapter 4). There has to be a high degree of trust in this individual(s): someone who is credible and persuasive.

The audit continues to consider all the elements of the Primary Colours approach, tasks and enablers. This audit is a true leadership audit, not a functional audit. The organisation chart typically allows a functional audit at a glance. The leadership audit requires much more persistence and skill. Whether such an audit is undertaken formally or informally, it needs to be conducted systematically, leaving nothing to chance. The leadership audit deploys all elements of the primary colours model: seven tasks and five enablers. The typical place of the enablers in the primary colours model is illustrated in Fig. 6.3.

Fig. 6.3 Tasks and enablers

Inspiration begins the process of creating alignment. It shows colleagues their place in a compelling future. Reinforcement, whether in the form of incentives or other actions, sustains alignment. Focus is the basis of planning and organisation. The leadership team that can remain focused makes planning and organisation easier, whoever is charged with formulating the plans or creating the organisation. Focus maintains a consistency of priorities around which other matters can take their place. An enabling top team helps foster team working. This is a team that is prepared to delegate and to take risks in giving trusted colleagues scope to make their own impressions and to have an impact. Learning genuinely sits at the heart of the model and the organisation. Learning has to be applied in all other areas: it transforms failures into successes and yesterday's performance into the foundation for greater success tomorrow. It banishes blame in order to foster both risk taking and reflection.

> Reinforcement, whether in the form of incentives or other actions, sustains alignment.

Leaders' Insights into Their Own Strengths

Regardless of who conducts a leadership audit, they must consider the degree of insight the boss has into his or her own strengths and limitations. The team leadership audit has to put the 'leader'/boss at the heart of it all, taking his or her self-awareness into account. New leaders often make the error of conducting a rough and ready assessment of the leadership team they have inherited and then considering how he or she may need to fit in themselves. We are suggesting this is the wrong way around. A wise leader understands and accepts his or her own strengths and limitations and considers what he or she needs in the team to be complementary.

The most effective form of such insight is likely to be derived from a systematic and objective assessment of the 'leader', rather than a crude self-assessment with its denials, self-deceptions and blind-spots. There is also evidence that the leaders of top teams (CEOs) are not very accurate in judging their own teams' effectiveness (Rosen and Adair 2007). The *Harvard Business Review* of 2007 carried their study conducted by Heidrick and Struggles in association with the University of Southern California's Centre for Effective Organizations. It examined the differences between the team effectiveness ratings of CEOs and those of their team members. It demonstrated among over 120 teams, that the CEOs typically overestimated the team's effectiveness, compared with the ratings of the team members themselves. Thus, the need for an external and more objective audit of these matters may be strong from time to time.

With the team leader, the same assessment needs to be conducted as with the other team members. But there are a few additional questions to be asked of him or her:

1. How accurate is the leader's self-perception? If the leader has an inflated view of his or her contributions, then the ability of the team to influence that leader will be reduced. This is a matter of judgement. An indication of his or her modesty is also helpful and this is a subscale on the NEO personality inventory.
2. How open is the leader to new ideas and practices? Leaders can be very conservative. They may even have achieved a leadership position precisely because they are regarded as a 'safe pair of hands' and a steadying influence. If this is the case, then the team's ability to suggest radical change will be reduced. The NEO also provides information about this, as does any 'Big 5' personality measure.
3. What are the leader's security needs? Coping with pressure is a key element of an assessment based on the Primary Colours Model, but it is

especially sensitive in the case of the team leader since he or she will often have the final say in most decisions. Leadership is often about coping with ambiguity and uncertainty and especially in the strategic domain where little is certain. Leaders who have a strong need for security may avoid risk to an unhealthy degree or become overly controlling. The MVPI, a psychometric questionnaire, provides insight about this and other motives and needs.

4. When the leader is under pressure, what is his or her likely pattern of reactions? Leaders can be derailed when a positive characteristic, such as confidence, becomes overplayed into arrogance, or when enthusiasm spills over into the volatility that switches from uniquely positive to uniquely negative perceptions. The leader needs to know those over-reactions to which he or she is most prone in order to advise the team how to take appropriate action (see chapter 8 in this volume and further reading is available in *Why CEOs Fail* by Dotlich and Cairo for more on this.)

Thus, the team leader is the foundation of the team upon which the team of leaders needs to be built. Subsequent analysis will consider where the team is strong and where there are gaps. Consider the following example based on a real team:

The CEO had not been to university and had only ever worked in one company since leaving the navy. He was assessed as being a good CEO but not especially strong either in strategic thinking or team working. The team had been assessed to be at least competent at their senior level in all aspects of the primary colours leadership model, though nobody was especially strong strategically except the HR director who had announced his intention to leave, when the time was right, to run his family business in a non-competing industry.

The CEO's personality profile showed him to be extremely modest, emotionally stable and open to new ideas. He was somewhat prone to arrogance when under pressure but was aware of it and asked his colleagues, genuinely, to let him know whenever he seemed not to be listening to them. He always responded positively to such feedback.

The prognosis for such a team is good. It is not perfect, nor is it complete, but the CEO makes it easy for the team to help him. He needs to recruit a more strategically minded colleague to lead in that aspect of the work of the organisation when the HR director moves on, or develop another team member in this area. He has time to do this. He also needs to allow his colleagues to take a lead in team working. He is open to their influence and accepts his strengths and limitations.

If the CEO had been shown to have an inflated view of his strengths, or denied his weaknesses, the prognosis would have been poor. Similarly, if the team had merely duplicated the CEO's strengths and limitations, the effort taken to make the team more complete would have been greater.

Creating and Maintaining Complementarity

There is a saying that 'safety is no accident', and in the same way, team complementarity is no accident: it has to be engineered into the team. If a new chief executive arrived to find there was no-one in the HR function, he or she would ensure they quickly recruited highly qualified HR professionals. Yet there could be a chronic shortage of leaders who can create alignment and no-one might know. Or there could be a surfeit of focusers and no enablers.

Awareness of the need for balanced and complementary leadership contributions and a broad repertoire does not happen at a point in time. It is an aspect of a more strategic leadership mindset. One of the key functions of leadership, according to Deborah Ancona of MIT, is sense-making. This is not only about the external environment but also about making the right sense of what is happening inside the organisation. Sense-making is on the one hand about detecting what is happening, but it is also about making the appropriate sense of it, and communicating that sense widely. Arguably, the need for sense-making is as strong inside the organisation and inside the leadership team as it is with respect to the external context.

Leadership teams need to notice that the plan they hatched yesterday is no longer current or that the organisational change they have agreed this afternoon has only a limited time before it is no longer fit for purpose. The world became spectacularly aware, during the 2008/9 financial crisis, that there had been a massive shift in the soundness of banks and the availability of credit. This was not hard to spot because the entire world's financial press was telling us about it. However, changing political, environmental, social or technological situations can often be much more subtle than this.

For example, a company needs to be aware of changes in technology in another sphere than its own that could have a profound effect on the soundness of its own business. With broadcasting, technology is becoming more and more miniaturised so that eventually networks of mobile phones could be used as a collective broadcasting device passing on TV signals as well as a receiving device for telecommunications. These technological changes, known as pico-cells or femto-cells, have to be monitored by those who broadcast through masts or satellites. The same is true of developments in the internet or social networking and their impacts on businesses such as the postal service or even newspapers and books. Businesses are constantly going to have to reinvent themselves and leadership teams are going to have to do the same thing. The balance established in a team can shift. Team members move on to other roles. Team members change as people: sensitivity can dull, motivation decrease and judgement deteriorate.

Keeping the leadership team healthy requires constant attention. It is not established once and for all, like digging the foundations of a house. It is much more similar to a moon shot: small corrections are needed frequently, and, occasionally, major course corrections have to be made boldly. Or perhaps the better analogy is a garden: constant care, nutrition, pruning and awareness of the conditions help the team remain healthy through all seasons.

The issue of balance is crucial in a constantly changing environment, less so when conditions are stable but this is increasingly rare. Differences, as we have seen, can be complementary or fractious: centripetal or centrifugal. Here the individual team leader does have a specific role: to maintain the balance and health of the leadership team: its cohesiveness and its responsiveness to the situation. He or she may not be sufficiently sensitive to discern when such corrections are required but he or she is usually the final arbiter of when such changes have to be made. In most teams it is difficult, though not impossible, for any other team member to take on this role. In some cooperative organisations, the leadership may, in every sense, be collective, but in more traditional organisations there is a hierarchy of influence.

Complementary leadership teams are no exception. Jazz ensembles are about as cooperative as it gets, but even they need someone to call the tune so that the ensemble can play. The minimum is usually for the group to know what they are playing, the tempo and the key. If they will accept these minimum constraints, then their virtuosity can be expressed fully and the audience are likely to enjoy a wonderful musical experience. Without this minimum adherence to shared discipline, they are not so much free as lost.

Creating a Positive Micro-Climate

According to research from the CLC, the greatest impact on employee engagement is the direct line manager. This means that anyone at any point in the organisation who leads others can take the approach outlined in this book. It is not necessary to be working for the perfect boss in order to be a good boss oneself. Even in a storm, anyone with an umbrella can create a discrete micro-climate in which others can shelter. Anyone who takes these ideas seriously can start to make sure that their team is in good shape. They can audit themselves, they can audit their team, they can run the ruler over whatever it is they do to make sure that it is adequately responding to all the factors we have been describing. We can be good leaders at any place in the organisation. Naturally, it is easier to be an effective leader in a complementary team working for an effective top team. The effect of the top team on employee engagement is quite a sizeable effect, but smaller than that of the direct manager. According to the CLC (2004), the relative difference is 25 % for the direct manager, compared with 17 % for the senior executives.

The creation of a micro-climate around a single manager is certainly possible but it requires either for him or her to have a considerable degree of discretion given by the organisation, or a tough-minded stance on his or her own part. In the civil service, for example, where good managers and leaders often feel constrained by the unwillingness of the organisation to tackle obstructive individuals, we have seen even good managers and leaders give up due to feeling unsupported in their push to remove someone whose impact on a team was entirely negative. Yet we have also seen outstanding examples of those who realised that they could take whatever actions they pleased, so long as they themselves were willing to take the consequences. Effective leaders frequently have to trade on their understanding that it is much easier to seek forgiveness than permission, and to do what they consider to be the right thing, even if it means bringing criticism upon themselves. Great leadership has always required an element of courage.

A Systematic Approach

Ensuring the effectiveness of a leadership team can now be undertaken systematically. A system typically comprises inputs, processes, outputs and outcomes arranged sequentially with later elements providing feedback to earlier elements. Thus, for example, when outcomes are not as envisaged, outputs, processes and inputs may be examined to discover why this may be so. In the following section, we describe how leadership may be regarded as a system, its elements and how to use such a system to maintain or enhance leadership team effectiveness (see Fig. 6.4).

Inputs, Processes, Outputs and Outcomes

Leadership occurs in a context. The context may include various historical, cultural and economic factors which would have implications for leadership in a current situation. Here, however, we regard the relevant input issues as to do with the leadership team itself, about which a number of questions may be asked:

- *Inputs*: who is included in the leadership team and what are their individual and collective strengths and limitations? This question may best be answered through a dispassionate assessment process using a model such as the Primary Colours Model as the framework against which the team's members are evaluated. By aggregating the data, an assessment of the team as a whole may be produced. The issue is how well

A systematic approach to leadership
(a leadership audit?)

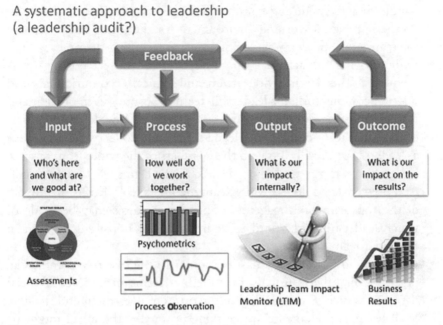

Fig. 6.4 A systematic approach to leadership

are the leadership tasks performed and what is the highest level of proficiency displayed by any of the team members? If the highest level is insufficient then action needs to be taken here first, either by developing the capability of individual team members or by recruiting a more capable individual on to the team.

- *Processes*: how well does this team work together? Some teams bring out the best in each other and others do the reverse, hindering and even disabling team members. Insights about this can come from two principal sources. First, psychometric profiling provides a powerful source of hypotheses. Teams with several members who are highly assertive will probably experience conflict, while teams with several highly conscientious members who score low in openness may be conservative and reject new ideas too quickly. Second, the best source of information about process is to observe it directly. When, where and how does the team set direction, create alignment, build relationships and the like? What is the emotional tone of the team? How do they handle disagreement and conflict? What are the norms and how well do they provide a working environment for the team? How well can the team move between exploring issues to resolving them?

- *Outputs*: what impact does this team have on those reporting to its members? This is the wider team and typically comprises around 50–60 people assuming a leadership team of around seven or eight and typical reporting ratios of around seven to one. How do the members of the wider team evaluate the leadership team's collective effectiveness as leaders? Specifically, how do the members of the wider team rate the leadership team's execution of the tasks in the Primary Colours Model? And how engaged do the wider team members feel? This is the impact of the top team on engagement and thus analysis may be made of which leadership tasks need to be improved to boost engagement in the wider team.[1]

- *Outcomes*: how is the organisation doing? In the case of a commercial organisation, this is usually measured in terms of various financial parameters such as turnover, profit, return on investment and the like. If all leadership elements are working optimally, the effect might be expected to show up in the bottom line of the organisation. Not all measures have to be financial at this level, but they should include the financial outcomes for a commercial organisation.

Measuring at these various levels and in the ways described makes it possible to develop the ability of any team to lead effectively. Improvement should become the systematic consequence of systematic analysis. Operating in this way can become a way of life and should not be thought of as a unique event. This system needs constant attention to keep the effectiveness of the leadership of an organisation at the high level typically required for the organisation to thrive. Yet such analysis is not complex and highly likely to pay handsome dividends both metaphorically and literally.

---

[1] The Edgecumbe Consulting Group has created a *brief* Leadership Team Impact Monitor (LTIM) to evaluate the impact of the leadership team in this way. It has the look and feel of a 360-degree feedback for teams rather than individuals and pinpoints areas where improvement needs to be made as well as areas where the leadership team's self-perception is misaligned with the views of the wider team.

Summary and Conclusion

1. The leader's repertoire responds to the forceful features of a situation to create direction.
2. The unpredictability of the situation favours a broad leadership repertoire just as the unpredictability of the natural environment favours a rich gene pool. The broader the repertoire of skills and attributes in the team, the broader range of challenges to which the team is likely to be able to respond successfully. Such a broad repertoire is more likely to be a feature of collective than individual leadership.
3. A healthy team may be created serendipitously but it is much likely that it will have been created and maintained by deliberate effort. Complementarity can be engineered into a team or fostered by more organic means over time. It begins with a realistic assessment of the strengths and limitations of each member and of their collective strength when all individual contributions are combined. This can be monitored regularly and systematically to produce increasingly effective leadership which maximises its impact and outcomes.

7

Do You Have to Be Smart
to Be a Leader?

The mind is not a vessel to be filled but a fire to be kindled.

Plutarch

I must have a prodigious quantity of mind; it takes me as much as a week sometimes to make it up.

Mark Twain

In the last few chapters we have described the various elements of leadership. We now turn to three related questions. In this chapter we consider the question of intelligence: do you have to be smart to be a leader, and, if so, in what way? In the chapter 8, we examine the evidence on personality and ask what are the characteristics most associated with effective leadership? In chapter 9 we consider what happens when it all goes wrong: when leaders fail and derail.

It is possible to speculate on these questions but we prefer to consider robust evidence. Accordingly, this chapter and the following two are a little more academic in nature and content. We want to be able to describe substantive studies and meta-analyses that combine the results from a wide range of investigations into a focused and authoritative resource. Such evidence does indeed exist. In 2004, Timothy Judge and colleagues conducted

© The Editor(s) (if applicable) and The Author(s) 2016
D. Pendleton, A. Furnham, *Leadership: All You Need To Know*
2nd edition, DOI 10.1057/978-1-137-55436-9_7

a meta-analysis to aggregate 151 independent samples from 96 sources to examine the relationship between intelligence and leadership. They found that the correlation between intelligence and leadership was either 0.21 or 0.27 depending on whether various statistical corrections were made in the analysis. They also state that 'perceptual measures of intelligence' (whether people are perceived to be intelligent—i.e., estimates) showed stronger correlations with leadership than paper and pencil (real) measures. Nevertheless, they concluded that the correlations between intelligence and leadership were considerably lower than originally thought, though the correlation was significant and in the expected direction. As intelligence rises, so does effective leadership but the association—though not random—is weak. It may also be that enough (intelligence) is enough.

If the Judge meta-analysis is correct, then only between 4 % and 7.5 % of leadership effectiveness is accounted for by differences in intelligence between leaders. The reasons for this relatively low correlation cannot be determined with any certainty from the study, but it is important to take on board the small size of the impact of intelligence on leadership. It may be because leadership effectiveness is less to do with solving complex problems and more about bringing the best out of people. Leadership is a contact sport and thus more dependent on social skills than purely cognitive acumen.

The impact of general intelligence on leadership effectiveness may be poorly researched, however, if there are several different types of intelligence to consider. Naturally, there are many definitions of intelligence. The simplest is that intelligence is what intelligence tests measure, though this is circular. More commonly, psychologists describe the difference between specific intelligences and their proposed common root ('g' or general intelligence) which is said to account for the correlations between intelligence measures of all kinds whether verbal, numerical, spatial and so on. If such specific intelligences do indeed exist, then the research aimed at establishing the relationship between intelligence and leadership would need to consider several different possible forms of intelligence and their varying impacts. In addition, we would need to consider in this book that there may be different forms of intelligence better suited to strategic leadership, operational leadership and interpersonal leadership.

In this chapter, we therefore consider the various claims about intelligence, both general and specific, and work through the insights they potentially provide on leadership. We will see that, despite many claims to the contrary, the argument for the existence of multiple intelligences is poor and the evidence weak.

Multiple Intelligences

Psychologists have long been interested in the idea of 'social intelligences'. These are nearly always put in 'inverted commas' because, strictly speaking, they are not intelligences but social skills, or our personality traits in action. The most investigated social intelligence is emotional intelligence, abbreviated frequently to EI or even EQ.

There are many explanations for interest in the social intelligences. One is that cognitive ability (academic intelligence) rarely explains more than a third to a half of the variance in any outcome measure, such as academic achievement, job performance or health. The question is, do the social intelligences predict leadership or management effectiveness better than simple IQ test results? A second reason is that intelligence is difficult to improve or teach, whereas the social intelligences—because they are more to do with skill—are improvable. Third, for over 20 years new advocates of 'multiple intelligences' have been enormously successful in persuading people both of their existence and importance, despite the poor quality of their empirical evidence.

Nick Mackintosh (1998) at Cambridge sees social intelligence as social competence and success in social interactions. He argues that social intelligence is adaptive and can be seen in other animal species. It allows people to understand others' hopes, fears, beliefs and wishes. He believes that is not too difficult to define social intelligence (mainly in terms of social skills) or indeed devise tests to measure it. But he doubts if these many social and interpersonal skills actually form a single dimension, and also whether they are related to standard IQ measures of cognitive ability. Thus, if social intelligence is uncorrelated with IQ, then it may not strictly be 'intelligence' at all, by definition.

Table 7.1 Fourteen intelligences?

Postulated Intelligence	Author	Year
1. Analytical	Sternberg	1997
2. Bodily-kinaesthetic	Gardner	1999
3. Creative	Sternberg	1997
4. Emotional	Salovey and Mayer	1990
5. Interpersonal	Gardner	1999
6. Intrapersonal	Gardner	1999
7. Mathematical	Gardner	1999
8. Musical	Gardner	1999
9. Naturalistic	Gardner	1999
10. Practical	Sternberg	1997
11. Sexual	Conrad and Milburn	2001
12. Spatial	Gardner	1999
13. Spiritual	Emmons	2000
14. Verbal	Gardner	1999

Various researchers believed social intelligence is multifactorial, relating to such issues as social sensitivity, social insight and communication. In other words it is much more of a social or personality variable than a cognitive variable. Thus, emotional intelligence or other social intelligences may be better conceived as a trait than an intelligence.

Since the 1990s there has been an explosion in the number of 'multiple intelligences' proposed. Table 7.1 shows 14 different so-called 'intelligences'.

The two people most powerfully involved with multiple intelligences are Sternberg (1997) and Gardner (1983, 1999). Gardner (1983) defined intelligence as 'the ability to solve problems or to create products that are valued within one or more cultural settings' (p. 11) and specified seven intelligences. He argued that *linguistic/verbal* and *logical/mathematical intelligences* are those typically valued in educational settings. Linguistic intelligence involves sensitivity to the spoken and written language and the ability to learn languages. Logical-mathematical intelligence involves the capacity to analyse problems logically, solve maths problems and investigate issues scientifically. These two types dominate intelligence tests.

Three other multiple intelligences are arts based: *musical intelligence* which refers to skill in the performance, composition and appreciation of musical patterns; *bodily kinaesthetic intelligence* which is based on the use of the whole or parts of the body to solve problems or to fashion products; and *spatial intelligence* which is the ability to recognise and manipulate patterns in space. There are also two personal intelligences: *interpersonal intelligence* which is the capacity to understand the intentions, motivations and desires of other people and to work effectively with them; and *intrapersonal intelligence* which is the capacity to understand oneself and to use this information effectively in regulating one's life.

However, in his later book Gardner (1999) defines intelligence as a 'biopsychological potential to process information that can be activated in a cultural setting to solve problems or create products that are of value in a culture' (pp. 33–4). In it, he introduces three possible new intelligences although he notes: 'The strength of the evidence for these varies, and whether or not to declare a certain human capacity another type of intelligence is certainly a judgement call' (p. 47). However, he only adds one new intelligence, namely *naturalistic intelligence* which is 'expertise in the recognition and classification of the numerous species—the flora and fauna—of his or her environment' (p. 43). It is the capacity to taxonomise: to recognise members of a group, to distinguish among members of a species and to chart the relations, formally or informally, among several species.

The other two potential new intelligences were spiritual and existential. *Spiritual intelligence* is the ability to master a set of diffuse and abstract concepts about being, but also mastering the craft of altering one's consciousness in attaining a certain state. This has recently become an issue of considerable debate (Emmons 2000). *Existential intelligence* is more difficult to define:

> the capacity to locate oneself with respect to the furthest reaches of the cosmos, the infinite and infinitesimal, and the related capacity to locate oneself with respect to such existential features of the human condition as the significance of life, the meaning of death, the ultimate fate of the physical and the psychological worlds and such profound experiences as love of another person or total immersion in a work of art. (p. 61)

Despite its popularity in educational circles, Gardner's theory has been consistently attacked and criticised by those working empirically in the area. Yet it seems quite obvious that leaders need multiple talents to succeed. They might not need to be able to sing and dance but they certainly need to understand themselves and others. So, there are multiple talents but are these intelligences?

Sternberg (1997) has also developed a multi-dimensional model known as the 'triarchic' theory of 'successful' intelligence. The key idea here is that human intelligence comprises three aspects: componential, experiential and contextual. The *componential* aspect refers to a person's ability to learn new things, to think analytically and to solve problems. This aspect of intelligence is manifested through better performance on standard intelligence tests, which require knowledge and ability in areas such as arithmetic and vocabulary. The *experiential* aspect refers to a person's ability to combine different experiences in unique and creative ways. It concerns original thinking and creativity in both the arts and the sciences. Finally, the *contextual* aspect refers to a person's ability to deal with practical aspects of the environment and to adapt to new and changing contexts. This aspect of intelligence resembles what laypeople sometimes refer to as 'street smarts'. Sternberg (1997) popularised these concepts and refers to them as analytic, creative and practical intelligence.

The idea of multiple intelligences seems to have been warmly embraced in the business world. Riggio, Murphy and Pirozzolo (2002) note that the multiple intelligence idea is intuitively appealing because it is self-evident that people require various areas of competence, other than only academic intelligence, to succeed at business leadership. Most organisations have competency frameworks used in selection, assessment and appraisal, and all comprise specific multiple competencies (often between six and eight) that are desirable or required to do the job. They nearly always involve cognitive ability and other skills.

The concept of multiple intelligences, particularly emotional intelligence, has become extremely popular. Leadership in the interpersonal domain in particular requires emotional literacy. The reason for HR specialists and others favouring the idea of multiple intelligences is partly due to caution about using traditional intelligence tests. With a trend towards increasing litigation concerning test bias and a general dislike of cognitive ability tests by those who have to take them—despite their proven validity—many have turned to multiple intelligence tests.

Emotional Intelligence (EI or EQ)

Of all the various postulated intelligences, it is the idea of *Emotional Intelligence* that has most captivated people's imaginations, but the 'story' of EI is told rather differently by different groups. Some claim EI was part of the 'multiple intelligence' movement dating back to the social intelligences of the 1920s (Petrides et al. 2004) or the impact of David McClelland who was responsible for other similar concepts like competency.

Daniel Goleman's (1995) international best-seller *Emotional Intelligence: Why it Can Matter more than IQ* and follow-up *Working with Emotional Intelligence* (Goleman 1998) propelled EI into the limelight and influenced most subsequent ideas of EI. Towards the latter half of the 1990s, the first EI measures started to appear. A difficulty arises, however, with deciding exactly which are the 'facets' or components of EI. As Petrides and Furnham (2001, p. 428) put it, 'asking what precisely should be part of a construct is like asking what sports should be in the Olympics; neither questions can be answered objectively' Petrides et al. (2004), however, listed facets of EQ that appear in different conceptualisations of the idea (see Table 7.2).

There are various other models suggesting different dimensions of EI showing how much disagreement there is still in the area. The optimist would say they are really very similar and all talking about the same thing. The pessimist would point out the muddle. Yet each has something to offer to the leader who recognises the social nature of his/her task. Consider the following summary of EI models in Table 7.3.

Unsurprisingly, with so many different formulations of EI, there are many measures of EI derived from the various approaches but they break down into two types: *ability* tests with right/wrong answers, and *preference* tests which look like personality questionnaires. There is a fierce debate among those who advocate these rather different types of measure as to which is more appropriate for purpose. The fact is, however, that they measure different things.

Table 7.2 Facets of EQ according to Petrides et al. (2004)

Facets	High scorers perceive themselves as ...
Adaptability	Flexible and willing to adapt to new conditions
Assertiveness	Forthright, frank, and willing to stand up for their rights
Emotional expression	Capable of communicating their feelings to others
Emotion management (others)	Capable of influencing others people's feelings
Emotion perception (self and others)	Clear about their own and other people's feelings
Emotion regulation	Capable of controlling their emotions
Impulsiveness (low)	Reflective and less likely to give in to their urges
Relationship skills	Capable of having fulfilling personal relationships
Self-esteem	Successful and self-confident
Self-motivation	Driven and unlikely to give up in the face of adversity
Social competence	Accomplished networkers with excellent social skills
Stress management	Capable of withstanding pressure and regulating stress
Trait empathy	Capable of taking someone else's perspective
Trait happiness	Cheerful and satisfied with their lives
Trait optimism	Confident and likely to 'look on the bright side' of life

Emotional Intelligence at Work

It was no doubt Goleman's book that electrified the public and popularised the term EI. He has tried to recapture attention more recently with *Social Intelligence* (Goleman 2006). In his second book on the subject, *Emotional Intelligence at Work,* he extended his ideas to the workplace. Now he has as many as 26 facets subsumed under five domains. Anyone inspecting this system (see below) may become confused, and for good reason. Traits, like conscientiousness, are subsumed under the domain of self-regulation. Equally psychological concepts like initiative and optimism are both classified under motivation though no more than marginally related. It seems difficult, in fact, to determine what is *not* a facet of EI. The layman might ask if the concept has become boundary-less and

Table 7.3 Summary of EI models

Authors	Elements of their approaches	
Salovey and Mayer (1990)	Appraisal and expression of emotion Utilisation of emotion	Regulation of emotion
Goleman (1995)	Self-awareness Self-regulation Self-motivation	Empathy Handling relationships
Mayer and Salovey (1997)	Perception, appraisal, and expression of emotion Emotional facilitation of thinking Understanding and analysing emotions; employing emotional knowledge	Reflective regulation of emotions to promote emotional and intellectual growth
Bar-On (1997)	Intrapersonal Emotional self-awareness Assertiveness Self-regard Self-actualisation Independence Interpersonal Empathy Interpersonal relationship Social responsibility	Adaptation Problem solving Reality testing Flexibility Stress management Stress tolerance Impulse control General Happiness Optimism
Cooper and Sawaf (1997)	Emotional literacy Emotional fitness	Emotional depth Emotional alchemy
Goleman (1998)	Self-awareness Emotional self-awareness Accurate self-assessment Self-confidence Self-regulation Self-control Trustworthiness Conscientiousness Adaptability Innovation Self-motivation Achievement orientation Commitment Initiative Optimism	Empathy Empathy Organisational awareness Service orientation Developing others Leveraging diversity Social skills Leadership Communication Influence Change catalyst Conflict management Building bonds Collaboration and co-operation Team capabilities

(continued)

Table 7.3 (continued)

Authors	Elements of their approaches	
Weisinger (1998)	Self-awareness	Effective communication skills
	Emotional management	Interpersonal expertise
	Self-motivation	Emotional coaching
Higgs and Dulewicz (1999)	Drivers	Enablers
	Motivation	Self-awareness
	Intuitiveness	Interpersonal sensitivity
	Constrainers	Influence
	Conscientiousness	Trait
	Emotional resilience	

thus devoid of precision: meaning all things to all people. The psychologist asks: does the concept of EQ have any divergent validity?

Here are Goleman's 26 Emotional Intelligences organised under their five domains:

Personal: competencies that determine how we manage ourselves:

- *Self-awareness*: knowing one's internal states, preferences, resources and intuitions
- *Emotional awareness*: recognising emotions and their effects
- *Accurate self-assessment*: knowing own strengths and limits
- *Self-confidence*: strong sense of self-worth and capabilities

Self-Regulation: managing one's internal states, impulses and resources

- *Self-control*: keeping disruptive emotions and impulses in check
- *Trustworthiness*: maintaining standards of honesty and integrity
- *Conscientiousness*: taking responsibility for personal performance
- *Adaptability*: flexibility in handling change
- *Innovation*: being comfortable with novel ideas, approaches and new information

Motivation: emotional tendencies that guide or facilitate reaching goals

- *Achievement drive*: striving to improve or meet a standard of excellence
- *Commitment*: aligning with the goals of the group or organisation

- *Initiative*: readiness to act on opportunities
- *Optimism*: persistence in pursuing goals despite obstacles or setbacks

Empathy: awareness of others' feelings, needs and concerns

- *Understanding others*: sensing others' feelings and perspectives and taking an active interest in their concerns
- *Developing others*: sensing others' development needs and bolstering their abilities
- *Service orientation*: anticipating, recognising and meeting customer needs
- *Leveraging diversity*: cultivating opportunities through different kinds of people
- *Political awareness*: reading a group's emotional currents and power relationships

Social Skills: adeptness at inducing desirable responses in others

- *Influence*: wielding effective tactics for persuasion
- *Communication*: listening openly and sending convincing messages
- *Conflict management*: negotiating and resolving disagreements
- *Leadership*: inspiring and guiding individuals and groups
- *Change catalyst*: initiating or managing change
- *Building bonds*: nurturing instrumental relationships
- *Collaboration and co-operation*: working with others toward shared goals
- *Team capabilities*: creating group synergy in pursuing collective goals

The book argues that, at work, relationship building is more important than technical skills. Goleman notes that technical training, in the essential job knowledge of any career, from accountancy to zoology, is easy compared to teaching EQ skills. That is, as an adult it is more straightforward to teach a person the technical aspects of the job than the soft skills. The idea seems to be that there is a critical period to acquire the bases of EI which is probably during adolescence.

To consider an example of how this might arise: a young person, often a male, may experience social anxiety, discomfort and rejection while attempting to interact with and influence others (specifically those they are attracted to). Hence they may, over time, find solace in computers and other activities with a high skills/low contact content. Thus, in early adulthood, they appear to be technically very competent in certain areas (e.g., IT, engineering) but still rather undeveloped in people skills and more specifically emotional awareness and regulation. They may even be 'phobic' about emotional issues and resistant to (social skills) training. It is also assumed that such people are less able to pick up EI skills as well as less willing to try. To acquire technical skills often requires considerable dedication and time, and in this way opportunities to acquire social skills (EQ) are, therefore, reduced. Consequently the low EQ person chooses technology rather than people for fun, comfort or a source of ideas because they do not understand emotions. Low EQ becomes self-sustaining in the same way that high EQ does and the sub-populations diverge.

In the workplace, the argument goes that failed and derailed managers tend to be rigid, with poor self-control, poor social skills and are weak at building bonds (see chapter 9). Understanding and using emotions/feelings are at the heart of business and indeed of being human. It is, says Goleman (1998) no accident that the words 'motive' and 'emotion' share the same Latin root meaning 'to move' … great work starts with great feeling.

> Understanding and using emotions/feelings are at the heart of business and indeed of being human.

Goleman has either captured or created a zeitgeist. In their book entitled *Executive EQ*, Cooper and Sawaf (1997) put forth the four cornerstones of EI at the executive level: *emotional literacy* (involving the knowledge and understanding of one's own emotions and how they function); *emotional fitness* (involving trustworthiness and emotional hardiness and flexibility); *emotional depth* (involving emotional growth and intensity) and *emotional alchemy* (involving using emotions to discover creative opportunities). There are many others with broadly similar themes and conclusions.

Zeidner et al. (2004), three world-class academics working in the area, provided a useful critical overview of the role of EQ in the workplace. Business people prefer to talk about emotional competencies (rather than traits or abilities) which are essentially *learned capabilities*. In this sense, EQ is 'the potential to become skilled at learning certain emotional responses' (p. 377). It, therefore, does not ensure that individuals will (as opposed to can) manifest competent behaviours at work. Thus, EQ is an index of potential. However, emotional competence does, it is argued, assist in learning (soft) interpersonal skills.

Perhaps more accurately, emotional competence is an *element* of interpersonal skills or social skills. Yet if one is to include older related concepts—like social skills or interpersonal competencies—then it is possible to find a literature dating back 30 years showing that these skills predict occupational effectiveness and success. Furthermore, there is convincing empirical research which suggests that these skills can be improved and learned.

> emotional competence is an *element* of interpersonal skills or social skills

However Zeidner et al. (2004) are quite rightly eager to squash the IQ vs EQ myth. They note (our italics):

> *several unsubstantiated claims* have appeared in the popular literature and the media about the significance of EI in the workplace. Thus, EI has been claimed to validly predict a variety of successful behaviours at work, at a level exceeding that of intelligence … Of note, however, Goleman is unable to cite empirical data supporting any causal link between EI and any of its supposed, positive effects. (p. 380)

Zeidner and colleagues review studies which provide positive, mixed and negative results. Quite rightly they offer critiques of the studies which purport to show EQ linked to work success. Typical problems include:

- The psychometric properties of the EQ measure
- Not controlling for intelligence (cognitive ability) or personality factors
- Not having very robust measures of work-related behaviour

- Not being able to disentangle the direction of causality through using longitudinal studies
- Having too many impressionistic, anecdotal studies and few published in peer-reviewed journals.

The authors are also interested in the explanation for the process. Thus *if* EQ does predict satisfaction, productivity, team work and so on, the question is what is the *process* or *mechanism* that accounts for this? It seems in the literature, there are various speculations to account for this:

- High-EQ people are better at communicating their ideas, intentions and goals. They are more articulate, assertive and sensitive
- EQ is closely associated with teamwork social skills which are very important at work
- Business leaders, high in EQ, build supportive climates which increase organisational commitment which in turn leads to success
- High-EQ leaders are perceptive and know their own and their teams' strengths and weaknesses which enable them to leverage the former and compensate for the latter
- EQ is related to effective and efficient coping skills which enable people to deal with demands, pressure and stress better
- High-EQ leaders can accurately identify what followers feel and need, as well as being more inspiring and supportive. They generate more excitement, enthusiasm and optimism
- High-EQ managers, unlike their low-EQ companions, are less prone to negative, defensive and destructive coping and decision-making styles

Zeidner et al. (2004) summarise as follows:

> our review suggests that the current excitement surrounding the potential benefits from the use of EI in the workplace may be premature or even misplaced. Whereas EI appears related to performance and affective outcomes, the evidence for performance is very limited and often contradictory. Much of the predictive validity of questionnaire measures of EI may be a product of their overlap with standard personality factors. Furthermore,

the literature is replete with unsubstantiated generalisations, with much of the existing evidence bearing on the role of EI in occupational success either anecdotal or impressionistic and/or based on unpublished or in-house research. Thus, a number of basic questions still loom large: Do emotionally intelligent employees produce greater profits for the organisation? Does EI enhance well-being at the workplace? Are the effects of training in EI likely to result in increases in job performance and/or work satisfaction? (p. 380)

In order to provide both good theory and evidence to support the use of EQ in organisational settings, Zeidner et al. (2004) recommend that the measures have to be reliable and valid, matched to the job and clearly related to outcomes. They conclude:

Despite the important role attributed to a wide array of emotional competencies in the workplace, there is currently only a modicum of research supporting the meaningful role attributed to EI (and nested emotional competencies) in determining occupational success. Many of the popular claims presented in the literature regarding the role of EI in determining work success and well-being are rather misleading in that they seem to present scientific studies supporting their claims, while in fact failing to do so. In short, despite some rather fantastic claims to the contrary, the guiding principle appears presently as 'caveat emptor'. (p. 393)

The claims about EI and leadership are all subject to this same caveat.

Business or Managerial Intelligence

In a study of in-patriate managers, Harvey, Novicevic and Kiessling (2002) listed eight 'managerial intelligences'. They took as their starting point Sternberg's (1985) triarchic theory of intelligence, but split the three intelligences further. Thus *analytic* intelligence is split into cognitive and emotional intelligence; *practical* intelligence into political, sociocultural, organisational and network intelligence; and *creative* intelligence into innovative and intuitive intelligence. Clearly this classification is controversial: as we have seen, emotional intelligence is not part of general or cognitive intelligence.

The authors argue that cognitive IQ is the 'g' factor of general intelligence that measures problem-solving abilities. They categorise emotional intelligence within the analytic category because 'emotional development and maturity are viewed as necessary to allow managers to effectively utilise their cognitive abilities. The importance of emotional intelligence increases with the level of authority in an organisation'.

The four practical intelligences are, inevitably, more controversial. *Political IQ* is defined as:

the ability to gain resources through exercising political power in situations where ambiguity and accountability levels allow for a shaping (i.e., spin) of attitudes and images among those being influenced ... A high political IQ refers to having a sense about the social infrastructure and the individuals that occupy key positions that can be instrumental in exercising influence to change resource, allocation or direction of the decision making. (p. 506)

Socio-cultural IQ is really cultural knowledge and ability to translate or integrate specific cues about culture. *Organisational intelligence* is knowledge of how things are done via policies, procedures, planning processes and audits. It is an understanding of the official formal rules of the organisation and the ability to get things done in a specific organisational context. *Network intelligence* is essentially about interorganisational management, while organisational IQ is about intraorganisational IQ. *Management IQ* is based on the size, structure and centrality of a person's personal relationships crossing organisations.

According to Harvey and colleagues, the two creative intelligences are innovative and intuitive. *Innovative intelligence* is defined as:

the ability to think in abstract terms, to develop business ideas and concepts that have not been conceptualised by others, constitutes business innovation. The embodiment of ideas/concepts into new processes, products, services and technologies is a valuable outcome of innovation. (p. 511)

Intuitive intelligence seems harder to define, and the authors talk about its subconscious origin, tacit nature, sixth sense and gut knowledge.

The authors provide a profile that allows anyone to score individuals on their eight intelligences. They do *not*, however, provide any data for their theory that supports the threefold classification. More importantly, they make little attempt to distinguish between abilities and traits or to consider whether it is possible to train or develop these intelligences. Interestingly nearly all the measures they propose for each of the IQs, save cognitive intelligence, are measured by self-report questionnaires about preferences, rather than power-based ability tests. Nevertheless, people recognise these different abilities/skills and traits (Table 7.4).

Table 7.4 Eight managerial intelligences according to Harvey et al. 2002

Type of IQ	Description
Cognitive	The traditional measure of intellectual ability. This IQ measures the ability to reason, learn and think analytically
Emotional	The ability to use one's own affective state to tap the affective state of others to accomplish objectives. The ability to display an appropriate emotional state and to respond to others' emotions in an effective manner
Political	The ability to use the formal and informal power in the company to accomplish objectives The ability to know how to prudently, judiciously and artfully use power in the organisation
Sociocultural	The extent to which one is adequately socialised in a society, an organisation, or a subculture. Recognition and understanding of roles, norms, routines and taboos, in various setting
Organisational	Having a detailed and accurate understanding of how the organisation operates both functionally and the time that is needed to accomplish certain tasks in the company. The detailed knowledge of how to 'get things done' in the company
Network	The ability to get things done with multiple organisational units. Accomplishing the goals of the company effectively by recognising, understanding and managing interorganisational relations
Creative	The ability to diverge/innovate in thinking and create fresh novel ideas and solutions to problems. The ability to address problems/issues with insight and resourcefulness and to find unique solutions
Intuitive	The ability to have quick insights into how to solve problems or to address situations without past experience of the problem, and without formally processing information (e.g., street-smart)

The concept of business IQ—at least as outlined by Harvey et al.—has not, as yet, attracted much attention. Certainly there remains little evidence of the separate 'unique' existence of these intelligences or indeed evidence that they predict anything. One of the advantages of Harvey, Novicevic and Kiessling's (2002) description of managerial intelligences is that they use psychological and psychometric concepts and translate them into the language of business. Clearly there are elements of problem solving in leadership. There are also social and political elements and a need to understand human motivation. The concepts are relevant to leadership, but here we are demanding much more. We want to see the evidence of the impact, and the *size* of the impact of these proposed intelligences on leadership effectiveness.

Once again although this idea is immensely appealing to consultants and managers, it is essentially misleading to label these 'intelligences'. It would be more sensible, however, to call these competencies. The question, rarely asked but nevertheless very important, concerns the origin of such 'intelligences'/competencies. How and when are they acquired? Can they easily be taught? Are there systematic—for example gender—differences in these competencies? How are they measured? Are people accurate at self-assessment? Are they linked in any systematic way, that is, is there an underlying structure to these beliefs? And, most importantly, what is their relationship with cognitive ability as measured by conventional power tests of intelligence?

Yet More Quotients of 'Intelligence'

Eichinger and Lombardo (2004) identified what they call the '"6 Qs of Leadership' and an explanation for how they combined to lead to success or failure. On the face of it, these different quotients could account for different degrees of success in our Primary Colours Model. The 6 Qs are:

- *Intelligence Quotient (IQ)*: Information processing, a good memory and ability to learn; the definition of IQ. It's very important and easy to assess. Managers who can handle large amounts of information, see patterns and trends, and can multitask best.

- *Technical/Operational Quotient (TQ)*: It measures how able managers are to manage ideas and projects, understand salient technology and operations and, in short, get things done. Those who fail may be too overdependent on a single competency or poor at initialising or following through. Again it's easy to measure by on-the-job measures of success. It is therefore particularly important early on in a career.
- *Motivational Quotient (MQ)*: This is the desire to achieve, lead and succeed and be prepared to sacrifice quality of life and work–life balance for it. It is about perseverance, getting, results and a focused compulsion to master the tasks at hand. It's about energy, commitment and goal setting. The high-MQ manager pursues stretching goals which get them out of their comfort zone.
- *Experience Quotient (XQ)*: This refers to amount and kinds (quality and quantity) of experiences managers have had. Some experiences are more 'developmental' than others. They learn more from personal experience than from the stories of others and they can be taught to benefit from experience. So, working abroad, making changes in scope, size, area, starting something from scratch are all relevant. It's about dealing with hardships and setbacks. Some bosses help by giving their staff wide experience of different problem domains. For XQ, more is better and broader is better.
- *People Quotient (PQ)*: This is about self-management and self-awareness of motives, emotions and actions on subsequent behaviour and others. Next there is a curiosity and openness with others. This is the essential, inspirational, charming stuff. Building strong bonds, strong teams, keeping the troops happy, being open and sensitive to others. Those with low PQ don't, can't or won't appropriately delegate or empower others. It is working with and through others, not moving away from or against them. Low PQ means poor, shallow relationships. It's really EQ relabelled.
- *Learning Quotient (LQ)*: This is learning agility: learning to think, manage and solve problems in a different way. It's 'street smarts'. People with higher IQ cope better with ambiguity and complexity; they experiment and handle new ideas deftly. They are characterised by curiosity and imagination. They seize opportunities and adapt well to new situations. They learn to adapt and hence survive. 'Know it alls'

who resist feedback and don't share knowledge fail. This skill is best tested in new assignments, ventures, Mergers and Acquisitions and responding to new competitors. Learning agility is the ability to make the most of experience.

Note that these authors talk of quotients not 'intelligences'. That is, they are measureable but not necessarily to be thought of as intelligence.

Summary and Conclusion

1. Many proposed intelligences purport to be related to leadership effectiveness. Most are not intelligences at all: they are competencies or capabilities. These are interpersonal skills that are measurable and learnable but they are not measures of purely *cognitive* acumen.
2. In terms of the Primary Colours Model, there are not different types of intelligence at work, but there may be different competencies that are related to success in the various aspects of leadership. Hence we spoke of ripple intelligence, problem solving and emotional intelligence in the context of the strategic, operational and interpersonal domains in chapter 1 but these are really competency differences.
3. When attempts are made to measure the impact of IQ or traditional intelligence on leadership, correlational techniques tend to be used. Strictly, these do not measure causality but merely association. We are thus left with the stark finding that the size of the association between leadership and intelligence is small and accounts for no more than 7.5 % of the variance in leadership effectiveness.

In chapter 8 we examine the power of personality measures to predict leadership effectiveness or rather the association between them. We see that the effect is much bigger than the impact of intelligence but, as we conclude this chapter on intelligence and leadership, we can state that there is a positive and significant correlation between leadership and intelligence though the relationship is weak. To answer the question in this chapter's title: you don't have to be smart to be a leader, but it helps.

8

The Impact of Personality on Leadership

Chapter 7 has demonstrated that the relationship between intelligence and leadership is counter-intuitive. It would seem reasonable to expect that intelligence would have a strong correlation with leadership effectiveness, yet the effect, as we have seen, is weak and accounts for no more than 7.5 % of the variance in leadership effectiveness. In the case of personality and leadership, we might expect that the effect would be considerably less than that of intelligence, and yet we shall see here that the effect is much stronger for personality. Personality accounts for 23 % of the variance in leadership emergence and effectiveness together though just 16 % for effectiveness alone (Judge et al. 2002; Hogan and Kaiser 2005). Though personality does not account for the majority of the variance, personality is something like three times more powerful than intelligence in explaining leadership emergence (who becomes a leader) and leadership effectiveness, and twice as powerful as intelligence in predicting leadership effectiveness alone.

In order to explain the findings for personality we will first consider what personality is and then consider its impact on leadership. We will examine in particular the dominant personality theory, dubbed the

© The Editor(s) (if applicable) and The Author(s) 2016
D. Pendleton, A. Furnham, *Leadership: All You Need To Know*
2nd edition, DOI 10.1057/978-1-137-55436-9_8

Five-Factor Model (or FFM). In chapter 9 we then examine the evidence on how over-reactions to pressure can derail otherwise effective leaders when the pressure mounts.

What is Personality?

Personality might simply be described as a predisposition to act, think and feel in certain ways. People described as kind have a predisposition to act generously; those described as sociable to spend time with people; those described as curious to investigate and experiment and so on. Personality has elements that are almost certainly genetically determined, such as anxiety, and those that are more probably acquired, such as self-discipline. Yet by adulthood personality is relatively unchanging: the mix of genetic and learned influences has stabilised and the patterns have been established. Personality is not invariant but it is slow to change. Yet personality does not influence behaviour in a manner that is strongly predetermined. It is not like the laws of physics whose effects can be predicted with great accuracy. Personality affects the *probability* that a certain behaviour will follow, but the probability seldom approaches anything like 100 %. In addition, personality interacts with the situation in which the individual is located, affecting both how the situation is perceived and the situation's effects on the individual. Behaviour in any situation is a function of the interaction between the person (personality) and the situation itself.

At one level, this all seems very simple and straightforward, and yet for a hundred years psychologists have tried to describe as parsimoniously and as scientifically as possible the nature of personality. There are almost 20,000 personality trait words in English. Some are used by psychologists in a 'technical' sense, and others are almost ignored by personality researchers. Words like stoicism, fortitude and integrity are strangely missing from most personality profiles. Laypeople describe and explain behaviour they see (in others) by the use of trait words, for example, 'He is an extrovert', 'She is impulsive', 'They are neurotic', even 'He has no personality', though this cannot be true in a technical sense. Personality descriptions come naturally to most of us and the attempt to understand personality has been a part of both lay language and scientific enquiry for thousands of years. Darwin would almost certainly have argued that there is survival value in being able to predict the behaviour of others and personality descriptions are part of this attempt to predict behaviour accurately for all of us.

One of the earliest documented attempts to produce a systematic theory of what we now refer to as personality was that of the ancient Greeks, typified by Galen (see Fig. 8.1). Galen was a Roman but of Greek ethnicity and continued the Greek traditional approach to medicine and other disciplines known as humourism which dated back to Hippocrates. The idea was that the body was made up of four basic elements or humours and all ill-health or personality problems originated from an imbalance between the four humours. Strange as this sounds to modern ears, this formulation was only finally abandoned in the mid-nineteenth century with the discovery of cellular pathology.

Galen's formulation goes back to AD 200 and his work *On the Temperaments*. He postulated that all people were governed by humours or bodily fluids that led to four temperaments—choleric, melancholic,

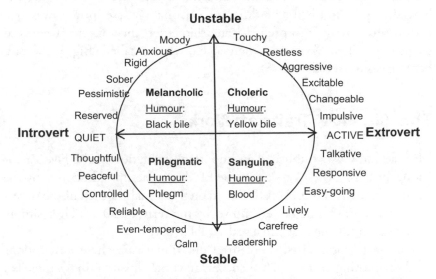

Fig. 8.1 The four humours according to Galen (AD 200) and two modern personality dimensions

phlegmatic and sanguine: words that are still part of our contemporary vocabulary and still to be found in novels and newspapers, though not in textbooks on personality. His theory can be mapped on to twenty-first-century personality dimensions, such as Extroversion–Introversion and Stable–Unstable, as in the Fig. 8.1. It is also clear that the temperaments described in the Myers-Briggs Type Indicator (MBTI) are similar to the humours where sanguine is essentially the SP temperament in the MBTI, Choleric is the NF temperament, Melancholic is SJ and Phlegmatic is NT.

In contemporary psychology traits are a central concept. Traits are distinguishing qualities or characteristics and are thought to be the more enduring aspects of personality as distinct from states which are, by definition, more transient. There have been many different trait-based approaches to personality, but there is growing consensus that personality is best described as comprising five 'super-traits' or factors. Since the 1980s personality theory has been dominated by this so-called Five-Factor Model (FFM).

This has had an important effect on the research investigating the relationship between personality and leadership. Before this time, the bewildering multiplicity of different personality descriptions was one reason why attempts to predict leadership emergence or effectiveness so frequently failed. With the emergence of the so-called 'Big 5' the task became easier (see chapter 5).

The 'Big Five' Traits at Work

McCrae and Costa published an important validation of the Five-Factor Model in 1987. Their version of the FFM is sometimes described by the acronym OCEAN or CANOE (based on the initials of each of the super-traits) but tends to be better known by the term NEO which is simply the acronym for the first three scales (Table 8.1).

For most pragmatists, the central question is: do these descriptions predict anything useful, such as success at work? Unsurprisingly, there is a considerable body of research to help answer the question. Generally, the answer is yes but with qualification—specific job success is best predicted

Table 8.1 The Big 5 traits

Traits (and synonyms)	Low scores	Average scores	High scores
Neuroticism (Emotionality, Emotional Control, Affect, Stability)	Secure, hardy and generally relaxed, even under stressful conditions	Generally calm and able to deal with stress, but sometimes experience feelings of guilt, anger or sadness	Sensitive, emotional, and prone to experience feelings that are upsetting
Extroversion (Social Adaptability, Surgency, Assertiveness, Power)	Introverted, reserved and serious. Prefer to be alone or with a few close friends	Moderate in activity and enthusiasm. Enjoy the company of others but also value privacy	Extroverted, outgoing, active and high-spirited. Prefer to be around people most of the time
Openness (Enquiring Intellect, Culture, Intelligence, Intellect)	Down-to-earth, practical, traditional and pretty much set in their ways	Practical but willing to consider new ways of doing things. Seek a balance between the old and the new	Open to new experiences. Have broad interests and are very imaginative
Agreeableness (Conformity, Love, Likeability, Friendly Compliance)	Hard-headed, sceptical, proud and competitive. Tend to express anger directly	Generally warm, trusting and agreeable but can sometimes be stubborn and competitive	Compassionate, good-natured and eager to cooperate and avoid conflict
Conscientiousness (Will to Achieve, Responsibility)	Easy-going, not very well organised, and sometimes careless. Prefer not to make plans	Dependable and moderately well organised. Generally have clear goals but are able to set work aside	Conscientious and well organised. Have high standards and always strive to achieve goals

by some traits rather than others, though generally success at work is predicted by Intelligence (not a personality trait), Emotional Stability and Conscientiousness *together* suggesting that success at work is rendered more achievable by such qualities as diligence, calmness in a crisis and the ability to solve problems quickly and accurately.

There have been many studies of these matters but one which is particularly powerful was published by Jesus Salgado in 1997. He undertook a meta-analytic study of the validity of the FFM for the prediction of job performance using studies conducted in Europe. Conscientiousness showed the highest predictive validity and Emotional Stability (Neuroticism) was almost as powerful a predictor. Openness to Experience was found to be a valid predictor of the ability to benefit from training. A positive correlation was found between Extroversion and two occupations in which interpersonal characteristics were likely to be important. Finally, the results for Agreeableness suggested that this factor may be relevant to predicting benefit from training but not for other aspects of success at work. Salgado concluded that it would be more powerful to use FFM-based personality approaches for selection than those that were not based on the Five-Factor Model.

Since the start of the new millennium, researchers and reviewers have been investigating the relationship between the 'Big Five' traits and various aspects of behaviour in organisations. Judge et al. (2002) chose to look at *leadership* in particular. In their set out below it seems clear that leaders are stable Extroverts who are both Open and Conscientious. We will consider this in more detail later. Further, the 'Big Five' have been linked to job satisfaction with quite clear results. Conscientious, Agreeable, Extroverts seem to experience and express more job satisfaction. Neurotics seem consistently dissatisfied, while Openness has little impact on satisfaction.

It is not difficult to provide an (albeit post-hoc) explanation for these findings. Conscientious people work hard: hard work is usually rewarded by salary increases, promotion and other forms of recognition which add to job satisfaction. Extroverts tend to be dispositionally happy, and have good social support networks. They also tend to have higher emotional intelligence which helps their interaction with superiors, peers and subordinates. Agreeable people are liked and admired for their cooperativeness, empathy and willingness to trust. They are the sort who tend to be helpful and 'happy with their lot'.

Those who score high on Neuroticism are dispositionally unhappy: they tend to be gloomy and to worry. Many studies have shown that they are prone to anxiety, depression and hypochondriasis: they are often very sensitive to, and unhappy about, hygiene factors at work. Of all the 'Big Five' factors that seem most logically and consistently related to all aspects of work behaviour it is Conscientiousness (positively) and Neuroticism (negatively) that exercise the most powerful effects.

Yet most of us would recognise that specific characteristics tend to combine with others to produce more complex effects. An anxious introvert might be quite different from a stable and relaxed introvert; someone who is altruistic *and* diligent might have a quite different impact in the workplace from someone who, though diligent, is unconcerned for other people. There is good research evidence for this also. Ones and her colleagues (2005) have argued from their meta-analyses that combinations of personality characteristics can predict outcomes in the workplace more powerfully than single characteristics. When those traits that do have predictive validity are combined with others, the results are impressive pushing validities to over 40. This is a very important and often overlooked point. Specific personality characteristics tend to be elements in a more complex picture and a personality is a combination of traits that interact. This is the significance of a more complete description of personality such as a personality *profile*.

> Specific personality characteristics tend to be elements in a more complex picture and a personality is a combination of traits that interact.

Barrick and Mount (2005) say personality matters at work for many reasons and provide sensible guidance on how to think about the evidence gleaned so far on these matters. They urge us to think about traits intelligently accepting that Neuroticism is only likely to predict negative behaviours (such as absenteeism) rather than positive behaviours such as productivity. They also recognise that there are sound measures of personality and those that are unsound from a technical point of view and also that there are good and poor indicators of workplace success. There is little to be gained from seeking to relate poor measures of either kind to each other and the attempt may be futile for purely technical reasons. Nonetheless they point out:

> In light of the research evidence, it simply is not feasible to suggest that being hard working and persistent doesn't matter, or that being co-operative or considerate is not relevant in team settings, or that being ambitious and sociable is unimportant. (p. 383)

Personality and Leadership

One of the most enduring questions about personality and leadership is 'are leaders born or made?' The answer is unequivocal: both. Research on the matter is clear from studies of many kinds but some of the most powerful tend to come from behavioural genetics and twin studies. Identical twins separated at birth, as well as fraternal twins and other siblings provide invaluable research possibilities.

Behavioural Genetics

In this tradition, Arvey et al. (2006) tested a simple model that genetic differences lead to specific chemical (hormonal), physiological (height/shape) and psychological factors which lead to four important factors for leadership: cognitive functioning, personality, interests and values and physical capacities. In their study they looked at the number of professional associations where participants played a leadership role and the number of leadership roles they held. This was a study of leadership emergence rather than effectiveness, nevertheless, the results were clear: a third (actually 30 %) of leadership can be attributed to genetics. They say that this is an important and powerful finding which supports the 'trait' leadership position.

Higher Order Factors

In a widely quoted article, Locke (1997) identified various leadership traits, which he regarded as *timeless* and *universal*. Locke organised the trait correlates of leadership onto higher-order factors. Thus he conceptualised 'cognitive ability and thinking modes' (e.g., active mind, intelligence and vision), 'motivation, values and action' (e.g., action commitment, ambition and effort and tenacity), and attitudinal variables, namely 'attitudes toward subordinates' (respect for ability and commitment to justice). In this model it is easy to see the factors affecting effectiveness in the domains of the Primary Colours Model proposed in chapter 3. Cognitive ability relates to effectiveness in the Strategic Domain, Motivation, Values and Action are more to do with the Operational Domain, and Attitudes towards Employees relates to the Interpersonal Domain. Locke's leadership traits are described in Table 8.2.

Table 8.2 Locke's (1997) leadership traits

Cognitive ability and thinking modes	Motivation, values and action	Attitudes toward employees (subordinates)
(1) *Reality focus*: not susceptible to evasions and delusions, but facing reality however grim it may be	(7) *Egoistic passion for work*: intrinsic motivation, workaholic	(11) *Respect for ability*: hiring and developing people with drive, talent and right attitudes
(2) *Honesty*: realistic assessment (accurate insight) of one's and others' abilities and weaknesses	(8) *Action commitment*: doing (not just thinking)	(12) *Commitment to justice*: Rewarding (and punishing) people appropriately
(3) *Independence/self-confidence*: 'thinking outside the box', innovating, breaking new ground	(9) *Ambition*: personal drive and desire to achieve expertise and responsibility	
(4) *Active mind*: constantly searching for new ideas and solutions	(10) *Effort and tenacity*: Hard-working, resilient, not discouraged by failure	
(5) *Intelligence* (IQ): ability to reason, learn, and acquire knowledge		
(6) *Vision*: Innovative, long-term plan, 'thinking ahead'		

Source: Adapted from Locke (1997) and Chamorro-Premuzic and Furnham (2005)

Five-Factor Model (FFM)

The re-emergence of the trait approach to personality and leadership since 2000 has largely been due to the adoption of the Five-Factor Model of personality and a great deal of research has been carried out in this tradition. It seems reasonable to suggest that, in modern organisations, leaders are more likely to be stable, extroverted, open and conscientious than are their followers. Leaders tend to show:

- higher levels of emotional balance, adjustment, and confidence (all of which are emblematic of low rather than high Neuroticism scores)
- higher levels of dominance and sociability (which characterise Extroversion rather than Introversion),
- higher intelligence and creativity (which are typical of higher rather than lower Openness)
- high levels of responsibility, achievement striving, and ethical conduct (which refer to individual differences in Conscientiousness).

The relationship between leadership and Agreeableness is not so clear. Higher social awareness and compassion (which are typical of high Agreeableness) might help with leadership but then so might the ability to take hard decisions and to be challenging (which are typical of low Agreeableness).

Silversthorne (2001) noted that effective leaders tended to score significantly higher on Extroversion, Agreeableness and Conscientiousness, and lower on Neuroticism, than non-effective leaders in US as well as Chinese samples. However, previous studies had suggested slightly different conclusions. Conscientiousness and Emotional Stability (low Neuroticism) tend to represent socially desirable traits in almost every culture, whereas Extroversion (with its elements of assertiveness and dominance) is less likely to be regarded as a virtue in Eastern cultures rather than Western cultures (Redding and Wong 1986).

Perhaps the most influential and definitive study since 2000 has been that published by Timothy Judge and his colleagues in 2002. They reviewed the extensive literature on personality and leadership. Ten writers, mainly from the 1990s, had listed what they regarded as intrinsic

Table 8.3 The ten previous studies

Study	Traits
Stogdill (1948)	Dependability, sociability, initiative, persistence, self-confidence, alertness, cooperativeness, adaptability
Mann (1959)	Adjustment, extroversion, dominance, masculinity, conservatism
Bass (1990)	Adjustment, adaptability, aggressiveness, alertness, ascendance, dominance, emotional balance, control, independence, nonconformity, originality, creativity, integrity, self-confidence
Kirkpatrick and Locke (1991)	Drive (achievement, ambition, energy, tenacity, initiative), honesty/integrity, self-confidence (emotional stability)
Yukl and Van Fleet (1992)	Emotional maturity, integrity, self-confidence, high energy level, stress tolerance
Hogan et al. (1994)	Extroversion, Agreeableness, Conscientiousness, Emotional Stability
House and Aditya (1997)	Achievement motivation, pro-social influence motivation, adjustment, self-confidence
Northouse (1997)	Self-confidence, determination, integrity, sociability
Yukl (1998)	Energy level and stress tolerance, self-confidence, internal locus of control, emotional maturity, personal integrity, socialised power motivation, achievement orientation, low need for affiliation
Daft (1999)	Alertness, originality, creativity, personal integrity, confidence

Adapted from Judge et al. (2002)

traits of effective or emergent and effective leaders. Judge and colleagues observed considerable overlap, such that most writers included self-confidence, adjustment, sociability and integrity, while a minority also listed persistence and masculinity. The Table 8.3 shows the ten previous studies considered.

After this *qualitative* analysis of the literature, Judge and colleagues performed a large-scale *quantitative* meta-analysis, which included 222 correlations from 73 studies. Results showed that Emotional Stability, Extroversion, Openness and Consciousness were all positively correlated with both leadership emergence (perceived leadership) and effectiveness (leadership performance). The results demonstrated that Neuroticism correlated with Leadership .24, Extroversion .31, Openness .24, Agreeableness .08, Conscientiousness .28. They concluded that Extroversion is the strongest predictor of both leadership *emergence and effectiveness*, almost certainly because of the assertiveness, dominance and sociability of extroverts. The multiple correlation for all five factors was 0.48 for leadership and personality when personality is measured by the FFM. This accounts for 23 % of the variance in leadership emergence and effectiveness together and 16 % in effectiveness alone.

However, the authors accept that the research does not always explain *why* these traits relate to leadership. It is possible that anxious individuals are unlikely to attempt leadership but are they also likely to be less inspirational? Extroversion may be related to leadership simply because extroverts talk more, but it could also be that people expect leaders to be more sociable and assertive than other folk. Or it could be that positive emotions are contagious, especially when someone is also quite expressive (both aspects of Extroversion)? Possibly Openness is favoured because this is associated with greater creativity or vision, or could it be to do with the fact that Openness is associated with greater risk taking? Agreeableness is both a hindrance and a help, so this may explain why its correlation with leadership is weak. Finally, is Conscientiousness related to leadership because conscientious individuals have integrity and engender trust because they excel at process aspects of leadership, such as setting goals, or because they are more likely to have initiative and persist in the face of obstacles? The authors conclude: 'Our study cannot address these process oriented issues, but future research should attempt to explain the linkages between the *Big Five* traits and leadership' (Judge et al. 2002, p. 774).

Some of the more recent studies have distinguished between different types of leadership like transformational and transactional leadership (see chapter 1). Bono and Judge (2004), for example, found stable extraversion most strongly related to transformational leadership. Personality was a strong predictor of leadership charisma and intellectual stimulation.

In our view, the most influential and important thinker in this area is Robert Hogan and his writings have influenced us greatly on the relationship between personality and leadership. The model he developed with Robert Kaiser (2004) (Fig. 8.2) states that a leader's personality has a direct impact on his/her leadership style which in turn strongly influences both employees' attitudes and team functioning, which together have an

Fig. 8.2 Hogan and Kaiser's model of the impact of leader personality on organisation performance

impact on work performance. The question, of course, is the power of these associations and the other factors involved. Certainly there is good evidence for each of these steps: the question is the strength of that association. Nevertheless it does seem logical that a leader's personality has a direct impact on those around him or her which in turn influences the performance of the organisation as a whole. It is also important to reiterate that the effect of leadership on the performance of their organisations or teams is not direct but indirect: mediated by the effect of leaders on those they lead.

Now, in chapter 5, we made the case that it is hard for any leader to be strongly capable in all aspects of leadership. The reasons, we argued, are partly due to the fact that different aspects of leadership are best served by different elements of personality. Yet here we have cited evidence that there are clear benefits to being Stable, Extroverted, Open-minded and Conscientious. Yet there is no contradiction since only 23 % of the variance in leadership emergence and effectiveness is accountable for by these personality characteristics and only 16 % of the variance in leadership effectiveness. Thus, whereas certain characteristics seem to help in most aspects of leadership to a moderate extent, there is a great deal more about leadership effectiveness to explain. Similarly, if Locke is right in distinguishing between 'cognitive ability and thinking modes', 'motivation, values and action' and 'attitudes toward subordinates' then we can see how these characteristics play differentially into our three domains of leadership.

A Word about Introverted Leaders

Whereas the balance of the evidence suggests that leadership favours extroversion, there are many effective introverted leaders and many studies that demonstrate the power of introversion in leadership. The figures of Gandhi and Abraham Lincoln are frequently cited examples of introverts whose leadership is legendary. There are many others. The qualities of thoughtfulness, objectivity, focus and lack of ego are hugely valued in leaders and these tend to characterise introverts more than extroverts. The strong case for introverted leaders was made by Jim Collins in 2001 in his article on 'Level Five Leadership' in 2001, without focusing on introversion specifically but on humility and determination in the transformation from good to great organisations. Arguably, he was evoking the power of introversion, agreeableness, conscientiousness and low openness.

> The qualities of thoughtfulness, objectivity, focus and lack of ego are hugely valued in leaders.

Introverts seem more likely to practice an empowering style of leadership since they are less desirous of being in the spotlight and less likely to dominate conversations. It is unsurprising that introverted leaders can do especially well when leading proactive employees. This was confirmed in a study in the *Harvard Business Review* in 2010. In a study of pizza stores, the article's authors found that, in stores where employees exhibited more proactivity, introverted leaders led them to significantly higher profits. In stores where the employees were less proactive, extroverted leaders were more effective in terms of delivering bottom-line results (Grant et al. 2010).

Agreeableness and introversion can have very positive effects in certain contexts. In a study in 224 stores of a US retail organisation, Emily Hunter and colleagues demonstrated that leader agreeableness was positively, and extroversion negatively, associated with so-called servant leadership which inspired followers to help each other with task and interpersonal matters, made them less likely to want to leave and had a positive effect on their feelings of engagement (Hunter et al. 2013).

The great difficulty for many introverts is that the world of work seems to favour extroverts. Whereas half the population are introverts, the selection of executives so favours extroverts that over 90 % of US executives are extroverts and the situation is apparently more acute with increasing seniority. Thus introverts are at a disadvantage when it comes to becoming leaders. Once they have been appointed, moreover, the unwitting conspiracy continues. Extroverts think out loud, introverts can think without moving their lips! Extroverts, it is said, don't know what they think until they hear what they say! So brainstorming, open-plan offices and even committees can seem great ideas to extroverts but purgatory and redundant to introverts. What is more, the presumption can easily be made that extroverts can do better at certain social tasks but, where the evidence is available, it contradicts such easy assumptions. The relationship between sales and introversion/extroversion, for example, shows a curvilinear relationship, thus favouring 'ambiverts' or those between introvert and extrovert (Grant 2013).

The flag of introversion has recently been flown to great effect by Susan Cain, notably a lawyer rather than a psychologist, whose 2012 book *Quiet* has the subtitle: the power of introverts in a world that can't stop talking. Cain provides perceptive insights into the situation of introverts in an extroverted corporate environment based on both the available evidence and her personal experience as an introvert. She also provides helpful guidance on how to maximise potential for an introvert by taking such steps as being selective about the leadership opportunities you accept, carving out restorative niches in your workday to replenish your energy and focusing more on one-to-one interactions when socialising. Similar resources can be found online through such websites as http://www.introvertedleaders.co.uk which is a powerful resource and toolkit for introverted leaders, but also sheds light on introversion for those extroverted leaders who want to understand their colleagues better and play to their strengths.

Personality and Behaviour

Implicit in the research we have described about personality is the idea that personality influences behaviour. Indeed, the very definition of personality suggests that this is the case. So we should consider the possibility that behaviour alone is all that needs to be measured to predict leader effectiveness. At first sight, the evidence for this is compelling. Meta-analyses (our favourite source of evidence on these matters) suggest that behaviour is an important predictor in its own right (e.g., Judge and Piccolo 2004; Judge et al. 2004).

Yet, one of the most recent meta-analytic studies shows that it is possible to predict leader effectiveness most powerfully of all by combining the effect of personality traits, intelligence and leader behaviour. This combination accounts for 31 % of the variance in leader effectiveness according to Scott Derue and colleagues (2011). They argued that many of the studies on this subject to date have not looked broadly enough at the possible predictors to establish whether the various effects are truly independent. It may be, for example, that those leaders whose style was transactional (rather than transformational) had different personality traits from the transformational leaders. In other words, it could be that, to some extent, they were accounting for the same variance by measuring traits as by measuring behaviours.

The authors developed a simple model which proposed that leader traits (demographics, traits related to task competence and interpersonal attributes) influenced leader behaviours (oriented towards task processes, relationship dynamics or change) and that these influenced leader effectiveness. They then tested this model empirically by meta-analysis of published research studies. To examine the power of traits they concentrated on gender, intelligence and the Big 5 personality traits.

The authors conclude that there is considerable support for combining the effects of personality traits, gender and intelligence with the effect of leader behaviours to explain leader effectiveness. They state:

> In general, leader traits associated with task competence related to task-oriented leader behaviours, which improve performance-related leadership outcomes. In contrast, leaders' interpersonal attributes were associated with relational-oriented behaviours, which improve affective criteria such as follower satisfaction with leader. As predicted, both task competence and interpersonal attributes predicted, at least marginally, leaders' change-oriented behaviours. Finally, passive leader behaviours were negatively associated with effectiveness and mediated some of the key relationships. (p. 37)

The contention in chapter 5—that it is hard for any leader to be strongly competent in all aspects of leadership—thus gains recent support. Task-oriented leader behaviours, which improve performance-related leadership outcomes, are characteristic of leadership in the operational domain of the Primary Colours Model. Relational-oriented behaviours, which improve affective criteria such as follower satisfaction, are the province of our interpersonal domain. The attributes associated with these different leadership approaches and effects belong to different kinds of people: differently oriented and capable leaders.

Drawing the Evidence on Personality Together

From chapter 7 we can see that successful leaders have 'emotional intelligence' and that this may best be regarded as a personality variable rather than anything to do with intelligence at all. They understand their own and others' emotions and are able to change their behaviour and that of others appropriately. Successful leaders are sensitive; derailed ones oversensitive. Successful leaders *do* worry; *do* get depressed, *do* become anxious … but only occasionally and appropriate to the circumstances. They also have healthily adaptive coping strategies. The unsuccessful leaders worry all the time. Their moodiness, fickleness and prickliness cause real problems at work.

This chapter has demonstrated that a manager's personality is powerfully implicated in their emergence as a leader and their success in leadership. Successful leaders appear to have a fairly typical profile and tend to avoid extremes in their reactions and personality characteristics:

- Successful leaders are nearly always *emotionally stable*. Derailed leaders are frequently emotionally vulnerable. Certainly failure at work may increase neurosis but it is more likely to be caused by it. One needs to be hardy, resilient, even stoical to succeed at work. This does not mean being emotionally illiterate: far from it.
- Successful leaders are *conscientious*. They work smart and hard. They tend to follow instructions and are orderly. They are diligent and prudent. Unsuccessful leaders don't have the work ethic and tend to be

clock-watchers. Occasionally excessive conscientiousness is the undo-ing of a leader, as with many over-reactions. Fanatical workaholism is as much associated with derailment as being very low in conscientious-ness. There is a period in all leaders' careers when they simply have to work very hard, be well organised and diligent. There is an optimal amount of conscientiousness required at work. People often do not make it to senior positions if they do not have enough.

- Successful leaders are *open to new experiences*. They have to anticipate and embrace change. They need to be original and creative, but they also have to be practical. Few people make it to senior management with very low openness scores. They tend to be too dull, conventional and traditional to lead with imagination. But very high scores can eas-ily derail leaders. Very high scores in this dimension maybe dreamers and very impractical. They may be prone to wasting large amounts of time and sums of money on 'white elephants', namely projects that go badly wrong. They may err too frequently on the side of aesthetic appeal rather than practical function.

- Successful leaders need to learn to behave as if they were extroverted even if they are not. They need to be socially confident and interper-sonally skilled and relaxed. The higher you go in organisations the less you do; the more you work through others. Extreme introverts do not enjoy many of the tasks of senior management: running interminable meetings, doing PR appearances, hosting parties. Good leaders know it has to be done and do it. Very extroverted leaders need 'back-up' to temper their natural ways of behaving. While they may enjoy the social aspects of the job, they may neglect the serious strategy and analysis that is equally important.

- Do successful leaders need to be agreeable? At times. To do well in business a leader also needs to be tough at times: competitive, egocen-tric, arrogant, even occasionally political, achieving goals through indirect means. Probably what characterises the successful leaders is that they can act agreeably with their own staff, but disagreeably from time to time with the competition.

- These generaliseable leadership attributes predict leadership emergence and effectiveness but there are more refined predictions for leadership in the three domains of the Primary Colours Model.

Summary and Conclusion

1. Successful leaders tend to be stable, medium or high in conscientiousness, openness and extroversion and medium to low in agreeableness. Yet these attributes have their impact on effectiveness through the *behaviour* of the leaders.

2. Those whose attributes are not ideal for leadership are able to learn to do the right things to some extent. Personality is not a prison or a straitjacket: it is a help or hindrance which can be worked on, though, if the hindrances are too large, a work-around solution may be the best option.

3. The case for working with people who demonstrate complementary differences in order to create complete leadership remains strong.

But what happens when leaders fail, when it all goes wrong? How and why do leaders derail? That is the subject of chapter 9.

9

When It All Goes Wrong:
Leaders Who Fail and Derail

Success breeds complacency. Complacency breeds failure. Only the paranoid survive.

Andy Grove

In previous chapters, we have focused on leadership success: how it is to be defined, explained and encouraged. Here, we turn to the opposite: leadership failure. How and why does it go wrong and what might be done to prevent it?

Of the over 70,000 books in the English language on leadership, surprisingly few focus on those leaders who fail and derail. Some get sacked, others resign, some preside over the dramatic decline of their organisation. Often we are told about the early setbacks and failures of a leader who learnt a great deal from these experiences and 'triumphed' in the end. Yet, still there have remained, until relatively recently, few books on leadership failure (Furnham 2010, 2015).

There are a surprisingly large number of leaders who fail and derail. The data suggest the number is around 50 % (Hogan 2007; Furnham 2010;). Thus, failure is as common as success. There are of course different types of failure but the point remains valid. A British politician once said that

© The Editor(s) (if applicable) and The Author(s) 2016
D. Pendleton, A. Furnham, *Leadership: All You Need To Know*
2nd edition, DOI 10.1057/978-1-137-55436-9_9

every political career ends in failure and it seems that a very high number of those in positions of high organisational leadership also fail. Failure can be a spur to success and a frequent experience on the path to success in a story of apparently happy endings. Failure can also come from seeds sown at the height of success: its consequence rather than its antecedent.

Failure and derailment often come as surprises to those who have been regarded as high flyers and in the talent group. Many have had 'stellar careers' with considerable early success and have built a good reputation. This may be because those very characteristics that help people succeed, like self-confidence and fearlessness, when taken to extremes, are the major causes of failure.

However, failure is not exclusively due to individual factors. Psychologists and psychiatrists have rightly been accused of 'pathologisation' and being too eager to explain failure in terms of individual, rather than contextual factors. Two other factors play an important role. The first is organisational culture or processes which can allow, even encourage, management failure. The second is employees or followers who are prepared to go along with—and obey—the derailing leader.

> there is unlikely to be leadership derailment unless there are leaders with
> a derailment profile, people who are prepared to follow derailing leaders
> and environments which 'allow it'.

There are clearly many factors that account for why potentially derailing leaders make it to the top. As we pointed out in chapter 1, there has been a recent focus on the role of followers in both leaders' success and failure. Just as three components are needed for fire, namely heat, oxygen and fuel, so there is unlikely to be leadership derailment unless there are leaders with a derailment profile, people who are prepared to follow derailing leaders and environments which 'allow it'.

Many people have challenged the trait approach to leadership derailment by stressing the nature of leader–follower dynamics while at the same time emphasising the role of overplayed strengths or, what has become known as, the dark side of personality. Ouimet (2010) noted three factors:

1. Cultural Factors: There are national and corporate cultural factors that favour the dark-side manager making it to the top. Further, if the

organisation promotes and trumpets values like immediate results, audacity, ambition, individual initiative, financial success, professional prestige and social celebrity, they become a breeding ground for dark side leaders (Ouimet 2010). Inevitably, dark-side types are drawn to organisations in which they can thrive. This is particularly the case for organisations in sectors which are fast moving and poorly regulated.

2. Environmental Factors: There is considerable historical evidence that dark side leaders emerge in times of political and economic crisis. Where people perceive an imagined or real and significant threat to their wellbeing and livelihood they are often drawn to the heroic leader who promises them he or she can save them. People are drawn to the rhetoric, the self-confidence and the bravado of leaders who can mobilise people and give them confidence.

3. Structural Factors: All organisations, for historical but also legal reasons, have processes and procedures which can, in effect, facilitate or frustrate the emergence of a dark-side leader. Some place serious restrictions on an individual's power and freedom to make decisions. Some organisations have strict rules and procedures about group decision-making and the keeping of records. Others are more relaxed. Furthermore, most organisations have rules about corporate governance. There may be non-executive directors whose explicit task it is to 'keep an eye on' maverick leaders and their decisions. There may also be rules about reports and statements and shareholders meetings which make all sort of procedures public. In short, the better the corporate governance, the less opportunity the dark-side leader has to emerge There is a great deal of literature which supports the idea that some environments inhibit and others almost encourage illegal behaviour.

Incompetence versus Derailment

It is important to make the distinction between leadership incompetence and derailment. Essentially the *incompetent* manager is lacking something. Most are simply over-promoted, others are there because of favouritism or poor selection. They do not have the skills, the energy, the courage or perhaps the insight to do that which is required of a good leader. Nepotism, poor selection techniques and complacency often account for the appointment of an incompetent leader: a leader with a deficit of some kind. *Derailment* on the other hand is usually the consequence of having too much of a *good* thing: an excess of a strength, which overused, becomes a weakness.

Incompetence and derailment are sometimes difficult to differentiate because the consequences in the business are often similar. They usually include declining customer service, morale and profits, high employee turnover and negative media coverage, as well as a lack of strategic clarity or simple operational matters such as inadequate quality control and stock flow. Yet they stem from different causes and are to be tackled in vastly different ways.

In the management literature, *derailment* has come to mean the demise of an otherwise successful leader who seems to have too much of a good thing: like the self-confidence, boldness or courage that got them appointed. However, the strengths became weaknesses possibly because of the way they were overused and rewarded.

Dark-Side Traits

Leaders and managers are interested in behaviour at work. Psychologists and psychiatrists have a great deal to say about the same issue but with different emphases. Psychologists are interested in personality traits; psychiatrists in personality disorders. Personality factors in general relate to how people think, feel and act. It is where a person's behaviour deviates *markedly* from the expectations of the individual's culture that the disorder is manifested. The psychiatric manual is very clear that 'odd behaviour' is not simply an expression of habits, customs, religious or political values professed or shown by a people of particular cultural origin.

The manuals go to great lengths to point out that some of the personality disorders look like other disorders: anxiety, mood, psychosis, substance-abuse and the like, but have unique features. The essence of the argument is that personality disorders must be distinguished from personality traits that do not reach the threshold to be described as a personality disorder. Personality traits are diagnosed as a personality disorder when they are inflexible, maladaptive and persisting and cause significant functional impairment or distress.

One of the most important ways to differentiate personal style from personality disorder is flexibility. There are lots of difficult people at work but relatively few whose rigid, maladaptive behaviours mean they continually have disruptive, troubled lives. It is their inflexible, repetitive, poor stress-coping responses that are marks of disorder.

Personality disorders influence the sense of self: the way people think and feel about themselves and how other people see them. The disorders often powerfully influence relationships. They reveal themselves in how people 'complete tasks, take and/or give orders, make decisions, plan, handle external and internal demands, take or give criticism, obey rules, take and delegate responsibility, and co-operate with people' (Oldham and Morris 1991, p. 24). The anti-social, obsessive, compulsive, passive-aggressive and dependent types are particularly problematic in the workplace. People with personality disorders have difficulty expressing and understanding emotions. It is the intensity with which they express them and their variability that makes them odd. More importantly they often have serious problems with self-control.

Perhaps the greatest progress in this area occurred when the Hogans developed the Hogan Development Survey (HDS) (Hogan and Hogan 1997). Their idea was to use the categories of the personality disorders but to conceive of 'dark-side' tendencies rather than disorders. The test, now widely used, contains 168 true/false items that assess dysfunctional interpersonal themes. These dysfunctional dispositions reflect one's distorted beliefs about others that emerge when people encounter stress or stop considering how their actions affect others. Over time, these dispositions may become associated with a person's reputation and can impede job performance and career success. The HDS is not a medical or clinical assessment. It does not measure personality disorders, which are manifestations of mental disorder. Instead, the HDS assesses self-defeating expressions of normal personality. The American Psychological Association's *Diagnostic and Statistical Manual*, more commonly known as DSM IV, is a diagnostic aid. It makes this same distinction between behavioural traits and disorders—self-defeating behaviours, such as those predicted by the HDS, come and go depending on the context whereas, personality disorders are enduring and pervasive across contexts. Table 9.1 compares DSM IV and the HDS.

Table 9.1 The DSM IV and the HDS

DSM-IV personality disorder		HDS themes	
Borderline	Inappropriate anger; unstable and intense relationships alternating between idealisation and devaluation	Excitable	Moody and hard to please; intense but short-lived enthusiasm for people, projects or things
Paranoid	Distrustful and suspicious of others; motives are interpreted as malevolent	Sceptical	Cynical, distrustful and doubting others' true intentions
Avoidant	Social inhibition; feelings of inadequacy, and hypersensitivity to criticism or rejection	Cautious	Reluctant to take risks for fear of being rejected or negatively evaluated
Schizoid	Emotional coldness and detachment from social relationships; indifferent to praise and criticism	Reserved	Aloof, detached and uncommunicative; lacking interest in, or awareness of, the feelings of others
Passive-aggressive	Passive resistance to adequate social and occupational performance; irritated when asked to do something he/she does not want to	Leisurely	Independent; ignoring people's requests and becoming irritated or argumentative if they persist
Narcissistic	Arrogant and haughty behaviours or attitudes; grandiose sense of self-importance and entitlement	Bold	Unusually self-confident; feelings of grandiosity and entitlement; over-valuation of one's capabilities
Antisocial	Disregard for the truth; impulsivity and failure to plan ahead; failure to conform with social norms	Mischievous	Enjoying risk taking and testing the limits; needing excitement; manipulative, deceitful, cunning and exploitative
Histrionic	Excessive emotionality and attention seeking; self-dramatising, theatrical and exaggerated emotional expression	Colourful	Expressive, animated and dramatic; wanting to be noticed and needing to be the centre of attention

(continued)

Table 9.1 (continued)

DSM-IV personality disorder		HDS themes	
Schizotypal	Odd beliefs or magical thinking; behaviour or speech that is odd, eccentric, or peculiar	Imaginative	Acting and thinking in creative and sometimes odd or unusual ways
Obsessive-compulsive	Preoccupations with orderliness, rules, perfectionism and control; over-conscientious and inflexible	Diligent	Meticulous, precise and perfectionistic, inflexible about rules and procedures; critical of others' performance
Dependent	Difficulty making everyday decisions without excessive advice and reassurance; difficulty expressing disagreement out of fear of loss of support or approval	Dutiful	Eager to please and reliant on others for support and guidance; reluctant to take independent action or go against popular opinion

Both the DSM IV and the Hogan measures also find that these scales tend to cluster into sub-groups. In the case of the Hogan scales, they describe three such clusters. The first cluster is to do with Moving Away and comprises Excitable, Sceptical, Cautious, Reserved and Leisurely. These scales describe a response to anxiety that maintains distance and pushes others away. The second cluster comprises Bold, Mischievous, Colourful and Imaginative. These responses help people manage anxiety by manipulating or controlling others. The third cluster comprises Diligent and Dutiful and represents the management of anxiety by building alliances with others.

The Hogans came to important conclusions in 2001 on these matters which are still relevant:

1. There is substantial agreement regarding the dysfunctional dispositions or traits associated with management incompetence and derailment.
2. Many derailed managers have impressive social skills, which is why their disorders are not spotted at selection but only later by their subordinates.

3. Bad managers are a major cause of misbehaviour by staff such as theft, absenteeism or high staff turnover. It is poor treatment that often makes staff resentful.
4. It is important to describe the personality disorders from the point of view of those who have to deal with them.

There is certainly evidence that a person's dark-side profile relates, independently of their skills and values, to the jobs they are attracted to and thrive in. With respect to the private vs the public sector (Furnham et al. 2014), the pattern is predictable: those in the public sector tend to score highly on Moving Away (Sceptical, Reserved) and Moving Toward (Diligent, Dutiful) but lower on Moving Against (Bold, Mischievous, Colourful) than those in the private sector.

There have been some interesting smaller-scale studies in this area. Winsborough and Sambath (2013), cited in chapter 5, looked at 117 New Zealand CEOs and the relationship between their dark side and leadership. They found three significant correlations. Those who were rated high on transformational leadership tended to be low on the Cautious and Reserved but high on the Colourful scale. They also found that being Bold was associated with Inspirational Motivation which they argued was the result of dramatisation of issues used by those with charisma.

In a much bigger study Carson et al. (2012) looked at 1,796 in a global retail organisation. They were particularly interested in how two of the higher order dark-side factors namely Moving Against and Moving Away related to such things as job tenure, being fired and leaving the organisation. The results showed, as predicted, that those managers with dysfunctional Moving Against tendencies were more likely to leave, either being fired or resigning.

One central question is when, why and how (if ever) dark-side traits are associated with leadership. An article by Judge et al. (2006) looked at the relationship between leadership and Narcissism. Results, as we might have expected, confirmed that Narcissism was positively related to self-ratings of leadership but negatively linked to others' ratings. Moreover, when others' ratings are used to assess leadership, narcissism correlated negatively with performance. These results provide evidence in support of the Hogans' view that there is an underlying 'dark side' to many leaders.

Many have made the point that 'moderate' scores on the dark-side traits tend to be associated with leadership success, while extreme scores predict failure and derailment (Kaiser et al. 2014). Thus extremes were related to Enabling, Strategic and Operational leadership. The Moving Against leaders were good at making bold moves, setting direction and supporting innovation (our *strategic domain*) but weak at monitoring performance, focusing resources and getting the details right (our *operational domain*). There is a cost benefit analysis with dark-side traits.

In an important meta-analysis, Gaddis and Foster (2013) looked at the relationship between the dark-side factors and overall managerial performance, as well as eight managerial behaviours including trustworthiness, work attitudes, leading others, decisionmaking and problem-solving, achievement orientation, dependability, adaptability/flexibility and interpersonal skills. They found that the tendency to Move Away under stress was almost always negatively associated with performance. Some of the Move Against pattern, however, specifically attention-seeking Colourful behaviour, was more controversial: positively predicting performance but negatively associated with trustworthiness and other behaviours.

Spain et al. (2013) summarised the dark-side traits at work. *Some* of the findings and displayed in Table 9.2:

Table 9.2 The dark-side traits at work

Job performance	There is a negative relationship for most traits
Citizenship behaviour	With few exceptions (Dependent Personality) dark-side traits are associated with *low* communal, citizenship behaviour
Counter-productive behaviour at work	This is positively related to many dark-side traits
Creative performance	There is often a *positive* relationship though the relationship is non-linear
Training	Many dark-side traits are associated with overconfidence and low learning and development
Interviewing	Many dark-side traits are associated with interviewing success
Leadership	They can play a role in both success and failure
Managerial derailment	There are many cases of this
Abusive supervision	This is clearly linked to callous, malicious and destructive traits

More and more studies are emerging to suggest that the personality disorders account of derailment has considerable merit. The question then arises as to why it is that people with significant character flaws actually get selected or promoted. Indeed, the very characteristics that help people up the 'greasy pole of management' are also the cause of their derailment (Furnham et al. 2013).

Recently, a different type of personality-related issue has been postulated, though the empirical evidence base is not yet strong. Lord David Owen, a former physician and politician, was the UK Foreign Secretary from 1977 to 1979. He has witnessed at first hand many people in political power whose behaviour has become maladaptive. These people have all fallen victim to what Owen has dubbed 'The Hubris Syndrome' (Owen 2008) to which people in power are thought to be especially prone. Owen argues that leaders who exercise power are prone to it and the more power they exercise, the more prone they are to developing hubris leading to nemesis. He also argues that it is less likely to develop in people who retain a personal modesty, remain open to criticism, have a degree of cynicism or well-developed sense of humour. Four heads of government in the last 100 years are singled out as having developed hubris syndrome: David Lloyd George, Margaret Thatcher, George W. Bush and Tony Blair. The 'symptoms' appear to be related to narcissism and involve exaggerated self-belief and 'a belief that, rather than being accountable to the mundane court of colleagues or public opinion, the real court to which they answer is much greater: History or God; often accompanied by an unshakeable belief that in that court they will be vindicated.' This particular syndrome, however, as hypothesised by Owen, is thought to abate once power has been relinquished.

Altogether more disconcertingly, there are psychopaths who become business leaders. Indeed one psychoanalyst at a European business school, Manfred Kets de Vries, has made describing the manifestation of personality disorder among business people his life's work (1984, 1994, 2006). He has concentrated on psychopathic managers who cause great damage. Most researchers in this area believe it is psychopaths that are the most common and dangerous at work (Babiak and Hare 2006).

Kets de Vries has described many different leadership profiles that are fraught with difficulties as well as benefits. He has identified, inter alia:

- The narcissistic leader who has a grandiose sense of self-importance that needs to be fed by constant admiration.
- The controlling leader who is rigid and excessively judgmental.
- The depressive leader who is joyless, dejected, apathetic and lacking in energy.
- The abrasive leader who is domineering and cruel and prone to outbursts of rage while being personally rigidly self-disciplined.
- The paranoid leader who is hypersensitive and reluctant to confide in others, self-righteous and unforgiving.
- The negativistic leader who is indecisive, passive, stubborn and fearful of commitment.
- The hypomanic charismatic leader who enjoys feelings of ease, strength, buoyancy, financial omnipotence and euphoria when in an upswing but who also crash into depression at other times.
- The neurotic imposter who has a constant dread of not living up to expectations and of being found out and tends to be a workaholic and a perfectionist.

Kets de Vries (2006) singles out a number of so-called virtues for special comment. One such is confidence which so easily becomes overconfidence. It is clear that organisations collude to nurture or indeed to amplify the inflated ambitions of those leaders whose overconfidence causes them to promise so much. Like others in this area, Kets de Vries recognises the double-edged sword of self-belief, self-confidence or narcissism in the business world. He writes:

> a solid dose of narcissism is a prerequisite for anyone who hopes to rise to the top of an organisation. Narcissism offers leaders a foundation for conviction about the righteousness of their cause. The narcissistic leader's conviction that his or her group, organisation, or country has a special mission inspires loyalty and group identification; the strength (and even inflexibility) of a narcissistic leader's worldview gives followers something to identify

with and hold on to. Narcissism is a toxic drug however. Although it is a key ingredient for success, it does not take much before a leader suffers from an overdose. (pp. 188–9)

Kets de Vries has achieved three things. *First* he has described the personality disorders in everyday language. *Second* he has shown that much odd dangerous and counter-productive behaviour of business people is due to their personality disorders. *Third* he has alerted people to 'tell-tale' signs of those problems (see below).

Spotting those at Risk: Three Crucial Indicators

The modern literature based on both psychological and psychiatric theory suggests that, underlying all the leader derailment (and all personality disorders), there are three very fundamental markers that might also be used to spot those at risk or beginning the path towards derailment.

1. Relationships: Can the person establish and maintain healthy, happy, long-term relationships with various sorts of people?

Leadership is done with—and through—people. It is almost impossible to conceive of a leadership position which does not involve groups and teams. The ability to form and maintain relationships starts early. People make friends at a very young age for various reasons and some keep them for very long periods. It is essential for mental health to be able to establish and maintain relationships.

While nearly all researchers have demonstrated that problems with interpersonal relationships are at the heart of the problem for derailing managers, it has been suggested that these are often complemented by self-defeating behaviours. These include being rigid, hostile, defensive, overcommitted, suspicious and defensive (Williams et al. 2013). However it seems the case that these self-defeating behaviours themselves play a big part in derailment because they are related to the inability to establish good relationships.

Often business people talk about *emotional competencies* (rather than traits or abilities) which are essentially learned. Emotional competencies include emotional self-awareness, emotional self-regulation, social–emotional awareness, understanding emotions in others and so on. If one is to include older related concepts like social skills or interpersonal competencies, then it is possible to find a literature dating back 30 years showing these skills predict occupational effectiveness and success. Further, there is convincing empirical evidence which suggests that these skills can be improved and learnt. By contrast, derailing managers tend to have problems with their clients, teams and direct reports and seem to be unable or unwilling to fix them.

2. Self-Awareness: Does the person have insight into themselves?

Self-awareness can be derived in many ways. Sometimes self-insight comes from a sudden epiphany in the classroom, on the couch or at an appraisal. More typically, self-awareness grows gradually with emotional maturity by understanding what others say and by observing our effects on those around us and vice versa. It comes out of success and failure.

Deliberate actions can facilitate the growth of self-awareness for most people in the workplace. Trying new tasks and experiences keeps us vigilant about ourselves, whereas confining ourselves to familiar tasks and territories seldom yields new insights. Seeking out *feedback* from others also provokes our self-awareness and self-acceptance. However, most derailed leaders are poorly informed about their strengths and weaknesses. They neither understand how they come across nor their effect on others.

> Trying new tasks and experiences keeps us vigilant about ourselves, whereas confining ourselves to familiar tasks and territories seldom yields new insights.

3. Adaptability: Does the person demonstrate the ability to learn from change or experience?

Charles Darwin pointed out that it is not the strongest or most intelligent that survive but those that adapt fastest to change. In most organisations, change is a constant that seems to be accelerating. At various times in a career, people have to learn to let go of old or dysfunctional assumptions and beliefs while acquiring new skills and ideas. This often means exposing oneself to learning situations that can be threatening and which may involve failure. People need to be adaptable and able to cope with change.

Some are clearly better at this than others. Those who show an inability to adapt, learn and grow are at risk themselves and put their teams and organisations at risk also.

Prevention

The central question for most organisations is how to prevent managerial derailment and failure, since it is so costly and wasteful. We suggest that attention is paid to selection and training.

Selection

Through job analysis, selectors usually have a list of competencies that they are looking for in selection. The aim is to accept the good applicant and reject the bad. However, there are two problems with this model:

1. The assumption of linearity. We assume that more is better. The more you have of a quality (intelligence, creativity, integrity) the better. Most jobs require an optimal amount rather than a maximal amount and the extreme may indicate a risk or danger. Extremes of self-confidence can be arrogance or even narcissism and extremes of creativity may be an indicator of schizotypal behaviour. Extreme strengths may suggest great weaknesses. Thus in the selection process it would be wise always to investigate those with very high scores to determine whether these are also indicators of current or impending problems.
2. We focus more on selecting what we want rather than rejecting what we do NOT want. Indeed, faced with a great strength, we can become blind to the down-side risks of selecting in to our organisation, those with traits or characteristics that are likely to prove harmful. The more important the job and the more the consequences of failure or derailment count, the more important it is to seek to assess potential derailers. Indeed the DSM IV or Hogan framework set out in the table above may be an excellent checklist to help people select out those who may be prone to fail.

Training

The second opportunity to intervene is with coaching, mentoring and training. A number of books give advice to people on how they should 'wrestle with their demons' once they know their dark-side profile. Table 9.3 contains Dotlich and Cairo's (2003) advice for each of the disorders:

Table 9.3 Dotlich and Cairo's (2003) advice

Arrogance	First determine if you really fit the arrogant profile
	Second find truth-tellers in your organisation and get them to give honest feedback
	Third, use setbacks that you may experience to cross back over the line before big failure hits
Melodrama	First, 'dial down the volume'
	Second, get someone to videotape you in action
	Third, identify the circumstances that cause you to cross the line
	Fourth, make time to reflect and really listen
Volatility	First, empower a 'trusted advisor' to give you a volatility alert
	Second, learn to take a step back, as well as where necessary forward
	Third, ask what is and is not happening and how I can influence the action
Excessive caution	First, prioritise and put you time and effort into the key matters
	Second, do something different and break routine
	Third, focus on past success to reduce the fear of failure
	Fourth, confront your fears by imagining worst case scenarios
Habitual distrust	First, analyses the 'why' behind the distrust of so many
	Second, reconfigure a key relationship and work on your suspicions
	Third, practice giving positive feedback to others
	Fourth, recognise how distrust is hurting your career
Aloofness	First, map out your network to determine allies (get savvy)
	Second, rehearse your messages so that people here clearly what you want to say
	Third, pay attention to your (lack) of impact and try harder to 'get through'
Mischievousness	First, take ownership of what you are really doing
	Second, determine which rules are (really) important to follow
	Third, role-play being on the receiving end of your mischief
	Fourth, confide in a coach and listen carefully to them

(continued)

Table 9.3 (continued)

Eccentricity	First, determine the price you are prepared to pay for your 'non-conformity
	Second, surround yourself with people who can execute your ideas
	Third, recognise the gap between your intention and the impact you want
Passive resistance	First, note the gap between how you are feeling and what you are saying/doing
	Second, put yourself in the place of people that you work with
	Third, work on potential areas of conflict
	Fourth, look to other successful leaders for models
Perfectionism	First, examine the costs of your approach and style: being stressed out and missing opportunities
	Second, prioritise the key jobs and learn to live with imperfection
	Third, give up the perfectionistic behaviour and your obsessiveness
Eagerness to please	First, identify what you really believe
	Second, pick a fight: a small-scale conflict
	Third, defend someone who is worth defending

Advice of this kind is seldom enough. To advise the perfectionist, for example, to 'give up the perfectionist behaviour and your obsessiveness' seems to deny the sense many feel of being trapped within their compulsions. Thus, many turn to coaches or even therapists to work on developing remedies over time. Expectations need to be managed carefully in this context and a blend of building insight, setting goals, provoking action and reflecting honestly on experience tends to require skilful coaches and determined clients. Significant progress is far from easy or rapid but progress can be made.

One of the key elements in this process is the appropriate mix of challenge and support. Unhelpfully, many conceive of this as a matter of balance as if challenge and support are at opposite ends of a continuum and the task for the coach is to find the sweet spot at which there is sufficient of each. A more helpful way of thinking about this is that the two dimensions are orthogonal as in Fig. 9.1. A great deal of challenge can be given *and* a great deal of support and this should probably be the aim both for leaders and coaches whose aim is development. Indeed, the greater the challenge, the greater the support required. Similarly, we

Fig. 9.1 Challenge and support are best regarded as orthogonal dimensions

should recognise that, with support, comes the opportunity to challenge and to provoke growth and development.

Key to this notion is that support and challenge need to be seen as a pair rather than independent elements. Too much support and insufficient challenge creates a therapy group. The reverse is an assault course aimed at weeding out the weak. When challenge and support are paired, too little of both tends to create disengagement.

Resilience

In an environment where change is constant and unpredictable and where the risk of failure is rife, resilience is to be prized. But first, resilience needs to be understood if it is to be pursued and nurtured. Essentially, there are two quite different approaches to thinking about resilience and they have rather different implications for leaders, managers and coaches. First, there is the notion of return and second of growth and adaptation.

Resilience comes from a Latin root *resilire*, which means 'to leap back or rebound from'. The bozo doll, when knocked over, bounces back to the vertical. Car bumpers (fenders), when they hit something gently, spring back into their original shape. This is a form of resilience based on stasis: return to the original state. But when the notion of resilience is applied to a person, we usually mean something far richer. Human beings have the capacity to use a setback or failure to learn, develop and grow. This is what Dr. Peter Gruenewald[1] calls 'Adaptive Resilience' to distinguish it from the more static version.

There are both nature and nurture factors in adaptive resilience. As chapter 8 on personality argued, there are individual differences in neuroticism. Some people are much more emotionally robust than others and there is a significant hereditary element in that. But, as people learn coping mechanisms, they are acquiring and developing resilience, whether these are learned in childhood or adulthood. There are also environments that promote adaptive resilience and others that inhibit its actions. Leadership, management, coaching and therapy all have the potential to enhance adaptive resilience if conducted skilfully.

Leaders need to consider—for themselves and their organisations— the extent to which they are able to promote reflection, learning and growth in the face of successes and failures. Since the 1990 publication of Peter Senge's book *The Fifth Discipline*, the term 'learning organisation' has become widely used but seldom practised systematically. Learning organisations promote adaptive resilience but there are more aspects to adaptive resilience than intellectual learning alone. Culture and climate play a part in promoting resilient individuals, teams and organisations. It is a matter of leadership.

Summary and Conclusion

1. For years the leadership failure and derailment was a hidden and under-researched area, thus it was not recognised quite how many went on to fail and derail.

---

[1] Dr. Peter Gruenewald is a physician who has created a range of practical techniques for developing Adaptive Resilience based on the notion of heart rate variability and creating heart–brain coherence http://www.adaptive-resilience.co.uk.

2. There are now well-developed tools and techniques to identify those at risk of failure and derailment and well-articulated understanding of the factors at work both in the individual (characteristics and traits) and in the context in which they operate.
3. Failure and derailment is neither inevitable nor unavoidable. Practical steps can be taken to prevent and to fix many of the issues at play, but all such actions need to start with an honest and accurate assessment of the individual and the situation.
4. Selection and development are key to prevention of failure and derailment. The ultimate aim is to foster adaptive resilience.

10

A Programme of Action

In the preceding chapters, we have set out four propositions. *First*, we have argued that leadership has to deal with the demands of three domains: strategic, operational and interpersonal. We have described these domains as overlapping and comprising *seven* capabilities as described by the Primary Colours Model.

Second, we have argued that it is hard, unlikely if not impossible, for any individual—however gifted—to be world-class in all three areas, let alone all seven capabilities. This is not just because the demands and characteristics required in the domains are different, but because in some cases, these demands are opposite. The broad thinking and appetite for new experiences associated with the personality trait of Openness, for example, seems to favour the strategic domain but the opposite tends to be true of the operational domain. In short, curious, open, creative people thrive in the 'big picture' activities, but may easily get bored with the details.

Third, the personality of the leader sets up a pattern of helps and hindrances in the establishment and maintenance of leadership capability. Based on this idea, we can distinguish between *natural* strengths, *potential* strengths, *fragile* strengths and *resistant* limitations. The leader tends

© The Editor(s) (if applicable) and The Author(s) 2016
D. Pendleton, A. Furnham, *Leadership: All You Need To Know*
2nd edition, DOI 10.1057/978-1-137-55436-9_10

to work with some confidence in the areas of his or her natural strengths. He or she can work *on* the potential strengths with some expectation of success but needs to continue to work *on* the fragile strengths so that they remain strong. In the area of resistant limitations, however, it may be more sensible to find a way to work *around* them since the likelihood of making progress here is small. The issue is where to invest time, effort and money to achieve the greatest results. For some time now it has been suggested that it is much more efficacious to work on (potential and fragile) strengths than weaknesses.

Fourth, complete leadership can come from incomplete individual leaders working together. To create the highest levels of leadership, teams need to comprise people who are each world class in *several* aspects of leadership, recognising where they are incomplete and seeking the contributions of colleagues whose capabilities are complementary.

> complete leadership can come from incomplete individual leaders working together.

In this final chapter we show how the actions that might be derived from these propositions can guide action at all stages of a leader's working life. We will tell a story to illustrate the points and include additional notes to show how several of the actions can be structured or put into practice. The story (case study) has a central character, Alan Franklin, who is entirely fictitious but is based on many executives we have seen and worked with. It covers his considering a job change, establishing himself in the new organisation and being promoted to the role of CEO. It tracks his progress through dealing with a downturn, re-emerging into a more positive phase and creating a future for the organisation that will lead to his leaving. It shows him getting things right, getting them wrong and learning from his experiences. It is a prototypic case: an allegory.

Alan Franklin's Story

Alan is a confident man, somewhat extroverted but not an extreme case. He likes the company of intelligent, active, articulate people and stays fit through regular exercise. He enjoys banter. He tends not to worry about much and is seldom troubled by stress, though he does become bored rather more easily than most when the pace of work or the level of challenge drops. At these times, he becomes restless and tends to tinker where he has delegated: dealing with his own frustration by increasing the frustration of his team.

Alan is not, as a result, very organised. He tries to be, but considers that he has a 'gene missing' and has slowly come to terms with the fact that he needs help to prevent his (and everyone else's) descent into chaos. He has finally figured out that his PA is part of the solution but has yet to learn to give her sufficiently free rein to help as much as she can.

Alan is very bright and loves the complexity that real strategic thinking requires. He is numerate and strong analytically and yet is also prepared to discuss and consider more unorthodox ideas—at least for a while. He gets on with a broad range of people, but becomes tetchy with those he considers to be bureaucrats, excessively conservative or, worst of all, dull. Most people like him for his wit, intelligence, energy and sense of fun. But that can also have a cost.

Considering a Job Change

He is 41 years old and has been working as a senior marketing manager in a large multinational company selling fast-moving consumer goods (FMCG) such as household cleaners, detergents and disinfectants. He has been in this role for 4 years and is ready for a change. He also wants to pursue a career in a different type of organisation and has become attracted to a new technology business that is advertising for a marketing director. He has discovered from the headhunter handling the assignment that this role could lead to being considered for the role of CEO in 18 months when the current CEO retires. Alan is ambitious enough to find the prospect of being a CEO attractive.

The headhunter asks Alan to undergo a psychological assessment as part of the recruitment process. Alan discovers a few 'home truths' through this process. His strengths are confirmed: he is a bright, strategic thinker, imaginative and energetic. He loves new ideas and gets on with most people. However, the psychologist points out that his strengths are *not operational*: he has insufficient attention to detail, tends not to plan well and needs to find a way to raise his game in this aspect of the work. It is a real Achilles heel and could cause him to fail unless it is addressed. Indeed it has caused issues in the past. The psychologist also points out that he is unlikely to make much progress by doing this himself since he seems to have a personality profile that is likely to be more of a hindrance than a help in this area.

Nobody had been quite so direct or honest with him about this before. It had always been a bit of a joke that Alan was to planning what George W. Bush was to scholarly debate. Now his lack of attention to detail and planning mattered and he considered he was unlikely to be given the job he wanted. So, imagine his surprise when the offer was made to meet the CEO, Sam.

Sam seemed unconcerned that Alan was not a detailed planner. He was taken by Alan's creativity, energy and intelligence. The CEO had been an operational specialist all his career and had made his name creating systems and processes that worked. He thought that he and Alan would be a good combination: one bringing creative energy and flair, the other ensuring that ideas were translated into sound processes and both getting on well with the rest of the team. Alan was offered, and accepted, the job of sales and marketing director, understanding that he had what they needed and vice versa.

What Does Psychological Assessment of an Executive Comprise?

Assessments hope to offer a dispassionate, third-party view of an executive's capability in specified areas. The techniques deployed vary a great deal but most now comprise a battery of psychological 'tests' (questionnaires) of personality, values and ability, an in-depth interview and usually a 360-degree feedback.

The psychological tests provide insights about various aspects of personality. General personality questionnaires provide an overview of character. We tend to recommend those measures designed to measure the Big 5 traits (see chapter 8) since these have been shown to predict leadership effectiveness significantly. We usually choose between the NEO-PI or the
(continued)

Hogan Personality Inventory (HPI). Both are designed from scratch as Big 5 measures and are valid, reliable and straightforward. Such general measures are sometimes called *Bright Side* measures because they ask about behaviour which is easy to see.

We also tend to add the Hogan Motives, Values and Preferences Inventory (MVPI) to consider what drives a person and is sometimes called the *Inside* of personality. Then there is the so-called *Dark Side* of personality revealed by the Hogan Development Survey (HDS). This examines likely maladaptive responses under pressure.

The in-depth interview concentrates initially on work: how it is done and how successfully. It also needs to produce a broader understanding of the person and so will include a semi-biographical section which might go into such matters as interests, home circumstances, education and upbringing. It attempts to understand where people are coming from, and hence where they may best be suited to go. It also determines the patterns and trends in a life story that may be used to extrapolate somewhat into the individual's future.

Reasoning measures may also be used. The most frequently deployed are verbal reasoning, numerical reasoning and/or a measure of general intelligence. This has the advantage of being very precise but may be subject to serious performance anxiety, so underestimating the true level of ability to some extent.

In addition, the use of a 360-degree questionnaire is a powerful means of creating a reality check since the personality questionnaires and interview all depend on the assessee's self-report. The 360 provides a measure of the *views of others* to set alongside the individual's own views. Different people know different things about people which means one can get a view on how it is like to *work for, with and around* various people.

All measures need to be constructed around or interpreted in light of any framework that will be used to write the report. The Primary Colours Model is one such framework, but there are others. All measures need to be related clearly and reproducibly to the underlying assessment framework.

Alan (S+ O– I+) and the CEO (S– O+ I+) quickly learned to value each other. They were interdependent, aware of the fact and comfortable with it. The rest of the team comprised a CFO, Anthony (S– O+ I–), who tended to work in the background and had a reputation for being spot-on with the numbers but also rather taciturn and private; a technology specialist, Peter (S– O+ I+), who had a keen eye for detail, was great with his team and was a real can-do manager, and an HR director, Chris (S– O+ I–), who was used to looking after the terms and conditions. Alan was the only really *broad thinker* about the market and the business as a whole: a strategy specialist, and it was a great relief to everyone that he was also a powerful and effective communicator.

Working with the Team

The problems for Alan were much more difficult with his sales and marketing team than with his peers and the CEO. This small company had had to compete for talent with a number of large employers in the area and had a less than impressive sales team. They had recruited from a variety of sources—few of them ideal—and there was a dearth of understanding in the sales team of the 'science' behind the products. This would not normally have mattered but for the fact that they had to sell to buyers who *did* understand the scientific issues. Their sales were thus relatively poor.

Alan quickly removed many of the sales team, replacing them with much brighter and scientifically sophisticated people. He had to pay a little more to attract them but considered this investment would pay for itself. As a sales manager he appointed a woman he could get along with, Terri, who was bright, lively and articulate, though a little disorganised like himself. This was his first significant mistake: hiring people you think are likely to work well with you because they are like you.

Within a few months the sales had improved but the sales team was restless and becoming more so. One or two left after a few months. Terri and Alan had frequently put together creative sales and marketing campaigns but they had too often descended into chaos due to poor planning and no amount of throwing more energy and 'can-do' attitude at them made up for the basic lack of detailed planning.

Terri had to go and Alan had to learn that recruiting in his own image was unwise. He set about recruiting a sales manager who was altogether different: less creative but more orderly and disciplined. Alan needed a *complementary* team member, not a *duplicate* with the same flaws and strengths. He appointed Sally, who was a bright science graduate with a background in sales gained through selling insurance where the need to be organised and relentless had been ingrained. Though straightforward, she was rather more introverted than Alan liked, and yet she had also learned the power of keeping her team briefed and of reviewing their performance weekly. She had described at interview her annual, monthly and weekly sales cycles and how she used them to set objectives, review the team's progress towards them and review individual performance.

Alan feared she might be somewhat compulsive or obsessional, but appointed her anyway and soon discovered her strengths were real and his fears unfounded. The team thought she was a breath of fresh air (S- O+ I+) who led sales through focus and clarity and with positive reinforcement. She was happy to leave the inspiration to Alan.

What to Look for to Identify Who is Capable and Motivated in the Leadership Capabilities Described in the Primary Colours Model:

When auditing the team or recruiting a new member, it is important to know what to look for and how to know when you have found it. Remember, we do not advocate looking for the complete individual leader but rather one who is strong in several areas and finds ways to *work on or around* those aspects of their leadership in which they need help. Each of the seven capabilities in the Primary Colours Model, and the capacity to cope with pressure, is identifiable. Here are some guidelines:

Setting Strategic Direction

Ask about and explore the strategic challenges facing their current organisation. Look for people who understand the market well, can describe how the organisation needs to respond as a whole and who are naturally curious about new trends and developments. Look for the capacity to make sense of apparently disparate events and communicate this clearly. Avoid people who are short-term or siloed in their thinking or ill-informed about the context in which the organisation is operating.

Creating Alignment

Explore recent attempts to persuade and influence people and to deal with resistance to an idea or plan. Look for people who can combine logical argument with passionate advocacy; people who listen and explore other people's points of view and can be assertive without dominating. Seek out those
(continued)

who involve people in order to build their commitment and engagement. It is important to have emotional intelligence, courage and the ability to confront people. Avoid those who dominate, use evidence or logic poorly, give in too easily or fail to identify with issues and express little enthusiasm.

Leading

Ask about the opportunities they have had to lead a department, team, project or initiative. Look for people who *coordinate* the contributions of others and *balance* the needs of the organisation with the needs of the team. Seek out those who are skilled in one or more of the five enablers: inspire, focus, enable, reinforce, learn. Favour those who know and accept that they cannot do all of this and invite others to contribute where they personally cannot. Avoid those who seek to do everything themselves and show poor self-awareness.

Planning and Organising

Ask how and when they plan and organise their work. Look for those people who can balance planning with flexibility, who schedule time for these activities and communicate the plans widely. Look also for people who express a need to remain organised at all times in order to be flexible, who have systems and methods that seem to work and who are tidy and self-disciplined. Avoid extremes, that is, people who are either inflexible and obsessional over details, or who are sloppy or casual about planning and organising: who do not allow time for these activities or who are lacking in discipline. Also avoid those who claim to be organised but cannot describe credibly how they do it.

Building and Sustaining Relationships

Ask about how they have built relationships with key people in the organisation, especially with their peers and those on whom their effectiveness depended. Look for people who have a rich vocabulary for describing people in their ambit: who can describe similarities and differences between people and who can describe how they used their understanding of the people they worked with to increase their effectiveness. Look for *psychological mindedness*, that is, being perceptive, intuitive, articulate and insightful about how people tick. Seek out those who made time for people and seemed to have relationships that were strong and resilient. Avoid those who avoid conflict, fail to make time for people or are preoccupied with those aspects of their work in which people are not involved.

Team Working

Ask about the various teams in which they have worked recently. Ask what is missing when they are not there and what they generally contribute to help the team function well. Ask them how they deal with disagreement in

(continued)

their team. Look for a strong narrative about getting work done in teams where each person knows what his or her contribution is expected to be. Look also for those who accept interdependencies and have found ways to make them work. Seek out those who show commitment to the team and the ability to challenge and support team members in equal measure and who work to sustain morale and motivation in the team. Avoid people whose egos seem to get in the way, who operate largely alone and who put their own needs ahead of the team's.

Delivering Results

Ask about his or her track record against any performance targets. Look for those who have regularly met or beaten their targets, even when they were stretched: people who are willing to do their utmost to meet deadlines, to push and assert, to meet schedules and to deliver within budgets. These are generally not comfortable people to be around but they understand the difference between assertion and aggression. Avoid bullies at all costs and those who seem too ready to offer excuses or who fail to accept accountability for their own performance.

Coping with Pressure

Ask about tough times in the job. Ask what they find difficult and also what stresses them. Ask them about their coping strategies and what works best for them and why. Ask also what they do to remain in good shape for their work and where they get the support they need. Look for those who understand their limitations and take steps to stay fit and well. Seek out those who can both give and receive support. Avoid the apparently invulnerable, and the extremely fragile unless you can offer them the support they will need.

After tripping up briefly over the appointment of a sales manager, things went well for Alan and, 18 months later, the CEO retired and Alan was offered the job. Unsurprisingly, he leapt at it.

Becoming the CEO

Alan finally had what he had wanted all along: his own company to run. He promoted Sally to sales and marketing director, looked around his new Executive team and thought that all was well in his world—and for a while it was, until Anthony retired about 6 months later. He needed a new CFO and moved quickly to appoint John (S+ O– I+), a former partner from a medium-sized accounting practice. John had demonstrated knowledge of the technology sector and had experience of raising finance for new ventures and acquisitions. This would serve the needs of the next stage in the company's development well. He was numerate and good with people too: a bonus after Anthony's taciturn character.

John became a great ally of Alan's and helped him hugely to think through the strategic moves that would help the company grow. There was a problem in that John struggled to satisfy his own team's need for detail, but he quickly rectified that by asking his financial controller to handle the detailed planning for the finance department.

The problem Alan faced was not John: it was Alan himself. The top team were used to working with an implementer who thoroughly considered how plans would be executed before unleashing them on the organisation. Alan did not: rather he moved at pace and expected everyone to be swept along with enthusiasm and confidence, but they found it hard to cope with Alan's lack of attention to how his ambitious plans would be made to happen.

Alan had to take a leaf from John's book and appoint someone to handle the operational matters. He needed a COO. He considered it overkill to appoint another senior executive when the company only had around 1000 employees, so he appointed Peter to take on his role along with his technology portfolio. Peter was grooming a successor in the technology group, so Alan was able to argue for Peter taking on a broader operational role. Peter agreed: problem solved.

Auditing the Team

Here is a series of questions to ask to help you audit a team against the Primary Colours Model:

1. How, where and when do we do the following?
    a. Set strategic direction
    b. Create alignment
    c. Ensure a balance of leadership contributions (lead)
    d. Plan and organise
    e. Build and sustain relationships
    f. Work together as a team
    g. Deliver results

2. How *well* do we do these things and how do we monitor our effectiveness?
3. Who is the most skilled team member in each of these seven aspects of leadership and how do we provide opportunities for him/her to lead when that contribution is most needed?
4. How, and how well, do we cope with pressure as a team and how resilient is each individual?
5. Are there factions in the team or do they truly work together effectively?

Each answer will suggest a possible need for a change of some kind. Usually, this will be a change of process. However, it could also be a change of personnel in the team or a need for one or two members to develop in some way.

Dealing with a Downturn

Alan's team had their work cut out roughly 2 years after he took over as CEO. The company made sensors for aero engines. Conflict in the Gulf drove up the price of fuel and terrorism fears made people reluctant to fly. These twin effects caused the two major aircraft manufacturers to cut their production to match the downturn in demand for air travel and the company's order book dried up significantly.

In such a crisis the company had little choice but to cut costs and the workforce. They had been measuring employee engagement on a regular (annual) basis and had used a Leadership Team Impact Monitor Six-Monthly. They therefore knew that there was a high level of commitment to the company and respect for the top team's leadership. Cutting the workforce was a drastic step to take, but there seemed to be little choice. By then, the company had grown to 1200 people and they recognised the need to reduce the workforce by as much as 20 % unless they could find another source of income fast.

Alan's team comprised a good blend of task-oriented and people-oriented executives. They considered the matter from many different angles. They embarked on a plan that was part surgery, part innovation but they knew that both elements had to be implemented rapidly.

Engagement in a Downturn and a Crisis: The Leadership Essentials

Leadership in the tough times is not so vastly different from leadership at other times. Consider the steps described in the models we have described:

1. Setting strategic direction: is a new direction required or merely new tactics, systems and processes?
2. Give considerable attention to alignment. Usually a crisis focuses attention powerfully and alignment follows. If it does not, be very clear what is required and consult rapidly about how changes are to be made. Never waste a good crisis: it can facilitate change because the 'burning platform' creates a widespread sense of urgency.
3. Keep the plans simple and widely communicated.
4. Attend to relationships between the top team and the rest of the organisation. Most people will have a keen sense of what is happening to orders, customers and the like. So, ensure the top team members are frequently visible, communicating, encouraging and singing from the same hymn sheet.
5. Continue to empower teams. They will frequently have more ideas than anyone gives them credit for. They are close to the customers. Use their ability to take decisions in the pursuit of very clear and agreed goals.
6. Deliver, deliver, deliver. Results count in a crisis and small increments in performance or efficiency may become hugely significant. Frequent successes, however small, keep the belief in the organisation that it is not powerless. Take drastic action, if required, celebrate successes and deal with performance shortfalls. This may be a time for tough love.
7. Lead as a team and ensure that the whole team plays to its collective strengths. As appealing as a hero may be in tough times, complete leadership is still unlikely to be found in an individual.

Once the basics have been attended to as in the steps delineated above, a simple mnemonic might be in the five leadership enablers:

- *Inspire* is largely a matter of inspiring confidence: the belief that we can affect what happens to us—we are not powerless. Take every opportunity to communicate and attend to the non-verbal messages. Now is a time to appear confident and steady under fire, however you may be feeling.
- *Focus* relentlessly on the (simple) plan and ensure everyone stays focused on its actions and priorities.
- *Enable* in this context means ensuring everyone knows what is expected of them, what decisions they can take *and* that they are unafraid to act.
- *Reinforce* those who take the right decisions, make the plan work and sustain the morale of their colleagues. Communicate their achievements

(continued)

- widely, recognise and celebrate them in a manner that is appropriate to the tough circumstances in which many may be struggling or losing their jobs.
- *Learn:* note the lessons the crisis or downturn is teaching, but don't spend too long reviewing. That is for later (and must not be skipped)— now is the time for action.

Alan and the team believed wisely in being visible in tough times. He and the top team visited their two plants on the same day to hold 'town hall' meetings. They described how they would have to lay off as many of 20 % of the workforce unless they could innovate rapidly, yet they also explained that they had decided not to take that simple option. They were planning to invite people to apply for voluntary redundancy or early retirement and apply a recruitment freeze in most parts of the business. They anticipated this would quickly reduce the workforce by 10 %. They would take a vote on a 10 % reduction in hours and working for those remaining. They were also going to create an innovations team to apply their technology to new markets and opportunities. That team would be expected to work flat-out for 6 months.

He divided his top team into two: half to run the business along with the workforce reduction, and half to lead the innovation. Ideally, he wanted to appoint Peter, the COO with an eye for organisation and detail, to run the business but Peter's technological innovation was even more sorely needed. So he asked John, the CFO, to run the business with the HR director, Chris, and the sales and marketing director, Sally. He asked them to meet him weekly to keep him informed and gave them a clear priority to be visible and to look after morale at this difficult time. Alan would also make sure he was visible and visit the plants weekly. Alan and Peter would look after the innovations required: Peter taking care of the technology and Alan searching out new markets. This was a gamble, but it was worth taking.

The top team was small and needed to co-opt a few from the next level of management to help. Peter drew together two other tech-nologists from his department to help him apply their sensing tech-nology to diesel car engines to help them run more smoothly and efficiently. Alan quickly learned of a small engineering firm about 50 miles away who had developed much of the diesel engine technology Peter had described. They decided a small acquisition was called for and so Alan handed that responsibility over to John and switched himself into the task of running the business while John managed the acquisition.

In all this, Alan had learned two important lessons. *First*, each sub-team needed balance and, *second*, that each person could lead in the area he or she was strongest. The task of running the business was largely a financial and operational task so John, Sally and Chris had all the bases covered: HR, sales and finance from a functional point of view and Strategic Leadership (John, though hardly required at all), Operational Leadership (Sally and Chris) and Interpersonal Leadership (Sally and John). In the innovations team: technology and marketing were represented and from a leadership perspective both Alan and Peter were strong interpersonally and between them could cover strategic and operational leadership also. When Alan and John switched, it was to move John into his area of M&A expertise without losing strategic or interpersonal leadership in the innovations team. In both teams, there was a great deal of focus on planning, organising and delivering results. The clear emergency was creating sufficient alignment, though there was a great need in both teams to take care of morale and to sustain engagement by consulting frequently on what could be done to achieve results quickly and inexpensively.

The strategic direction had been set. It was not going to be changed. The challenge was execution which required a great deal of operational and interpersonal focus and expertise. Alan had to take more of a back seat than is usual for a CEO to allow room for his team to do what they did best. If Alan's ego had not been held in check, he could have disabled the team by either trying to do too much himself or by leaping in to run the business from the start of the twin-team leadership approach. Instead, he got it broadly right by keeping himself in touch with the employees on key occasions and letting his operational specialists lead.

It took 3 years for the downturn to end. By then, the company had made its acquisition, broadened its offer to include sensors for diesel auto and marine engines and restored the salaries to their pre-downturn levels, as they had agreed at the start. The workforce was back at 1,200.

The Next Stage of the Journey

When salaries had been restored, there was a company-wide recognition that the downturn was over but the next stage of the journey had not been defined. That was the next task. Alan invited his team to a strategy retreat, joking at the ironic use of the term 'retreat' when it was designed to help them move forward.

Force Field Analysis (FFA)

FFA is a simple and powerful planning tool. It can be used for many purposes. We use it for helping a team conduct strategic planning and also for team development. In the case of strategic planning, it comprises five simple questions in a strict sequence. These are:

1. What are we planning to achieve together over the next 3–5 years?
2. Where are we now relative to these goals?
3. What is currently helping us (pushing us in the required direction)?
4. What is currently hindering us (pushing us off-course or holding us in our current state)?
5. What do we therefore need to do, especially to remove the hindrances?

At each stage we encourage very specific discussions and the avoidance of generalisations. Question 1 describes the preconditions for association. Any team member who cannot agree with the rest of the team about this first question, after it has been discussed, should consider his or her future. There may be no place for him or her on the team. At question 5, responsibilities need to be allocated and deadlines agreed to ensure delivery.

When used for team development, there is a new question introduced and the entire discussion is refocused. Once the team has agreed what they need to achieve together, a new question 2 is introduced: How do we need to lead together to deliver this agenda? The subsequent discussion is then refocused on the team and its collective leadership. To facilitate this, we tend to introduce assessments of the team members and the use of 360-degree feedback and psychometric measures (see above: box on Assessment) before the team workshop, so that the results can be fed into the workshop as part of the helping and hindering factors. This needs to be carefully led by a facilitator who is not a part of the team.

At the retreat, they conducted a Force Field Analysis to help them work out what they were aiming to achieve together over the next 3–5 years. Two decisions were clear at the end of the event. The first was public, the second private. Publicly, the top team had agreed that they had to focus over the next phase of their journey on driving down costs. They had to become a low-cost producer at the highest possible quality level in order to protect their margins. These priorities were in sales, technology and finance: the operation. This had set the strategic direction for a while. Privately, Alan had realised that these were not his own areas of strength. It would soon be time for him to go once he had decided the succession required for a smooth transition and the continuing success of the company.

His options to succeed him were relatively straightforward if he was not to recruit from outside the organisation. He had to choose between Peter, John and Sally. To make the choice, he discussed the matter extensively with the Chairman and they opted for Peter. The reasons included the fact that Peter had the confidence of the Board and the top team. He was an operational leader by inclination and was good at it. It was time for Alan to go and for Peter to begin again the task of balancing the top team around his own skills and leadership capabilities.

Peter was good with people and recognised his strategic limitations. John was happy to serve under him and to provide the strategic input as required. Sally would move up to COO and appoint a new head of sales and marketing with an emphasis on marketing. Peter's successor in technology (Marga) was ready for her directorship, though she had a great deal to learn about creating alignment. Since the strategic direction was clear, Peter had resolved to focus on getting the top team aligned before any other priorities.

In our story, Alan and Peter had come to see leadership issues clearly and the light that had been shed on them was made up of primary colours. They were incomplete alone but had learned how to act together so that the whole was greater than the sum of the parts.

Summary and Conclusion: Complete Leadership

Alan's story demonstrates that the four central propositions about leadership can guide action.

1. The Primary Colours Model describes the territory of leadership. Against its elements, leadership teams can be evaluated and around its principles they can be built.
2. Complete leadership is a real possibility provided it is seen as the province of the team (and not one individual) and appropriate for the circumstances the organisation is facing. Complete leadership is *complementary* leadership: each member of the leadership team bringing high levels of skill to part of the broader leadership capability set. In this way, a team can respond to the varying demands placed upon it.
3. Organisations are unlikely to find heroes who are deeply impressive in all aspects of leadership. They need leaders who know who they are, what they bring to leadership and what they need from others to cover all elements in the strategic, operational and interpersonal domains, and who, with their team, can cope with pressure.
4. Finally, complete leadership requires the balancing and coordination that is the province of 'leading' that lies at the heart of the Primary Colours Model. This ensures that the most appropriate aspects of leadership are deployed at the appropriate times from the broader team; and even *leading* can emerge from an effective leadership team.

There is a great deal one can know about leadership. The research literature is growing at a vast rate and popular books abound. There is also the learning that derives from observing leaders at work and from personal experience and feedback. This book is by no means all there is to know about leadership but it may be all you *need to* know.

Bibliography

Alimo-Metcalfe, B., Alban-Metcalfe, J., Bradley, M., Mariathasan, J. & Samele, C. (2008). 'The impact of engaging leadership on performance, attitudes to work and well-being at work: a longitudinal study'. *Journal of Health Organization & Management, 22,* 6, 586–598.

Ancona, D. Malone, T.W. Orlikowski, W.J. and Senge, P. (2007) In praise of the incomplete leader. *Harvard Business Review,* Feb 2007.

Alvarez, J.L., & Svejenova, S. (2005). *Sharing executive power: Roles and relationships at the top.* Cambridge: Cambridge University Press.

Avery, G. (2004). *Understanding Leadership.* London: Sage Publications.

Arvey, R., Rotundo, M., Johnson, W., Zhang, Z., & McGue, M. (2006) The determinants of leadership role occupancy: Genetic and personality factors. *Leadership Quarterly, 17,* 1–20.

Babiak., P., & Hare, R. (2006) *Snakes in Suits.* New York Regan Books.

Bales, R.F., & Slater, P.E. (1955). Role differentiation in small decision-making groups. In T. Parsons & R.F. Bales (Eds.), *Family, socialization and interaction process.* Glencoe, IL: The Free Press.

Bar-On, R. (1997). The Bar-On Emotional Quotient Inventory (EQ-i): A Test of Emotional Intelligence. Toronto, Canada: Multi-Health Systems.

Barrick, M., & Mount, M. (2005) Yes, personality matters: Moving on to more important matters. *Human performance, 18, 359–371.*

© The Editor(s) (if applicable) and The Author(s) 2016
D. Pendleton, A. Furnham, *Leadership: All You Need To Know*
2nd edition, DOI 10.1057/978-1-137-55436-9

Barrick, M., Day, D., Lord, R., & Alexander, R. (1991). Assessing the utility of executive leadership. *Leadership Quarterly*, 2, 9–22.

Bass, B. M. (1990). Bass and Stogdill's handbook of leadership: Theory, research and managerial applications. New York: The Free Press.

Bass, B.M., & Alvolio, B. J. (1990). *Multifactor Leadership Questionnaire for Research.* Palo Alto, Mind Garden.

Bassi, L., & McMurrer, D. (2007). Maximising your return on people. *Harvard Business Review*, 1–9.

Bennis, W. and Nanus, B. (1985) *Leaders: the strategies for taking charge.* NY, Harper and Row.

Bennis, W. G. (2003). *On Becoming a Leader.* New York: Basic Books.

Bono,J., & Judge, T. (2004) Personality and Transformational and Transactional Leadership: A Meta-Analysis. *Journal of Applied Psychology.* 89, 901–910.

Borrill, C., West, M.A., Shapiro, D., & Rees, A. (2000). Team working and effectiveness in health care. *British Journal of Health Care*, 6 (8), 364–371.

Borril, C. and West, M.A. (2002) *Team working and effectiveness in health care: findings from the healthcare team effectiveness project.* Birmingham, UK, Aston Centre for Health Service Organisation Research.

Briner, R. (2014) What is employee engagement and does it matter?: An evidence based approach London, Institute for Employment Studies.

Brown, S. and Leigh, T. (1996) A new look at psychological climate and its relationship to job involvement, effort, and performance. *Journal of Applied Psychology*, 81, 358–68.

Buchanan, D.A., Addicott, R., Fitzgerald, L., Ferlie, E., & Baeza, J.I. (2007). Nobody in charge: Distributed change agency in healthcare. *Human Relations*, 60(7), 1065–1090.

Burke, C.S., Fiore, S.M., & Salas, E. (2003). The role of shared cognition in enabling shared leadership and team adaptability. In C.L. Pearce & J.A. Conger (Eds.), *Shared leadership: Reframing the hows and whys of leadership.* Thousand Oaks, CA: Sage Publications.

Burns, J. (1978). *Leadership.* New York: Harper and Row.

Cain, S. (2012) *Quiet: the power of introverts in a world that can't stop talking.* New York: Crown.

Carson, M., Shanock, L., Heggestad, E., Andrew, A., Pugh, S., & Walter, M. (2012). The relationship between dysfunctional interpersonal tendencies, derailment potential behavior, and turnover. *Journal of Business and Psychology*, 27, 291–304.

Catlette, W. and Hadden, R. (1998) *Contented Cows Give Better Milk.* Germantown, TN. Saltillo Press.

Catlette, W. and Hadden, R. (2007) *Contented cows moove faster.* Germantown, TN. Saltillo Press.

Chamorro-Premuzic, T., & Furnham, A. (2005) *Personality and intellectual competence.* Mahwah: LEA.

Collins, J. (2001). Level 5 Leadership. *Harvard Business Review* Jan 2001.

Conrad S. and Milburn, M. (2001) *Sexual Intelligence,* New York, Crown.

Cooper, R., & Sawaf, A. (1997) *Executive EQ: Emotional Intelligence in Leadership and Organisations.* New York: Grosset Putnam.

Corporate Leadership Council (2004) *Driving performance and retention through employee engagement.* London, Corporate Leadership Council.

Daft, R.L. (1999) *Leadership: theory and practice.* Orlando, FL., Dryden Press.

Denis, J.-L., Langley, A. & Sergi, V. (2012) Leadership in the Plural. The Academy of Management Annals <u>6</u> (1) 2012, 211–283.

Derue, D. S., Nahrgang, J. D., Wellman, N., & Humphrey, S. E. (2011). Trait and behavioural theories of leadership: an integration and meta-analytic test of their relative validity. *Personnel Psychology 64,* 7–52.

Dotlich, D. L., & Cairo, P. C. (2003). *Why CEOs Fail: the eleven deadly sins and how NOT to commit them.* New York: Jossey Bass.

Doz, Y. L. & Kosonen, M. (2007) The new deal at the top. *Harvard Business Review* June 2007.

Eichinger & Lombardo, M. M. (2004). Patterns of rater accuracy in 360-degree feedback. *Human Resource Planning, 27* (4), 23–25.

Ellis, R., & Whittington, D. (1981). *A guide to Social Skills Training.* London: Crown, Helm.

Emmons, R. (2000) Is spirituality an intelligence? *International Journal for the Psychology of Religion, 10, 3–26.*

Fayol, H. (1917). Administration industrielle et générale: Prévoyance, organisation, commandement, coordination, contrôle. Paris: H. Dunod et E. Pinat.

Follett, M.P. (1949) *The Essentials of Leadership.* London: Management Publications Trust.

Furnham, A. (2006). Explaining the popularity of emotional intelligence. In K. Murphy (Ed). *A Critique of Emotional Intelligence.* New York: LEA, p.141–159.

Furnham, A. (2007) Rating a boss, a colleague, and a subordinate. *Journal of Managerial Psychology, 22,* 610–621.

Furnham, A. (2010). The elephant in the boardroom: The psychology of leadership derailment. Bracknell: Palgrave Macmillan.

Furnham, A., Crump, J., & Ritchie, W. (2013). What it takes: Ability, demographic, bright and dark side trait correlates of years to promotion. *Personality and Individual Differences, 55,* 952–956.

Furnham, A., Hyde, G., & Trickey, G. (2014). Do your dark side traits fit? Dysfunctional personalities in different work sectors. *Applied Psychology, 63,* 589–606.

Furnham, A. (2015). *Backstabbers and Bullies.* London: Bloomsbury.

Furnham, A., & Petrides, K. V. (2003). Trait emotional intelligence and happiness. *Social Behaviour and Personality, 31,* 815–823.

Furnham, A., & Petrides, K. V. (2004). Parental estimates of five types of intelligence. *Australian Journal of Psychology, 56,* 10–17.

Gaddis, B.H. and Foster J.L. (first published on line 2013) Meta-Analysis of Dark Side Personality Characteristics and Critical Work Behaviors among Leaders across the Globe: Findings and Implications for Leadership Development and Executive Coaching. *Applied Psychology* (2015) 64, 25–54.

Gallup (2003) cited in *Employee engagement: how to build a high performance workforce.* London, Chicago and Sydney Melcrum Research.

Gallup Path. in Coffman, C. and González Molina, G. (2002) Follow this path: how the world's greatest organizations drive growth by unleashing human potential. New York, Warner Books.

Gallup (2006) *Engagement predicts earnings per share.* Gallup Organisation.

Gallup (2006) Feeling Good Matters in the Workplace. *The Gallup Management Journal Online.*

Gardner, H. (1983) *Frames of Mind: The Theory of Multiple Intelligence.* New York: Basic Books.

Gardner, H. (1999). *Intelligence Reframed.* New York: Basic Books.

Gelade and Young (2005) Test of a Service Profit Chain Model in the Retail Banking Sector. *Journal of Occupational and Organizational Psychology, 78,* 1–22.

Gibb, C.A. (1954). Leadership. In G. Lindzay (Ed.), *Handbook of social psychology.* Reading, MA: Addison-Wesley.

Goffee, R. & Jones, G. (2000) Why should anyone be led by you? *Harvard Business Review* Sept-Oct 2000.

Goleman, D. (1995). *Emotional Intelligence: Why it can matter more than IQ.* New York: Bantam Books.

Goleman, D. (1998). *Working with emotional intelligence.* New York: Bantam Books.

Goleman, D (2000) Leadership that gets results. *Harvard Business Review.* March 2000.

Goleman, D. (2006). *Social Intelligence: The New Science of Human Relationships.* New York: Bantam Books.

Grant, A.M., Gino, F. & Hoffmann, D.A. (2010) Reversing the extraverted leadership advantage: the role of employee proactivity. *Academy of Management Journal* 54(3), 528–550.

Grant, A.M. (2013) Rethinking the extraverted sales ideal: the ambivert advantage. *Psychological Science* 24(6), 1024–1030.

Grint, K. (2000). *The arts of leadership*. Oxford University Press.

Hackman, J.R. (2010) What is this thing called leadership? In Nohria and Khurana (2010) ibid.

Hambrick, D. C., & Mason, P.A. 1984. Upper echelons: the organization as a reflection of its top managers. *Academy of Management Review*, 9: 193–206.

Harter, J.K., Schmidt, F., Kilham, E.A., Asplund, J.W. (2006) *Q12 meta-analysis*. The Gallup Organisation.

Harvey, M., Novicevic, M., & Kiessling, T. (2002) Development of multiple IQ maps for the use in the selection of impatriate managers. *International Journal of Intercultural Relations*, 26, 493–524.

Handy, C. (1991). *The Age of Unreason*. London: Century Hutchinson.

Heffernan, M. (2011) *Willful blindness*. NY, Walker and Co/Simon and Schuster.

Heifetz, R., & Laurie, D. (2001). The work of leadership. *Harvard Business Review*. Dec 2001.

Herzberg, F., Mausner, B., & Snyderman, B. (1959) *The Motivation to Work*. New York: Wiley.

Herzberg, F. (1975) One more time how do you motivate employees? IN *Business Classics: 15 key concepts for managerial success*. Cambridge, MA, Harvard University Press.

Higgs, M., and Dulewicz, S. (1999). *Making Sense of Emotional Intelligence*. Windsor, UK: NFER Nelson.

Hogan, R., Curphy, G., and Hogan, J. (1994) What we know about leadership *American Psychologist 1994 493–504*.

Hogan, R. and Hogan, J. (1997) *Hogan development survey manual*. Tulsa, OK., Hogan Assessment Systems.

Hogan, R., & Hogan, J. (2001). Assessing leadership: A view from the dark side. *International Journal of Selection and Assessment*, 9, 40–51.

Hogan R. and Kaiser, R. (*2005*) What we know about leadership. *Review of General Psychology* 2005, 9, 169–180.

Hogan, R. (2007). *Personality and the fate of organizations*. Mahwah, NJ: Lawrence Erlbaum.

Hogan, J., & Warrenfeltz, R. (2003). Educating the Modern Manager. *Academy of Management Learning and Education*, 2, 74–85.

House, R.J. and Aditya, R.N. (1997) The social scientific study of leadership: Quo vadis? *Journal of Management,* 23, 409–473.

House, R. J., & Podaskoff, P.M. (1994) *Leadership effectiveness: Past perspectives and future directions for research.* In Greenberg, J. (Eds) *Organisational Behaviour: The State of the Science.* Jillsdale, NJ: Lawrence Erlbaum Associates, pp.45–82.

Holland, J. (1973). *Making Vocational Choices.* Englewood Cliffs, NJ: Prentice Hall.

Hunter, E., Neubert, M., Perry, S., Witt, L., Penny, L. & Weinberger, E. (2013) Servant leaders inspire servant followers: antecedents and outcomes for employees and the organisation. *The Leadership Quarterly* 24, 316–331.

Huselid, M.A. 1995. The impact of human resource management practices on turnover, productivity, and corporate financial performance. *Academy of Management Journal,* 38, 635–672.

Huselid, M. A., & Becker, B. E. (1995) *The Strategic impact of high performance work systems.* Paper presented at the 1995 Academy of Management annual meetings, Vancouver, BC.

Jolton, J. and Hayes, B. (IBM 2014) Big data helps bust the top three myths of employee engagement and leadership. IBM Smarter Workforce Institute.

Judge, T.A. and Bono, J. (2000) Five factor model of personality and transformational leadership. *Journal of Applied Psychology,* 85, 751–765.

Judge, T.A. and Bono, J. (2001) Relationship of core self-evaluations traits – self-esteem, generalised self-efficacy, locus of control and emotional stability—with job satisfaction and performance: A meta-analysis. *Journal of Applied Psychology,* 86, 80–92.

Judge, T. A., Colbert, A. E., & Ilies, R. (2004). Intelligence and Leadership: A Quantitative Review and Test of Theoretical Propositions. *Journal of Applied Psychology, 89*(3), 542–552.

Judge, T.,Bono, J., Ilies, R., & Gerhert, M. (2002) Personality and leadership. *Journal of Applied Psychology, 87,* 765–780.

Judge, T. A., LePine, J. A., & Rich, B. L. (2006). The narcissistic personality: Relationship with inflated self-ratings of leadership and with task and contextual performance. *Journal of Applied Psychology, 91,* 762–776.

Judge, T. A., & Piccolo, R. (2004). Transformational and transactional leadership: A meta-analytic test of their relative validity. *Journal of Applied Psychology, 89,* 755–768.

Judge, T. A., Piccolo, R. F., & Ilies, R. (2004). The forgotten ones?: A re-examination of consideration, initiating structure, and leadership effectiveness. *Journal of Applied Psychology, 89,* 36–51.

Kaiser, R.B. (2004, November). *Rethinking Executive Assessment: Making Room for Overkill and Imbalance in Leaders*. Invited presentation given at the 20th semi-annual meeting of the North Carolina Society for Industrial and Organizational Psychology, Greensboro, NC.

Kaiser, R., LeBreton,J., & Hogan, J. (2014). The dark side of personality and extreme leader behaviour. Applied Psychology.

Kets de Vries, M. (1994) The leadership mystique. *Academy of Management Executives, 8,* 73–89.

Kets de Vries, M. (2004) Organisations on the couch. *European Management Journal. 22,* 183–200.

Kets de Vries, M. (2006). *The Leader on the Couch.* New York: Jossey Bass.

Kets de Vries, M. (2006) The spirit of despotism; understanding the tyrant within. *Human Relations, 59,* 195–220.

Kirkpatrick, S.A. & Locke, E.A. (1991) Leadership: do traits matter? *Academy of Management Executive, 5,* 48–60.

Kotter, J. P. (1990). *A force for Change: How leadership Differs from Management.* New York: Free Press.

Kouzes, J. and Posner, B. (2002) *The leadership challenge.* (3rd Ed) San Francisco, Jossey-Bass.

Lewin, K., Lippitt, R., and White, R. (1939). "Patterns of aggressive behavior in experimentally created social climates". *Journal of Social Psychology:* 271–301.

Lord, R. & Maher, K. (1991) *Leadership and Information Processing: Linking Perceptions and Performance.* Boston, Mass., Unwin Hyman.

Locke, E. (1997) Prime movers: The traits of great business leaders. In C. Cooper & S. Jackson (Eds). *Creating Tomorrow's Organisation.* Chichester: Wiley. pp 75–96.

Lieberson, S. & O'Connor, J. (1972) Leadership and organisational performance: a study of large corporations. *American Sociological Review* 1972, 37, 117–130.

Lopes, P., Salovey, P., & Straus, R. (2003). Emotional intelligence, personality and the perceived quality of social relationships. *Personality and Individual Differences, 35,* 641–658.

MacGregor Burns, J. (1978). *Leadership.* New York: Harper & Row.

Machiavelli, N. (originally 1513) *The Prince.* Chichester, Capstone (2010).

Mackintosh, N. (1998). *IQ and Human Intelligence.* Oxford University Press.

MacLeod, D. & Clarke, N. (2009) *Engaging For Success: enhancing performance through employee engagement.* London, Department for Business Innovation and Skills.

Mann, R. (1959) A review of the relationships between personality and performance in small groups. *Psychological Bulletin*, 56, 241–270.

Maslow, A. (1959). *Motivational Personality*. New York: Harper & Row.

Matthews, G., Zeidner, M., & Roberts, R. D. (2002). *Emotional intelligence: Science and myth*. Cambridge, MA: MIT Press.

Matthews, G., Zeidner, M., & Roberts, R. D. (2011). Measuring emotional intelligence: promises, pitfalls, solutions? In A. D. Ong, & M. van Dulmen (Eds.). *Handbook of methods in positive psychology*. Oxford University Press.

Mayer, J., & Salovey, P. (1997). What is emotional intelligence. In P. Salovey and D. Sluyter (eds) *Emotional Development and Emotional Intelligence*. New York: Basic Books.

Mayer, J. D., Salovey, P., & Caruso, D. R. (2002). *The Mayer-Salovey-Caruso Emotional Intelligence Test (MSCEIT): user's manual*. Toronto, Canada: Multi-Health Systems.

McCrae, R. R., & Costa, P.T. (1987). Validation of the five-factor model of personality across instruments and observers. *Journal of Personality and Social Psychology, 52* (1), 81–90.

McGregor, D. (1960). *The Human Side of Enterprise*. New York: McGraw-Hill.

Meindl, J.R., Ehrlich, S.B., & Dukerich, J.M. (1985). The romance of leadership. *Administrative Science Quarterly*, 30(1), 78–102.

Melcrum (2005) *Employee engagement: how to build a high performance workforce*. London, Chicago and Sydney Melcrum Research.

Mintzberg, H. (1973). *The Nature of Managerial Work*. New York, Harper and Row.

Murphy, K. (Ed). (2006). *A critique of emotional intelligence*. New York: LEA.

Nelis, D., Quoidbach, J., Mikolajczak, M., Hansenne, M. (2009). Increasing emotional intelligence: (How) is it possible? *Personality and Individual Differences, 47*, 36–41.

Nohria, N. and Khurana, R. (2010) *Handbook of Leadership Theory and Practice: A Harvard Business School Centennial Colloquium*. Boston, Mass., Harvard Business Press.

Northouse, P.G. (1997) *Leadership: Theory and Practice*. Thousand Oaks, Calif.: Sage.

Oldham, J., & Morris, L. (1991). *Personality self-portrait*. New York: Bantam.

Olivier, R. (2001) *Inspirational Leadership*. London, Spiro.

O'Reilly, C.A., and Pfeffer, J. (2000) Hidden Value: How Great Companies Achieve Extraordinary Results with Ordinary People. Boston: Harvard Business School Press.

Ones, D., Viswesvaran, C., & Dilchert, S. (2005) Personality at work: Raising awareness and correcting misconceptions. *Human Performance, 18, 389–404*

Ouimet, G. (2010). Dynamics of narcissistic leadership in organisations. Towards an integrated research model. *Journal of Managerial Psychology, 25,* 713–726.

Owen, D. (2008) *In sickness and in power.* London, Methuen.

Oxford Said Business School and Heidrick and Struggles (2014) *The CEO Report: Embracing the paradoxes of leadership and the power of doubt.*

Padilla, A., Hogan, R., & Kaiser, R. (2007). The toxic triangle: destructive leaders, susceptible followers and conducive environments. *Leadership Quarterly,* 18, 176–194.

Peter, L. and Hull, R. (1969) *The Peter Principle: why things go wrong.* NY, William Morrow.

Peterson, C., & Seligman, M. (2004). *Character Strengths and Virtues.* Washington, DC: APA Press.

Peterson, R. S., Smith, D. B., Martorana, P. V., & Owens, P. D. (2003). The Impact of Chief Executive Officer Personality on Top Management Team Dynamics: One Mechanism by Which Leadership Affects Organizational Performance. *Journal of Applied Psychology, 88* (5), 795–808.

Petrides, K. V., Frederickson, N., & Furnham, A. (2004). The role of trait emotional intelligence in academic performance and deviant behaviour at school. *Personality and Individual Differences, 36,* 277–293.

Petrides, K. V., Furnham, A., & Frederickson, N. (2004). Emotional intelligence. *The Psychologist, 17,* 574–577.

Petrides, K. V., & Furnham, A. (2001). Trait emotional intelligence: psychometric investigation with reference to established trait taxonomies. *European Journal of Personality, 15,* 425–448.

Petrides, K. V., Perez, J. C., & Furnham, A. (2006). On the criterion and incremental validity of Trait Emotional Intelligence. *Emotion and Cognition.*

Petrides, K. V., Furnham, A., & Mavroveti, S. (2006). Trait emotional intelligence: Moving forward in the field of EI. In G. Matthews, M. Zeidner, & R. Roberts (Eds) *Emotional Intelligence: Known and Unknowns.* Oxford: OUP.

Podolny, J.M. Khurana, R., and Besharov, M.L. (2010) Revisiting the meaning of leadership. In Nohria and Khurana (2010) ibid.

Porter, M., & Kramer, M. (2011), Creating shared value. *Harvard Business Review* Jan-Feb 2011.

Radcliffe, S. (2008). *Future Engage Deliver.* London, Troubador.

Rath, T. and Conchie, B. (2008) *Strengths based leadership.* Gallup Press.

Rooke, D. & Torbert, W.R. (2005) Seven transformations of leadership. *Harvard Business Review.* April 2005.

Rosen, R. and Adair, F. (2007) CEOs misperceive top teams' performance. *Harvard Business Review.* September 2007.

Redding, S.G. & Wong, G.Y.Y. (1986) The psychology of Chinese organizational behavior. In M.H. Bond (ed.), *The psychology of the Chinese people.* Hong Kong: University Press.

Riggio,R., Murphy, S., & Pirozollo, F. (2002). *Multiple Intelligence and Leadership.* Mahwah, NJ: LEA.

Roberts, R., Zeidner, M. R., & Matthews, G. (2001). Does emotional intelligence meet traditional standards for an intelligence. Some new data and conclusions. *Emotion, 1,* 243–248.

Rucci, A.J. Kim, S.P. and Quinn, R.T. (1998) The employee-customer profit chain at Sears'. *Harvard Business Review* Jan-Feb 1998.

Rynes, S.L., Gerhart, B. and Minette, K.A. (2004) The importance of pay in employee motivation: discrepancies between what people say and what they do. *Human Resource Management, 43,* 381–394.

Sachau, D. A. (2007) Resurrecting the Motivation-Hygiene theory: Hertzberg and the positive psychology movement. *Human Resource Development Review* 2007, 377–393.

Saklofske, D. H., Austin, E. J., & Minski, P. S. (2003). Factor structure and validity of a trait emotional intelligence measure. *Personality and Individual Differences, 34,* 707–721.

Salgado, J. (1997). The five factor model of personality and job performance in the European Community. *Journal of Applied Psychology, 82,* 30–43.

Salovey, P., & Mayer,J. (1990). Emotional Intelligence. *Imagination. Cognition and Personality,* 9, 185–211.

Sashkin, M., & Sashkin, M. G. (2003). *Leadership that matters.* San Francisco, CA: Berrett-Koehler

Schutte, N. S., Malouff, J. M. Hall, L. E., Haggerty, D. J., Cooper, J. T., Golden, C. J., et al. (1998). Development and validation of a measure of emotional intelligence. *Personality and Individual Differences, 25,* 167–177.

Seligman, M.(2002) *Authentic Happiness.* New York: Free Press.

Seymore, D. (2000). Emotional labour. *Hospitality Management, 19,* 159–171.

Silversthorne, S. (2001) Leadership effectiveness and personality: A cross-cultural evaluation. *Personality and individual differences, 30,* 303–309.

Sjoberg, L. (2001). Emotional intelligence: A psychometric analysis. *European Psychologist, 6,* 79–95.

Solansky, S. (2008). Leadership style and team processes in self-managed teams. *Journal of Leadership & Organizational Studies*, 14(4), 332–341.

Spain, S., Harms, P. and Lebreton, J (2013) The dark side of personality at work. *Journal of Organizational* Behavior 1–20.

Spillane, J.P., Camburn, E.M., & Pareja, A.S. (2007). Taking a distributed perspective to the principal's workday. *Leadership and Policy in Schools*, 6, 103–125.

Spillane, J.P., & Diamond, J.B. (2007). *Distributed leadership in practice*, Critical issues in Educational Leadership Series. New York: Teachers College, Columbia University.

Sternberg, R. (1985) *Beyond IQ: A triarchic theory of human intelligence.* New York: Cambridge University Press.

Sternberg, R. (1997). *Successful Intelligence.* Plume, New York.

Stogdill, R. M. (1948), Personal factors associated with leadership: A survey of literature. *Journal of Personality, 25*, 35–71.

Tamkin, P., Pearson, G., Hirsch, W., and Constable, S. (2010) *Exceeding Expectations: the principles of outstanding leadership.* London, The Work Foundation.

Taylor, F. (1911). *Principles of Scientific Management.* New York: Harper & Brothers.

Thorndike, E.L. (1911) *Animal intelligence.* NY, Macmillan.

Thomas, Alan Berkeley (1988) Does Leadership Make a Difference to Organizational Performance? *Administrative Science Quarterly* 33, 388–400.

Towers-Perrin-ISR (2006) *Employee engagement report.* London: Towers Perrin ISR.

Uhl-Bien, M., Graen, G.B. & Scandura, T.A. (2000) Implications of Leader-Member Exchange (LMX) for strategic human resource management systems: relationships as social capital for competitive advantage. *Research in Personnel and Human Resources Management* 18, 137–186.

Uhl-Bien, M., Riggio, R.E., Lowe, K.B. & Carsten, M.K. (2014) Followership theory: a review and research agenda. *The Leadership Quarterly.* 25 83–104.

Wasserman, N., Anand, B. & Nohria, N. (2010) When does leadership matter? A contingent opportunities view of CEO leadership. In Nohria and Khurana (2010) ibid.

Weisinger, H. (1998). *Emotional intelligence at work: The untapped edge for success.* San Francisco: Jossey-Bass.

Welford, A. (1981). Social skills and social class. *Psychological Reports, 48*, 847–852.

West, M. A. (1994). Reflexivity and work group effectiveness: A conceptual integration. In M.A. West (Ed). (1996). The handbook of work group psychology (pp. 555–579).Chichester, England: John Wiley & Sons Ltd.

West, M. A. (1994) *Effective teamwork*, Oxford Blackwell, Second edition 2003.

Williams, K. Y., & O'Reilly, C. A. (1998). Demography and diversity in organizations: A review of 40 years of research. In B. Staw & R. Sutton (Eds.), *Research in Organizational Behavior* 20, 77–140. Greenwich, CT: JAI Press.

Williams, F.I., Campbell, C., McCartney, W., & Gooding, C. (2013). Leader derailment: the impact of self-defeating behaviours. *Leadership & Organisation Development Journal, 34*, 85–97.

Winsborough, D.L. and Sambath, V. (2013) Not like us: and investigation into the personalities of New Zealand CEOs. *Consulting Psychology Journal: Practice and Research*, <u>65</u>(2), 87–107.

Yukl, G. (1998) *Leadership in Organisations.* Upper Saddle River, NJ. Prentice Hall.

Yukl, G., and Van Fleet, D.D. (1992) Theory and research on leadership in organisations. In M.D. Dunnette and L.M. Hough (eds) *Handbook of Industrial and Organisational Psychology* 3, 147–197. Palo Alto Calif.: Consulting Psychologists Press.

Zeidner, M., Matthews, G., & Roberts, R. (2004). Emotional intelligence in the workplace: A critical review. *Applied Psychology, 33*, 371–399.

Zeidner, & R. Roberts, R. (Eds) *Emotional Intelligence: Known and Unknowns.* Oxford: OUP.

Index

© The Editor(s) (if applicable) and The Author(s) 2016   **239**
D. Pendleton, A. Furnham, *Leadership: All You Need To Know
2nd edition*, DOI 10.1057/978-1-137-55436-9